WISE GUYS

STORIES OF MOBSTERS
FROM JERSEY TO VEGAS

WISE GUYS

STORIES OF MOBSTERS
FROM JERSEY TO VEGAS

EDITED BY CLINT WILLIS

Thunder's Mouth Press
New York

For
Dylan Hanley
and
Vanessa Hanley

with much love

contents

ix   **Introduction**

1   from *Joey the Hitman*
    by Joey with David Fisher

35   from *Wiseguy*
    by Nicholas Pileggi

45   from *The Godfather*
    by Mario Puzo

65   *The Black Hand*
    from *The Business of Crime*
    by Humbert S. Nelli

97   from *The Mafia in America*
    by Howard Abadinsky

139   *Life of Crime*
    by Richard Stratton

163   *Sparks*
    from *Gotti: Rise and Fall*
    by Jerry Capeci and Gene Mustain

177   *Men of Honor*
    by Richard Ben Cramer

207   *Tongs*
    from *Chinatown*
    by Gwen Kinkead

221   *Crimetown USA*
    by David Grann

243   *Blood Brothers*
    by John Sedgwick

269   from *Tin for Sale*
by John Manca and Vincent Cosgrove

279   from *Mobfather*
by George Anastasia

311   *The Sting*
by Elizabeth Gilbert

333   from *Hit 29*
by Joey with David Fisher

347   **Acknowledgments**

348   **Permissions**

350   **Bibliography**

Introduction

embers of the Mafia have been known to refer to organized crime as *La Cosa Nostra*—Italian for "this thing of ours." But the Mafia now exists largely as story, and as such it has come to belong to the rest of us, too. We've adopted a version of organized crime as a kind of cultural mascot. The Mafia reminds us that Americans who live in suburbs and drive boring cars can be gritty and ruthless. We may feel safer knowing that in a war these scary guys are on our side—they are for us and with us even if their regular job is to take from us.

Our stories about the Mafia also manage to suggest that even the worst of us—the killers and thugs—are essentially good guys; like other Americans, they're doing what it takes to get by in a world of snobs and hypocrites and the *real* low-lifes: people like Osama Bin Laden or Saddam Hussein. And so stories we tell ourselves about Michael Corleone and Tony Soprano and John Gotti and Lucky Luciano somehow get mixed up with how we respond to Arab terrorists or difficult U.N. delegates.

Why do we like these stories? It may be that there are times when we feel so trapped in our lives that we can't imagine real freedom, and so we look around us for notions of what freedom might look like and find it in surprising places. At moments, Tony Soprano and his pals at the Bada Bing are having a kind of fun that is not available to most of us: Their unrelenting self-involvement, their meaty vocabularies, their knee-jerk rages, their bad eating habits and their violence sometimes look like a certain kind of fun—even if we know these people are self-destructive, evil and ultimately tedious.

Reading a good story about organized crime is at moments like reading a good ghost story: You're so glad you're not there that you find yourself glad to be here. The stories also offer us a sense of who we are when we're not well-behaved; and they remind us that the worst of us—the most brutal and confused—are more familiar than we can easily explain.

The best stories about organized crime—about anything—ring true in part because they report back to us actual moments, imagined or experienced—moments familiar to us even if we've never buried anyone next to a highway or been to prison. Such moments remind us to keep moving; when the stories are good enough, we realize that if we stopped finding or experiencing stories we would die.

One reason is that stories carry the truth. Mobsters are some of the biggest liars around; if they faced the truth they would stop being mobsters. The best single scene in *The Sopranos* comes when Tony's wife Carmella goes to a shrink—an old man who apparently knows something about evil and its consequences. The psychiatrist tells Carmella that she must leave Tony and his money: There is no other way to get clean. She momentarily hears him—she knows he is telling her the truth—and then she goes back to hiding. But what the shrink also knows is that there is no way to hide from evil or its consequences; the story of her life will unfold regardless of whether Carmella has the courage to watch or believe it.

Mobsters don't mean to tell us the truth about themselves or about ourselves or about life itself. But they can't hide from the ways that intention and action lead to outcome—a process some Buddhists call karma. And so ultimately a mobster's blind behavior and its consequences can lead its witnesses to understanding, which often turns up where we are most surprised to find it. Whatever you expect to find in these stories, stay open to the chance that you will stumble upon wisdom.

—Clint Willis
Series Editor, Adrenaline Books

from Joey the Hitman
by Joey with David Fisher

The mob killer known to readers as Joey wrote his 1973

autobiography with David Fisher (born 1946). Like

Nicholas Pellegi's Wiseguy—*which came 12 years later—*

Joey the Hitman *offers a convincing and instructive look*

at mob culture.

was sitting in Patsy's Pizzeria reading the New York *Daily News* not so long ago when a numbers runner I know sat down at my table to ask if I wanted to bet with him. The headline of the paper stated that the police had caught the men who had kidnapped, and presumably killed, Carlo Gambino's nephew. He shook his head sadly. "Those guys are in some trouble."

I said, "No, they ain't, they're safe. It's the law that's got them. Carlo's wife and brother called the FBI when they got the ransom note."

He again shook his head sadly. "Ain't that a sorry situation when Carlo Gambino has to call the cops. This business is in a bad state."

This business. Our profession, organized crime. Organized crime is indeed a business. A business that happens to be illegal, but still a business. It is run better than the United States government or General

Motors and makes a bigger profit than United States Steel, Chrysler Corporation and Standard Oil combined. It is run very smoothly: We have no union problems, we don't pay overtime, we have no pension plan and we have enough work to keep everybody busy. Our profit-sharing plan is the best in the business world, and our customers usually are satisfied and happy. We—and by "we" I mean the 100,000 or so men in this country who can honestly claim they belong to the nationwide crime organization—we exist simply to serve the public. We give them what they want, we cater to their desires. We do things for our benefit, of course, but in doing them we give people what they want.

And what they want is a chance to make a bet, get some narcotics, borrow some money quickly and quietly, or the opportunity to buy first-class merchandise, from cigarettes to stockings, at good prices. We supply these things to your so-called honest citizen. We deliver on time, we stand behind our merchandise and we pay off when we lose.

Occasionally we use violence—but when we do, it is generally confined to people in the mob. Very rarely do we step out of our own realm to hurt somebody. The only people outside the organization who do get hurt are people who borrow our money and don't pay us, or bet with us and don't pay us, or make an agreement and don't pay us. These people are going to get hurt, no question about it. But the honest citizen has nothing to fear from us; we are not out to hurt him. Violence is expensive, killers cost a lot of money, musclemen command good fees, and so violence is only used as a last resort. The real money comes out of gambling and shylocking and narcotics and merchandising.

Most of the money made by organized crime today is made in areas that are legal in other countries—gambling and prostitution, for example. If there is one thing I'm going to stress in this book, it's that you cannot legislate morals; don't try. The people want prostitution, let them have prostitution. They want to gamble, get ready to take their money. As long as you let people do what they want, as long as they don't bother anyone else, then who is being hurt? Let man be the master of his own fate. The minute you tell a man he is not allowed to do something, you've just created a brand-new business. Because I'm gonna be there to help him do it—just as often as he can afford.

Prohibition is the best example of what I'm talking about. The bluenoses came in and said nobody drinks anymore. Boom. Organized crime was born. You made millionaires out of people who never figured to earn more than ten dollars a week. Today some of your most respected people are former bootleggers. The people who founded the "21 Club" in New York, bootleggers. Toots Shor was a bootlegger. These people made bathtub gin, or they ran the stuff in from Canada. Bootleggers spawned everything from shylocking to murder. Yet these people are idolized in the restaurant business today. What kind of morality is that?

The stupidity of the people in this country never ceases to amaze me. I'm supposed to be an evil man. I'm supposed to be eliminated so people can walk on the streets at night. Not only is that bullshit, that's the worst hypocrisy I've ever heard. Without your so-called honest citizen I would cease to exist. He's my customer and my employer. All the organization does is act as his supplier; whatever he wants, we get. As soon as the average American decides he's willing to pay the full price for merchandise, willing to follow all the laws, willing to stop gambling and playing around on the side, I'm gone. I can't survive.

But it will never happen. People are going to continue doing exactly what they want, and I'm sick and tired of being blamed for their faults. I used to work in the Cincinnati area in one of the most beautiful bust-out joints this side of Las Vegas. When I say bust-out joint I don't mean it was crooked, it was not. A real bust-out joint is a place where you come in and they take you up one side and down the other. This place was called the West Riviera Club, and you got as fair a shake there as you would anywhere else in the world. I was working there for Meyer Lansky, making sure nobody was pocketing his money. One night I met a customer from Omaha, Nebraska. He was the deacon of his church. I know because he kept telling me. Yet here he was 6 or 700 miles from home, shacking up with a broad he never saw before, drinking like gangbusters. So I said to him, "Listen, instead of coming all this way, why don't you just legalize it in your community?"

He says, "What! Are you crazy? I wouldn't subject my family to this!"

"If you're such a great family man," I asked him, "what the hell are you doing messing around with a girl young enough to be your daughter?" I mean, if he's gonna do it, what the hell difference does it make where he does it? This type of hypocrisy makes me sick. And that is another reason for this book.

I'm not saying that the mob is a branch of the Sisters of Mercy. These are men, some of them, who will kill you if you cross them. But the majority of the people who make their living in crime are simply out to provide for their families. They don't want to hurt anybody. There are a lot of people in the mob who will not pull the trigger, who will not break legs, who will not swing a pipe because they just don't have it in them. I mean, they're larceny-hearted, they're not violent.

But the only people who get to the top, as far as making good money, are the people who don't give a fuck, people who would just as soon blow your brains out as look at you, break your leg if it's a necessity, if you deserve it. Me, for example; I have no compunctions about doing anything. If there is money involved, I will do it. And, because of that, because of the fact that I do not flinch when I pull the trigger, I am a respected mob man.

Organized crime was well organized long before I got involved. The roots of crime as it is organized today were planted hundreds of years ago in Sicily, when the Italian people turned to a secret organization for protection from the land barons and feudal rulers. The first initials of the name of this society spelled out Mafia, which is why the group was called that. At first the Mafia was very popular with the Sicilians but then *it* began to get powerful. Eventually it was more powerful than the barons had ever been, and controlled everything from the stores to the Church. They even began to offer protection from the Mafia itself, which is how the extortion business got going.

The first Mafiosi came to America in the 1880s. Most of them left Sicily because the police were after them there. They figured what worked in Sicily would work in America. They were right. These Italian immigrants were very superstitious—they considered it bad luck to be beaten up—and the protection rackets started. Eventually the Mafia controlled a great deal of the illegal activities in the eastern United States.

At the same time the Italians were arriving other immigrant groups were streaming in too. The Irish and the Jews saw what the Italians were doing in their community, so they began doing it to their own people. At this point there was absolutely no organization. The Irish couldn't touch the Italians, and the Italians left the Irish alone. Everybody had their own territory and did their own thing.

That all changed when Prohibition began.

The original base of organization within crime came from an uncle or cousin of Al Capone's named Johnny Torrio. Torrio left Brooklyn and formed a crime cartel in Chicago, dealing in numbers, bookmaking, prostitution, things like that. When bootlegging became important he needed somebody to run the Chicago operation for him and he sent for Al Capone. A few years later a rival gang almost killed Torrio, and he decided he needed some fresh air, in another country, and Capone took over. That's when everything really started: the fight for territory, control, power and money. Your gang wars started here. (Eliot Ness. The so-called Untouchables.) Capone modernized mob thinking. He realized that communication and cooperation with other major mobs was not only necessary for business purposes, it was a good thing in general. As the years went by the old-timers, the people who had started it all, the Mustache Petes, had to go because they were stagnating, and your young turks began rising. By the mid 1930s almost every major city was controlled by a single mob which had outlasted and outfought its competitors. The city of Detroit was predominantly controlled by the Jewish mob. Cleveland was Jewish. The Irish owned the docks, and the Italians had part of New York and most of the East Coast. These people realized that Capone was right, they had to work with one another or be destroyed, so the organization was created. We organized because we finally realized we were all in the same business, and if engineers could organize and real-estate operators could organize, so could we, the people who worked in crime. Today people of almost every race, creed and nationality work in or for the organization. It is truly an American business.

It's funny, people blame all of organized crime on the Italians. They think that the Mafia is the same thing as organized crime. Not true. The Mafia is just part of the entire nationwide structure of the organization. Unfortunately for the Italians, they are the people who always get the publicity. But just to make sure the Italians don't get *all* the publicity, many Italian hoods, when they begin to make a name for themselves, make sure it's an Irish name. Jimmy Plumeri became Jimmy Doyle, and Thomas Eboli became Tommy Ryan, for example. I don't know why they do this, the Irish certainly don't need any help. *Today,* even, you have a strong Irish mob. You have a strong Jewish mob; Jews practically control gambling. You even have Chinese mobs. But everybody blames everything on the Italians. Now I don't want to take any credit from them away, they've done their fair share, but the hardest people to deal with, the most vicious killers in organized-crime history, were the Jews. It was Jews who founded and worked for an outfit called Murder Incorporated. This was originally started by a Jew named Abe Reles and had members like Louie Lepke Buchalter and even Bugsy Siegel.

Nobody thinks of the Chinese as members of organized crime and, in reality, they are not. They have their own gambling, their own money-lending, their own narcotics. This is all Chinese, no Caucasian in the world is going to get in there. If a white guy tried to get into New York or San Francisco's Chinatown mobs he would be blown away. I know these people. There's one guy in New York, a little old Chinaman by the name of Wu. This man controls fan-tan, Mah-Jongg and narcotics down there. He runs an organization comparable to any mob in the country. And he makes a lot of money because the Chinese are great gamblers, they'll bet on which of two cockroaches has more legs. The Chinese have their own political clubs, their own collections, their own connections. You do not dictate to them. They got their own setup and that's it, pal. People in the organization respect them because they went out and put their own thing together, they organized themselves, like everyone else did.

• • •

On a national scale organized crime, or the syndicate, or the mob, the hoods, the boys, whatever you want to call them, is actually very loosely organized. Each area is broken down into certain specific territories, and each of these territories is under the direction of a boss. You cannot operate within another man's territory without the permission of that boss. Let's take an area like the north Bronx. This area is controlled primarily by the Carmine Tramunti mob. The people in this area, the book makers, the shylocks, the numbers runners, any activity you want to mention, are beholden to him. Carmine has established this area as his domain. This will probably run from the tip of the north Bronx right to the end of Westchester County, as far south as the Parkchester area, approximately, and anyone doing business within these boundaries is doing so with the consent and protection of Carmine Tramunti.

In return for that permission and protection a percentage of every dollar made in that area goes to the so-called family. In New York there are five major families which control the city and all surrounding areas.

Internationally there is no worldwide crime oganization like television and the movies would have you believe, but there is a certain amount of cooperation between groups. Consider narcotics. We have to get it from somewhere. The trade was originally controlled by the Corsicans, but now most of it comes from South America by way of Europe and Asia. There are international working agreements, but there is no organization in the American sense of the word.

As far as American-built organizations expanding into other countries, you can forget that. The way we have successfully built an organization is by knowing how to operate within the American system—we know where we can do it, we know how we can do it, we know with whom we can do it. Other countries have totally different systems, and it would be impossible to adapt to them.

Only one Western country can say today that it doesn't have organized crime and that's England. They have crime there, spectacular crimes like bank holdups, train robberies, stuff like that. Gambling has been knocked off by being legalized, prostitution has been knocked off—it's not legal but they don't bother you—and the government's narcotics program has taken most of the profit out of that. England also has a very tough legal system to beat. They have uniformity of laws. There is no such thing as a law in London and another law in Manchester—each law is for the entire country. And finally, over there, from the time you are arrested to the day you go to trial, it's never more than three or four weeks. In other words, it's very difficult for a man to do a dishonest day's work in England.

Now take a look at a map of this country. Almost every state is broken up into areas like the north Bronx, some bigger, some smaller, but all organized the same way. A man gets to be boss of an area because he has been smart enough or strong enough to organize a group of people, which the newspapers will call a family. A family can consist of anywhere from 20 or 30 men to a few hundred.

The boss delegates some of his authority to certain men who will act as his lieutenants, or button men, as they're known. Let me explain a button man. A button man is an individual who will control a certain area, maybe a few blocks, maybe a whole neighborhood, for a boss. He is liable to have as many as 40 to 50 men, "soldiers," working under him in a specific area. The button man is responsible for making sure everything in his area runs smoothly and those people who are beholden pay their dues. All the money that comes from that area, after his people get paid, he will split right down the middle with the boss. This money will include receipts from shylocking, bookmaking, numbers, all illegal money. Legal activities might include food stores, bowling alleys (which are very big), bars and social clubs. (Social clubs are usually storefronts or apartments where you can always find a bookmaker, a shylock, a card game and a fence with almost any kind of stolen merchandise.)

As far as loyalty within a family there is not an extreme amount of it. Money has a very big mouth; it not only talks, it screams. Under normal circumstances, though, a man is loyal to a boss because (1) he is treated well, or (2) he is afraid of him or (3) he can earn a lot of money working for this particular individual.

A few big bosses command loyalty simply because they treat their button men and soldiers very well. A man like that will be able to ask his men to do anything for him. When I worked for Jack Dragna in California, for example, if he told me to go to hell I would have taken a shovel and started digging. I literally loved that man. He showed me how to make money, he showed me how to live good, he got me out of trouble when I stepped into it. He stopped me from drinking and taught me to control my violence. When I did something wrong he didn't yell and scream at me, he talked in a nice quiet voice, and explained right and wrong. And how to do wrong better.

At his peak Jack ran southern California. To put it bluntly, you couldn't take a shit in southern California unless Jack got a piece of the toilet paper. I don't know how he got to be a mob boss because he was in power when I first met him. But I assume he got there the same way everybody else did: by being a little tougher and a little more ruthless than anyone else around.

Physically he was about five foot eight, a little paunchy, and spoke with an Italian accent. He was what a mob boss should be: loved by his employees and feared by his enemies. He issued orders in a cold, calculating way and never left any room for discussion. The party was over when Jack said it was over.

One night the party took place in a little restaurant called Alex's or Alexander's in Los Angeles. Mickey Cohen had gotten out of jail and he wanted to reorganize bookmaking and various other activities so he could regain some lost power. So he called a meeting with Jack and about 20 other hoods. I went along as Jack's protection.

The food was wonderful. We started off with antipasto, shrimp cocktails and baked clams. Then they brought in the macaroni, spaghetti and ziti. Finally the main course, veal and chicken, was brought in. The restaurant I don't remember, the meal I can't forget.

Jack never did like Mickey or any of his associates very much, and he was quite happy with the status quo, so he was not fond of Mickey's reorganization plans. He waited until the dinner was over, until Mickey had made his proposals, and then he got up and began speaking. "You makea nice speech and you serva me nice meal and I'ma thankin' ya. I'm thankin' ya by tellin' ya somethin'. If I find anybody who'sa going south of LA on their way to Mexico, or they goin' west on a way to Arizona and they stoppa for anything but to take a piss and a cuppa coffee and gasoline, I'm a gonna kill 'em. Good-night, gennelmen." And then we left.

I originally met Jack through some people in New York. I was running muscle with Joey Gallo, just two young punks on the way up, and we had to go see a man about some money. This guy had an office on the first floor of the Strand Building, which was on Broadway between 47th and 48th. The guy started to give us a song and dance, and I just grabbed him and threw him over my shoulder. I figured I would just slam him around a little—unfortunately I threw him right out an open window. I said to Joey, "I think we had better take leave of this place," and he agreed. The guy wasn't really hurt, but a lot of people had seen him become a hit on Broadway.

We went back to see the guy who hired us, and the next thing I know I'm in a car going to Chicago. I had no idea why they wanted me out of town, but they were paying the bills so I agreed to go. They put me in the Maryland Hotel for four days and just kept sending up broads, booze and food. I figured, "What the hell, if I'm going to die, I might as well have a good time."

Eventually a man named Eddie Marlowe came to see me and gave me a plane ticket to Los Angeles, $100 and the address of a bar in San Pedro. I arrived, went to the bar and sat around waiting. I still didn't know what was supposed to happen. Inevitably I got into a fight with a guy at the bar. In those days I fought with just anybody. I didn't know any better. I had just finished opening up this guy's head with a beer bottle when Jack Dragna walked in. He smiled and told me who he was and explained that I would be working for him. The first thing he did was take me to a men's shop and buy me six new suits. Then he got me an apartment and a car. The first place I worked for him was in a bucket of blood, a whorehouse in Tijuana, Mexico, a place called the El Matador. Eventually he brought me back to LA to run certain things for him; smuggling, numbers, whatever came up. We had a wonderful relationship, he treated me more like a son than an employee. When Jack died—of an overdose of his own heroin—I felt like I lost my father. To this day I miss that man. As far as I'm concerned he was the finest mob boss who ever lived.

The Boss also has people he is responsible to—the Board of Directors. This "board" consists of all the bosses in a large area. The Commissioner is called the Boss of Bosses (in New York, for example, this is Carlo Gambino, who earned it through time, respect and survival). This board meets whenever an emergency arises, whenever somebody important has to be killed, or concerning a territorial dispute. It is up to this board to say either, "Yes, you can control this if you're good enough," or "No, you cannot step over into this territory." There is enough territory to go around, and to try to abuse someone else is only going to hurt everybody, so the board keeps control. Every major city, with the exception of Los Angeles which is almost mob-free today, is set up like this. If you wanted to do something in another city you would have to first obtain the permission of that city's Boss of Bosses. And that goes for Carlo Gambino as well as for me.

I have earned my right to do a lot of different things within the structure of the mob, but anything I do I'm still completely beholden to it. If I want to start an operation within an area I still have to contact the man who runs the area, tell him what I have in mind and take him in as a partner. A boss's territory is his own, and he directs everything that happens in it.

There is no single national leader, no one man who runs the whole show. Even Capone, at the height of his power, all he controlled was Cicero, Illinois. He didn't even really have the city of Chicago. There is no way in the world a man in organized crime could take over the entire country. It is just a physical impossibility. He would have to have the loyalty of more than 100,000 people; he would have to be the Fuehrer, a complete dictator. It can't be done.

The one man who has come closer to being a national boss than anyone else is Meyer Lansky. He is the man that the mob has more respect for, that the mob owes more to, than anyone else in the world.

I worked for Meyer for almost eight years. He is patient, easy to work for and brilliant. I firmly believe that if he had decided to be the president of the United States he could have made it. Instead he went after the world, and he made that. Meyer appreciates when you do things right. He lets you know it with a pat on the back, extra money, a broad, whatever you want. And he is the one man who has the total loyalty of the people who work for him.

Wherever you go in this country Meyer is known as "The Old Man." In this case this is a term of respect and affection, as well as a nickname. As the movies and print media have shown, nicknames add a great deal of glamour to the inhabitants of the world of organized crime. Not everybody has a nickname, of course. Some people pick them up as they go along, others never get one. Me, for example, I've had a lot of aliases, but I've never had a real nickname that was mine and mine alone.

The nicknames themselves come from everywhere. Some of them are based on an individual's real name, like a guy named Joe DeStephano becomes Joey Dee, or if his name was Frankie Zeno he would probably be Frankie Z. If a guy's first name is Frank he may become known as Cheech.

Other people get their names from their looks. Carmine the Snake got his name because he looked like a snake. Charlie the Bull was built like a bull. Alex the Beard had a beard. If a guy has a big nose he might become known as Big Nose.

Other people pick up names because they are directly opposite what they are supposed to be. Fat people are called Skinny, skinny people are known as Fats (so are some fat people, of course), and bald people are called Curly.

A physical handicap might be the basis for a guy's nickname. An individual with a bad arm would be known as Wingy; a bad leg, Gimpy; and a cross-eyed guy would be called Cockeye. There was one famous cross-eyed guy (actually he became famous when he went to the electric chair) by the name of Cockeye Dunn.

Some people are known by their ethnic background: Nick the Wop, Alex the Greek, Yiddy Stein. Others by the services they perform: One guy who used to work on the docks was called Charlie the Hook. If he didn't like you he would pick you up with his longshoreman's hook. A guy that's good with a knife may become The Blade. One guy I used to know who ran a string of flophouses was known as Louie Flop-house. A guy who is good with his muscle, a slugger, would probably be called The Club or something like that.

Others get their names from where they come from. Johnny Odo came from the Bathbeach section of Brooklyn, so he was Johnny Bath-beach. A guy from Pittsburgh was called Louie Pitt.

Certain names have very specific meanings. A man whose last name is Black represents death. He is either a hit man or he sets hits up. Just like the man who uses the name Costello is probably a gambler. It's just an association: Costello equals gambling. Also a guy whose name is Peppy would probably also be in the gambling phase. It's just something that's known, that's accepted.

A few guys got their names from their habits. This guy Funzi I know likes to eat pizza all the time, so everybody calls him Pizzaman. There was one guy who was always sniffling, so he was named Jimmy the Sniff, and I know one guy who used to take at least nine showers every single day and douse himself with bath powder after each one. He would put his hat on first, so he didn't get any powder in his hair. His nickname? Baby Blue.

If a man has one unusual thing happen to him in his career, that might be the basis of his nickname. Joey Gallo became Crazy Joey when he tried to plead temporary insanity to a burglary rap. Lucky Luciano became Lucky when they found him ventilated with bullet holes, but somehow still alive.

Finally, some people are so good at what they do that they are given a special nickname, and everyone knows them by that name. It's as much a term of respect as it is a nickname. The Fixer, for example, was

Frank Costello, which was a tribute to his tremendous political connections. Gil Beckley was known everywhere as The Brain because, when it came to figuring out odds, he could outthink a computer. When Frank Erickson was alive he was The Bookmaker's Bookmaker because people all over the country would lay off their action on him.

When you begin in the mob, you start right at the very bottom. Let's say you see that the numbers runner in the neighborhood is making a good salary and you decide that's what you want to do. First thing you do is find some people who want to start playing the numbers. You talk to these people and ask them if you can handle their action. For your own health you'd best make sure these people are not already playing with somebody else. After you have your customers you have to find a controller. A controller is the individual who runs the business end of a specific operation. They're not difficult to find, just ask your local bartender to put you in touch with his runner, almost every bar has one, and then explain the situation to the runner. He'll make the proper introductions. You tell the controller you got some customers you'd like to pick up for him. So now you've got a little franchise and you start progressing from there.

If you're sharp you look around for deals in which you can make money for the mob. You find out who's shying, who's booking, and you start bringing them customers. Of course, you're responsible for the people you bring in. From that point on it's just a matter of how ambitious you are, how much initiative you have. Eventually if a hit comes along and the mob feels you are capable of making it—you've shown you have muscle and are not afraid to use it—you may be approached, or you may even let the word out that you're interested. You can go as far as your balls and brains will take you.

What makes a good mob man? A lot of things. He's got to be an individual who can take the consequences of what he is doing without bellyaching; an individual who can show complete loyalty to the people he is with. Most of the people who have been at all successful are fairly intelligent. They have learned how to think, how to keep their mouths shut and how to observe. They learned, as I learned, that if you're not sure of something, or someone, you just pass on that particular job or deal.

Physically, a good organization man will be tough, a guy who isn't really afraid. Most people are afraid of jail, violence, death—but the guy who is really a hard case, the guy who can legitimately say he doesn't give a damn, he's the guy who is gonna move.

What keeps a man out of the organization? You'll find that junkies do not work in the organization. Dummies do not work in the organization. Loudmouths do not work in the organization. We don't want people with emotional hang-ups, because they cannot be trusted, people with sex problems, like homosexuals, because no one wants to work with them, and the bleeding-heart sentimentalists who are going to worry about what happens to the other guy.

Today it is difficult to pick the average mob guy out of a crowd. He looks like any other businessman or blue-collar worker. In the old days you lived the mob. Everything you did centered around the mob and mob business. That's not entirely true anymore. Today you got a lot of people like me who either work freelance or have their own small thing going and don't spend that much time with other people in the organization. If we go out among ourselves, which we don't do too often, it is generally for dinner and then to a sporting event, usually the fights. But the center of attraction is the food. Mob people are among the best eaters in the world. They just love to put it away.

Food and business go hand in hand. I would say 95 percent of all the business meetings I ever attended have taken place over a dinner. The choice of restaurant, as well as the honor of paying the bill, always belongs to the individual doing the inviting. I would say that the most popular restaurants in New York City, as far as my friends are concerned, are Patsy's Pizzeria on 118th Street and First Avenue, Delsomma's on West 47th Street, Rao's on 114th Street and Pleasant Avenue, Walsh's Steak House on East 23rd Street, and Manny Wolf's Chop House on East 49th and Third Avenue when it's not burned down.

I was in Patsy's one night for a business meeting. I went with a friend of mine who runs muscle by the name of Rocco. I had to go in back and see somebody, so I told Rocco to stay out front and have something to eat on me. I figured he would have a nice dinner, but when I came out his bill was $23. Twenty-three dollars in Patsy's is like $100 somewhere else. I asked the waiter, "What the hell did this guy eat?"

He consulted his check. "A dozen baked clams, two orders of ziti and clam sauce, veal, a pizza pie, some wine and six bottles of soda."

I looked at Rocco. "Had enough?"

He burped. "That'll tide me over until I get home."

My wife is a decent cook—she does all right with steaks and chops—but I'm the real chef in the family. Though I'm not Italian, I am an excellent Italian cook, an art I learned in self-defense. When I was doing a lot of collecting I was on the road all the time. One day in this city, two days in another, a few hours somewhere else. There was never enough time to discover the decent restaurants, so I would end up walking into some greasy joint and ordering a steak. The cook would throw it on the grill and it would slide off and onto the floor and he would pick it up, dust it off and put it back on the grill. This turned my stomach a little, so I went out and bought some cookbooks and taught myself. This is how I won Rocco's allegiance, incidentally. We were staying in a motel in Akron that had a little kitchenette, and I did my little thing with veal and a salad. After we finished Rocco laid down on the bed, burped, and said, "You tell the boss. Wherever you go—I go!"

I think the social aspects of mob membership began to fade when the organization became professional, when the old customs started dying. Funerals are a good example. Take Joey Gallo. A very small funeral. In the old days Joey would have rated dozens of big black flower cars and tens of limousines. But the people got smart, they realized funerals like that attracted a lot of attention, so they were dropped. We don't try to attract attention, we get enough without trying.

That doesn't mean we're heartless. We do go to funerals, but we just don't make a big deal out of it. I went to a funeral in 1971 for an acquaintance of mine who died of lead poisoning—he was shot full of it. This man will remain nameless, but it was a very nice service. The priest really eulogized this guy. He said things that were just unreal. Finally he says, "This man should not have died in the prime of life."

"If this guy was as good as that priest said he was," I told the guy I was with, "he would *not* have died in the prime of life."

In the old days the mob was much more family and community oriented. One family—and by that I mean a group of men working under a boss, not only blood relations—might include brothers and cousins and uncles and brothers-in-law, and they would be tied together by blood as much as by choice and money. When the boss died his son would be there to pick up the reins. Not anymore. Today a "family" is just a business organization. Generally you'll find that when a man is strong enough to hold it together, his kid ain't got the guts to pick up a rubber ball and throw it against a wall. A lot of bosses don't keep their children in the business; for the most part they try to keep them away. Albert Anastasia, for example, was extremely powerful when he died. Yet his son, Al Junior, couldn't do a thing. Joe Colombo's son is having a very hard time holding it together too.

Another way things have changed for the worse. In the old days mob people used to live in the same area in which they worked, and they used to work out in the open, on the streets. I'll tell you something: In those days the streets were safe. Until the Kefauver Committee started attacking the mob, which took the runners and shylocks off the corners, you could walk the streets at night without being afraid some punk was going to come along and mug you. The mobs did not want people being hurt in their domain. People who got hurt were people who could not come out to bet or buy. So these punks were simply not allowed to operate. As tough as I was as a kid, if the man who worked on the corner told me to get home, my only question was how fast. Wherever the mob operated, the streets were safe for honest people. Even today you're safer in Little Italy in New York City than you are in your mother's arms. That is the way almost all big cities used to be.

Yeah, things have changed in the last 15 years. The mob has become modernized, more professional. A lot of the excitement, the so-called romantic aspects of crime, have gone the way of the famous "Kiss of

Death." I have to admit missing some of the old stuff, but, on the other hand, business is both better and safer than ever.

I've seen the changes take place and I've been able to adapt to the changes. I used to make the major portion of my income from physical work: muscle jobs, hits and protection. Now most of my money comes from more sedate things like running card games, smuggling cigarettes, bootlegging different items and, just to keep it interesting, an occasional hit.

I learned a long time ago that it is vitally important to keep up with the times. That's the first lesson any good businessman learns.

Mario Puzo's book *The Godfather*, and the movie they made from it, did for the organization what silicone does for tits. They both make their respective subjects stand out. We needed *The Godfather* like Joey Gallo needed another portion of clams. Many people think because they saw the movie or read the book they know everything there is to know about organized crime. This is like saying you know everything there is to know about politicians because you watch *Let's Make a Deal*. One thing has absolutely nothing to do with the other.

Don't misunderstand me, I thoroughly enjoyed *The Godfather*. I thought it was a very entertaining, very funny movie. It was also a wonderful piece of fiction. Things just don't happen in real life like they did to Marlon Brando and family.

Let us begin at the beginning. The whole thing starts when Sollozzo goes to see Don Corleone to get financing and political protection for a narcotics operation. He's got the whole fucking mob backing him up, so what does he need Corleone for? The political connections? Any man in his business who is politically connected will help anybody else. That's why it's called an organization. What does this mean to Corleone? The politicians on his payroll do what he tells them to do. Why such a big deal? Besides, Sollozzo did not need Corleone's contacts that badly, he could have gone out and bought his own.

Second, all of a sudden Corleone gets some morals and decides that he doesn't want to deal in narcotics. Ridiculous. When you are controlling a family there is no such thing as not getting involved. Isn't it kind of stupid? Here's a man into bookmaking, shylocking, numbers, fixing, a man who will kill everybody and his brother, and yet he's not willing to sell narcotics. These people are in business to make money, and any man that is a big boss, a controller, he doesn't give one fuck where the money comes from. He'd love narcotics because there's more money being made there than in anything else.

Third, assuming he didn't want to sell narcotics, which no one with his head on his shoulders will believe, he is simply not going to go against a commission meeting, a meeting of the Board of Directors. If a certain thing has been decided there is no reason in the world he's gonna go out of his way to cross them. The commission is too powerful; if it wants something to happen, believe me, it happens.

Next, the shooting of Don Corleone. In every instance I have ever known that a boss was shot, it is because his bodyguard double-crossed him. And a bodyguard does not double-cross him by calling up and saying he is sick. He is there when you get killed. All he does is step aside. He does not leave himself in a position where he will be killed by his own family. Any boss that I've ever known got killed because his bodyguard helped to get him, because he had been offered an improvement in his financial status.

Fifth, the bit about the hired guns "taking to the mattresses." That just doesn't make any sense at all. I couldn't stay locked up in a room with eight other guys for one day, and neither could anybody else. You've got eight tense personalities crammed together waiting for a gunfight, how long can you play gin rummy or poker without going crazy?

During a gang war most people live at home. They just kind of lie low and stay as close to the house as possible. During the Colombo-Gallo War, for example, I met this old friend of mine who was hooked up with the Colombo people. He said, "Why don't you come out to the house for dinner this week? I'm home every night now. But I hope you don't mind if I don't walk you to your car." The home is a sanctuary. You can hit people outside the house, but you can't go inside; it's just not considered proper etiquette.

Even more, no family can afford to keep hired guns locked up in a room for any length of time. An organization that is not earning cannot afford to pay its people, and in order for you to earn you've got to be out on the street. What do you think is going to happen if they stop working and stop earning money? Listen, if people can't earn they leave you. Now, in this so-called gang war they had, these people who "hit the mattresses" were not earning any money. And there is just not enough money to continue paying these men.

Another thing, you are not gonna kill a cop, no matter how crooked he is, and get away with it. No matter how bad he is. There is simply no way in the world the police department is going to allow it. They will hunt you down, they will get informers on the street, they will pay money, they will get you no matter how long it takes. You are not going to kill a cop; believe me, you are not going to do it and get away with it. The cops who get gunned down in the city are hit by crazy addicts, black-power people and other nuts.

Now we come to the murder of Sonny Corleone. To refresh your memory they drew him to a deserted toll-booth area and then about a dozen guys all armed with submachine guns popped out from behind the booth and killed him. Wrong. No way in the world you're going to have that many guys there when a murder is committed. You want as few people as possible to know you're connected with the crime to begin with. Then, if you're going to set up a guy you don't have to go through all that planning, like taking over an entire roadway. There are so many different ways to hit a man. Any professional will pick his time and place; he can sucker you out, find you out or seek you out. You don't have to go through an elaborate plan to hit a man. It's very simple to catch him leaving a barbershop, or catch him coming out of his girlfriend's house or catch him having dinner in a restaurant. Nobody is going to be able to stay behind walls forever, and when he comes out you've got him.

If you remember your book and movie, after Sonny got it the Corleone family killed all the other bosses. No way. It cannot be done. As ruthless as you want to be, you wouldn't last. I don't care how careful your plans are, it is a physical impossibility. And no one can afford to hire an entire army of killers to do the job. The price is just prohibitive. The planning is incredible and the undercover work, getting to every bodyguard, is impossible. When that many people know something is going to happen, it doesn't happen. In 1931 the young turks eliminated many of the old bosses in one day and night. That was more than 40 years ago and simply could not happen again today.

I thought the most convincing character was Sollozzo, the guy who tried to force the issue of narcotics. He epitomized what a man is in this business, completely ruthless, he doesn't give a fuck.

The character of the Godfather himself, Don Corleone, was a composite of a number of people I know. (I personally thought Brando was good despite the line going around that "The Italian who played Marlon Brando did a good job.") But there were some problems in his portrayal. No boss wants to be referred to as a Godfather. Most people prefer to be anonymous. The men in this business who have gone to prison are men who have allowed themselves to become too well known. The quieter a man lives, the better off he is. And when a boss does have an affair, like the Corleone wedding, he tries to hold it in an out-of-the-way place. He does not invite public figures to these affairs, because he knows the embarrassment it would cause them.

Even the relationship between Corleone and his button men, in particular Clemenza, was ridiculous. A button man is in control of an area and he may see his boss once a week, if that often.

I rated it three stars, a great comedy, and almost everybody I know in the mob agreed. For a while the movie was the main topic of conversation. Everybody was running around threatening to "make you an offer you couldn't refuse." The most popular joke in the mob had this guy Funzi asking his friend Tony, "Have you seen *The Godfather?*"

And Tony answered, "No, I went over to his place but he wasn't home."

A big game that everybody was playing was trying to figure out who the different characters were supposed to be. There was one character I had no problem recognizing: the horse who had his head cut off. I think I bet on him out at Aqueduct the day before I saw the movie.

We shall now see how it is done in real life.

Everybody loves gang wars whether via television, radio, newspapers, magazines or movies. Everybody, that is, except the gangs. While the general public finds gang wars exciting and fascinating, the gangs find them expensive and dangerous. They could live without them, so to speak. But they do erupt, and when they do there is little anyone can do but try to finish on his feet.

Gang wars are caused by many things: young hotshots trying to push older people out, personal dislikes and, most of all, territorial disputes. In most cases these wars can be settled relatively peacefully, but sometimes both honor and money are involved, and then you have people shooting other people. The biggest war of all time, the one which set the standard by which gang wars are judged, was Chicago's Al Capone–Bugsy Moran War during Prohibition, which lasted until the entire Moran organization was destroyed. In reality there have not been too many real out-and-out fights since I've been in the business. The last big one, the Colombo–Persico–Gallo War, had all the elements of the classic gang confrontation and made headlines all over the country. As far as I know, the entire story has never been told from beginning to end. I was there, I was approached by all three parties and I know exactly what happened.

This thing had been building for years and there had been some fighting a few times earlier. It actually started in 1957 when Joey Gallo killed Albert Anastasia under a contract let out by Joseph Profaci. As a reward Profaci gave Joey some territory in south Brooklyn. But Joey was very ambitious and wanted a bigger area. In 1959 the Gallo group, headed by Joey and his older brother Larry, broke away from the Profaci organization and started to fight. Although the

Gallos were badly outnumbered they fought pretty tough, and bodies kept turning up until 1962.

Actually Joey and his eventual enemy, Joseph Colombo, had started out together in the Profaci organization. They even worked together on a few hits. They both did good work and climbed up the ladder until they split into different factions and organized their own small groups. In 1959 Colombo stayed loyal to Profaci when the Gallos split with him.

At the same time Carmine (the Snake) Persico was also starting to get some power. He was known as a man who could be depended on, even though he blew one of his biggest jobs: Profaci gave him the contract on Larry Gallo and he messed it up. He had suckered Larry into a bar in Brooklyn and was strangling him when a police sergeant happened to accidentally walk in. This was the biggest break I ever heard a man getting. But this attempt caused a great deal of bitter hatred between the Gallos and the rest of the Profaci organization.

Normally the police don't care what happens in these things, unless innocent people get hurt, but they brought this one to a halt by getting Joey on an extortion rap. Peace was more or less made before Joey went to the can, and the shooting stopped. I always felt that Colombo and Persico could have avoided a lot of problems by hitting Joey at this time, which they could have done because he just didn't have that many people. They would have saved themselves a lot of grief.

Of the three of them, I knew Joey Gallo best. Joey was one of the shrewdest and funniest people I ever met, and he was far from crazy. He knew rackets. He knew what made money and what didn't make money. He knew what he wanted to control. And he knew how to convince people that his way of thinking was best.

He once kept a lion in the basement of his social club on President Street in south Brooklyn. If a guy was giving him a hard time, or if someone defaulted or came up short, he would bring them into the cellar where the lion was tied. He would explain what solution he had in mind and then say, "If it doesn't work out, guess who's coming to dinner?" and laugh like crazy.

Joey was short, about five foot six, and had a medium build, and he was a very violent man. But it was controlled violence; he always knew what he was doing. And he was funny, a lot of laughs to be with, what you'd call good company. Years ago, when I was just getting started, we ran some muscle together. I remember one day I was driving along and I look at him and he's staring into the rear-view mirror. He kept contorting his face into the meanest looks he could make. "Hey, moron," I said to him, "what the fuck do you think you're doing?" He looked at me with a sneer splitting his face and said, "What do you think I'm doing? I'm practicing to look tough!"

He didn't have to practice too hard, he was tough. But his problem was that, from the very beginning, he wanted power. He needed it desperately. When I left New York to go to California he was just on his way up. A few years later he made a big splash when he killed Anastasia. He never talked about the killing, but I knew he had done it.

He had one thing in him that somewhere along the line I've lost: Joey could hate. He was a brutal ruthless man when he hated somebody, and he found it easy to hate anybody who got in his way. I once saw him work a guy over. He really put his heart and his muscle into it. He just kicked this guy until his eye popped out of his head, and then he kicked him in the balls maybe 30 times. He just made himself hate this poor sucker.

We were friendly until the day he died. One of the last times we had dinner together he seemed very wistful. I think he knew he didn't have long to live. "I wish you had thrown in with me," he said. "We could have done some great things together."

I said, "Joey, you went your way, I went mine. You've done good and I've done good and everybody's happy." Joey never really made it as big as he wanted to; he didn't really control too much when he died. But right up until the very end he was trying. That's the thing you always remember about Joey, he never knew when to lay off.

When Joey went to prison in 1962 Larry took over the President Street mob and the south Brooklyn area. Larry could have handled things until Joey got out because he was tough and smart and people respected him. Unfortunately, he died of cancer and the third brother, Albert, took over. Albert just didn't have the power or strength or the smarts to keep control. When he first took over they called him Kid Blast . . . after a while it became Kid Blister.

Meanwhile, sitting quietly on the sidelines, carefully watching all this, slowly gathering the real power, was Carlo Gambino. He had been in competition with Profaci and when Profaci died in the summer of 1962 he just kind of eased in and took it. He took over whatever he wanted and consolidated his gains because there was no one to stop him—everybody was busy fighting within the mob. Finally it got to a point where it was a toss-up who was more powerful, Gambino or Vito Genovese.

Vito Genovese was the most ruthless man I have ever known. He desperately wanted to be the Boss of Bosses and was willing to kill anybody who got in his way. He set up the Albert Anastasia hit (which helped Gambino, an Anastasia lieutenant, move into power) and also tried to get Frank Costello. Chin Gigante did the job, but his shot just wounded Costello and he recovered. It didn't matter, Frank knew enough to take the hint and he retired, leaving Vito in the top spot.

Even after Vito went to prison for 15 years on a narcotics conspiracy rap he wouldn't give up any of his power. Anthony Strollo, better known as Tony Bender, tried to take a little and one night he went out for a newspaper and never came back. Vito gave the order from his cell.

Anyway, Genovese and Gambino were the big bosses of the New York area in the early 1960s. Between the two of them they controlled everything there was to control. They also had enough influence to make things happen anywhere else in the country, but even they had to first receive the permission of whoever the boss of the territory was.

The period just after Joey went to jail saw a lot of power changing hands. Colombo was busy building an organization out of what had been the Profaci family, Persico emerged as the most powerful group within the Colombo organization, with his own men and area, and Vito Genovese went to jail, leaving the active control to Carlo Gambino.

Although there was some maneuvering for power, things generally stayed quiet while Joey was in prison.

In April 1970 Colombo's son, Joseph, Jr., was arrested by the federal government and charged with melting down silver coins, a federal offense.

This is where it all started again. Claiming that his son was innocent and his entire family was being persecuted because they were Italian, Joe Colombo announced the formation of the Italian-American Civil Rights League. This idea, this "League," had been discussed beforehand with Gambino, with Buster Aloi (Alloy), Carmine Tramunti, Tony "Ducks" Corallo, and almost anybody else of importance in the New York organization. The deal was that Colombo would be the titular head of the whole thing. The income was to be derived from memberships, which cost ten dollars per person. The idea was to get every Italian in New York to join, which could come out to be a couple of million people, or $20 million.

The $20 million was what the whole thing was all about. The League was more or less a shakedown operation, and a lot of people were convinced to join and pay their ten dollars. The money was to be split among the New York families.

Mr. Colombo's problems began when he forgot that there was a Carlo Gambino, Buster Aloi, Tramunti and Corallo, and he put the money in his own pocket. The newspapers wrote that the mob was angry because the Civil Rights League was attracting publicity to its operations, but that was bullshit. The League was a laughing fucking joke. Nobody cared about the publicity; organized crime had gotten publicity for years, whether we wanted it or not. Anyway this was good publicity, you might say. What got them mad was they weren't getting their fair shares. They were getting double-crossed, and they kept warning Colombo that there was going to be serious trouble if he didn't come through with the coin. While this was going on, Joey Gallo got out of jail.

In public Gallo said he had been reformed in prison, that he had read a lot of books and learned a great deal, and that from now on he was going to play it straight if the mob would let him. In private the first thing he did was go to see Carlo Gambino. "Listen," he told him, "south Brooklyn is mine and I ain't giving it up." He wanted the dock area, the President Street area, the bookmaking, the shylocking, the muscles, everything he had before he went to prison. The old man agreed, and Joe Colombo agreed. Colombo was not thrilled but he had no choice. Gambino said that was the way it was going to be, and you do not go against Gambino and live too awfully long.

The final straw with Colombo and Gambino came when an audit of the League's books showed it was bankrupt. Everybody knew there was plenty of money around and it was obvious that Colombo was keeping it. A meeting was held at Buster Aloi's house and word filtered back to me that Carlo sat there and said very explicitly, "I want Joe Colombo hit in the head like a pig."

Guess who they offered the job to? Joey Gallo would have given anything to set this deal up and so he was given the contract. Joey did not instigate this at all, he didn't have the power. Only bosses can approve the killing of another boss. But Colombo had to go because he had gotten to the point where he believed he was bigger than the mob, that he was indestructible. Wrong.

Hitting a boss is a very complicated undertaking, if you'll excuse the expresssion. In order to get him you have to have people within his own organization who are willing to double-cross him. Joe Colombo's chief bodyguard at this time was a man by the name of Gennaro (Fat Jerry) Ciprio, and he was the man who had to be gotten to put Colombo in a position where he could be assassinated. He agreed—I assume he was promised more money and power—and the arrangements were made through him. Colombo was to be killed at his own giant Civil Rights League rally in Columbus Circle, right in the middle of Manhattan. They decided on the rally because it was the perfect place to cause mass confusion, which was exactly what they wanted.

Gallo also had to find a man to pull the trigger. He didn't want to use one of his own people because he knew there was no way the killer could get away after the shooting. Through the connections Gallo made while he was in prison he was able to find a black man stupid enough to believe that he was going to get $100,000 or so for committing this particular crime. In reality all he was going to get for his efforts was a bullet in the head. He was dead the minute he agreed to do the job. The mob couldn't afford to let him live, he simply knew too much. It was a real sucker job.

Ciprio, Colombo's bodyguard, was responsible for the actual details of the plan. It took about a month to set the whole thing up. Ciprio had to get press credentials for Jerome Johnson, the killer, to get through the dozens of cops that were in the area. Again, these credentials had to be provided by someone with the organization. And Ciprio had to maneuver Colombo into a position where Johnson would have a clean, clear shot at him. Usually, if you're a bodyguard you shield your man with your own body. If you are out to let him get hit you step aside. Ciprio stayed up on the grandstand and watched the whole thing happen. Colombo should have been killed but he wasn't—although for all practical purposes he's dead because he isn't anything but a vegetable now. Johnson blew the job (the consequences of hiring an amateur) but he didn't live long enough to know that.

The minute he pulled the trigger Ciprio leaped off the stand and headed for him. A New York City cop, who had no knowledge of the plan, wrestled the gun away from Johnson and had him on the ground. The cop never saw Ciprio come up from behind and blow Johnson's brains out. If that cop had been a little quicker, or Ciprio a little slower, Johnson would have lived to tell a very interesting story.

When the shooting took place both Gallo and Gambino were miles and miles away from Columbus Circle. All they had to do was sweat it out that everything went right. Fortunately for them, it did. But there was no doubt who set the whole thing up, and had Gambino not backed Gallo, Joey would have been dead within 48 hours. There is no doubt about that. But the fact that Gallo was seen with Gambino after the shooting was enough to stop everybody. No matter how much people would have liked to take care of Joey they didn't dare. It was obvious he had the old man's approval and therefore had to be left alone.

That didn't mean there wasn't going to be a fight. As I said, some potential wars are settled peacefully, but this one didn't have a chance once Joe Colombo got hit. Forget about it. Blood had to run. It had to.

But not right away. Gang wars are expensive and people go out of their way to avoid them. So a very uneasy peace settled over the New York organization. Joey, of course, started getting more powerful. He was busy pretending he had gotten out of the rackets, he was on parole at the time, which had something to do with that act, and was getting chummy with show-business people. According to newspaper columnists, he was also writing a book. As he should have realized, the worst thing you can do in this business is become publicity-conscious. Unfortunately, Joey Gallo liked to read about himself in the newspapers.

Businesswise Joey started to consolidate his gains. Now he had had a hardon for Carmine Persico ever since Junior (the Snake) had tried to kill his brother. So Joey cried no tears when Carmine got 14 years in a federal penitentiary for hijacking. Now the positions were reversed, Joey was out and the Persico mob was being run by Alphonse Persico and Lenny Dell. Joey simply told them he was taking over. The Persico people realized there was nothing they could do, they weren't strong enough to hold the organization together without Junior. So they went to see Carlo Gambino.

Gambino owed Joey something, so when Dell and Persico went to see him he just shrugged his shoulders and said that this was between Gallo and them. That was his way of protecting Joey, his way of letting the Persico people know that he wasn't going to help them, that Joey would be allowed to do whatever he was strong enough to do. He didn't believe for a second they would be strong enough to knock Joey off and he figured, like everyone else, that they would have to capitulate and give it all up. It didn't work that way.

The Persico people went to Tony Colombo and Joe Colombo, Jr., and acting boss Joseph Yacovelli and explained the situation. The way I understand the conversation, they told the Colombo people that if Gallo took over Persico's organization he would be strong enough to take over the Colombo people next. This made a great deal of sense all around, and both groups went back to the old man. If Gallo took them over, they said, he would eventually have to go after Gambino. And everyone knew Joey was a very ambitious man. They finally told the old man that they were going to fight Joey Gallo and, if they did, they would fight him too. That's when Carlo decided he could live without Joey. Colombo and Persico were threatening all-out war, and since he, Gambino, was fighting extradition at that moment, all-out war was something he could do without. So he agreed to let them kill Gallo.

But the Colombo people wanted more than permission. They knew they were now doing Gambino a favor and, in return, wanted the names of the people within the Colombo organization who had set up Joe Colombo to be killed. This was their price, and Carlo agreed it was a fair one.

I was told Joey Gallo was going to be killed about three weeks before it happened. I was sitting in an Italian restaurant on 86th Street in Brooklyn, and Lenny Dell said to me, "There's going to be an open contract on Gallo. Do you want it?"

I said, "No, I'm not thrilled about it."

He said, "Okay, but then we're gonna need guns, you like to come to work?"

No way. "Look, Lenny, let's be realistic," I told him. "I know you and I know Joey and I know the Colombo people. I've been doing business with you people in one form or another for years. I don't want to offend nobody. If I take sides now, that means I got to take sides for the rest of my life. I just don't want to do it." I had the right to refuse the job, which I did. But it is also understood that I must keep my mouth shut; I can't discuss the fact that the contract was out with any-body. An open contract means that anybody who has the balls can do it, and anybody with brains shuts up about it.

I wasn't afraid to see Joey Gallo, even though I knew there was a contract out on him, because when Joey went out in public he always had at least one bodyguard with him who could be trusted. Number two, I always carried a cannon, and number three, the man was my friend. So what was I going to do? I had dinner with Joey twice between the time I knew the contract was out and the night the actual hit took place. I never even felt an urge to tell him what was happening. I didn't have to, he knew something was up. I just looked at him and thought, "Well, sucker, you took your best shot, now they're going to take theirs." I never even thought about telling him. I figured he had to know they were looking to hurt him, but he made the same mistake Colombo made, he figured he was Joey Gallo and nobody would dare do anything to him.

His real mistake was not keeping closer tabs on Gambino. He figured Carlo was his man, and he was, but Carlo just didn't want a big war breaking out. What Joey should have done was, instead of talking with Dell and Persico, he should have killed them. Had he done that he would have eliminated all his problems. Their people would have either walked away or come into his organization. Remember, all most men want is a chance to earn a living and he really doesn't care much who gives it to him.

Again, if you are going to hit a boss you have to have help. Even if you are going to hit Joey Gallo. Now, when Joey was killed his bodyguard Pete the Greek was with him and made a legitimate attempt to guard him. Pete used to be with Colombo, but since he himself was wounded and did some shooting trying to defend Joey, it's obvious where his loyalties were. But there was a second bodyguard, a guy named Bobby, who had also been to the Copa with Joey and Pete and Joey's family that night. When he was asked to go along to Umberto's Clam House he refused, saying he was going with some broads. I would have to say this was probably when the phone call was made telling where Joey Gallo would be.

To this day I really don't know who did the job. The story seems to be that this guy Luparelli saw Gallo going into the restaurant and went to the social club where he picked up Carmine DiBiase. They contacted Yacovelli, who was running the Colombo mob and making the payment, and he said go ahead. DiBiase, or whoever, then walked into Umberto's, killed Gallo, and shot Pete the Greek. After finishing the job, he ran out and hopped into the car Luparelli claims he was driving. They drove to Nyack, New York, and laid low.

Eventually Luparelli got the idea that they were trying to poison him in his hideout and split.

I can't buy this whole story, there are just too many contradictions in it. I'm not saying DiBiase didn't pull the trigger, I just doubt it happened like Luparelli says it did. Believe me, I'm not trying to defend DiBiase. He and I almost had it out in a social club on Mulberry Street one sunny afternoon.

I didn't really know Carmine very well, but we had both been involved in a business deal and it annoyed him that I kept the best piece for myself. When we were making the cash split he made some nasty remarks about my ethnic background and I smacked him in the mouth. Then I went home.

The next day I got a message that Carmine was sitting around his social club threatening to kill me. I could see that if he tried to follow through it would put a terrific strain on our friendship, so I decided to beat him to the punch, so to speak. I picked up my .357 magnum, which is one mighty big cap gun, and I drove down to the social club. I walked in and pulled the gun out of my belt and stuck it right between his eyes. "I understand you don't like me," I said.

One look at Carmine's eyes told me he was upset that this rumor had gotten around and he felt this was the proper time to dispel it. "Like you?" he replied. "Like you? I love you!"

It was nice to know the rumors were unfounded. "Fine," I said, "and if I were you, I'd make sure the romance lasts."

So you understand I never received my membership card in the Carmine DiBiase Fan Club. But let us assume you have a hit going. I'm sitting in my social club and you come and tell me so-and-so is in such a place. Now, I have to get permission before I can go ahead, so I'm gonna pick up the phone and call a man at his home or at his girlfriend's, right? Wrong. Wherever he is, no two ways about it, that phone has got to be tapped. Second, I'm not gonna have you sitting in the car while I go inside and shoot it out myself. Third, I'm not gonna take you to a hideout I got and, all of a sudden, try and kill you. And if I was going to kill you, why would I bother poisoning you? What the fuck do I want to do that for when I can just as easily pull the trigger? I mean, the whole story doesn't hold water with me. But I don't know a better version. It doesn't really matter anyway; the end result was the same. So long, Joey.

The newspapers made a big deal out of the fact that Gallo was hit in front of his wife and daughter, which is a clear violation of mob rules. But they forgot that Joe Colombo was hit in front of his family. Tit for tat. One thing about the mob, they'll even things up, one way or another.

The shooting really started after Joey was killed. I met with one of the Gallo people who asked me if I wanted to throw in with them until the shooting was over. "I turned the other people down," I said, "why should I join you?" I wanted nothing to do with it. What did I need it for? I'm not some young punk looking to make a reputation.

Normally it is easy to recruit guns during a war. First of all, you know the people who have worked with guns before and you contact them. You offer them X dollars to remain with your people for the length of the shooting. It's not going to last more than a couple of months because there is nobody that can afford it; it's a physical impossibility. You hire a good gun and you're going to have to pay him a minimum of $5000 a week plus a bonus for everybody he shoots, $20,000 or so, just to keep him there. No professional will risk his life—which is what he is doing—for less. And business is severely curtailed during the fighting. You have to send someone around to protect your people as they make their rounds, and even then they may see only half their regular customers. And you've got to have some people patrolling the neighborhood, riding around making sure there are no strange faces in the area. A gang war is when you find out who your friends are.

During a war everybody in the organization automatically becomes a gun, even though they really can't handle anything. But on paper they are considered a gun. Plus you have whatever you can grab. You try to have 30 or 40 people who can pull the trigger, and if you're paying them $5000 a week it is going to get very expensive. So it won't last too long.

Once the war breaks out it's easy to see who is siding with who. Just take a ride through their territory and see who's hanging out in the area. And as for the people who have been paying off one boss, if they stop he knows they can't be working with him. That only leaves one other side.

As it turned out the Gallo people couldn't get enough men together to make a fight of it. You have to have something to pay people with, and they evidently didn't have it. There is no longer a Gallo organization. It was completely destroyed when Joey died. It was taken over by Colombo-Persico. The people in Joey's group were drafted, almost like they do in sports, first one family making a selection and then the other and so on. The Gallo people had two choices: either do business with the new people or be completely cut out. Albert Gallo, for example, threw in with Colombo. Business, as they say, is business.

In all, a total of about 12 people went down. They were turning up in car trunks and vacant lots all over the city. Once they had the names, it was a simple process for the Colombo people to eliminate those men within their own organization who had double-crossed Joe Colombo.

The day before Gallo was killed Thomas Edwards (Tommy Ernst) was shot to death on his father-in-law's porch.

That same day Bruno Carnevale was shot in Queens. He had $14,000 on him when the cops found him.

Ciprio was shot three days after Gallo died. He owned a restaurant in Brooklyn and he walked out one night and was gunned down.

Richard Grossman, who I never heard of and who I doubt was involved in this thing, was found the same day, stuffed in a trunk of an abandoned car in Brooklyn.

Frank Ferriano went down the same day.

William Della Russo went down five days later.

Rosario Stabile was shot in his car a day after Della Russo.

I think you get the point. Gang wars are about as much fun as walking through a plate-glass window. There is no excitement, no adventure, only a lot of time spent laying low. It always seemed to me that if your average citizen finds them so exciting, he should choose up sides and go at it himself. But please leave me out of it.

from **Wiseguy**
by **Nicholas Pileggi**

*Crime reporter Nicholas Pileggi's (born 1933) 1985 col-
laboration with ex-wiseguy Henry Hill helped popularize
mobster realism. Like Tony Soprano, Henry and his pals
must endure mob-style versions of familiar problems—
family, money, work.*

For most of the guys the killings were just accepted. They were a
part of every day. They were routine. I remember how proud
Tommy DeSimone was when he brought Jimmy's kid, Frankie, on
his first hit. Frankie Burke was just a timid little kid. Jimmy used
to complain that the kid wet his bed all the time and that Jimmy had
to beat the shit out of him almost every night. Jimmy even sent him to
some military school to toughen him up. Frankie must have been sixteen or seventeen when Tommy took him on the hit, and Tommy
said the kid held up great. Jimmy walked around real proud. You'd
have thought the kid had won a medal.

"Murder was the only way everybody stayed in line. It was the ultimate weapon. Nobody was immune. You got out of line, you got
whacked. Everyone knew the rules, but still people got out of line and
people kept getting whacked. Johnny Mazzolla, the guy I used to go

cashing counterfeit twenties with when I was a kid, his own son was killed because the kid wouldn't stop holding up local card games and bookmakers. The kid was warned a hundred times. They warned the father to keep the kid under wraps. They told him if the kid had to stick up bookmakers, he should go stick up foreign bookmakers. It was only because of Johnny that they let the kid live until he was nineteen. But the kid apparently couldn't believe he would ever get killed. The dead ones never did. He couldn't believe it until the end when he got two, close range, in the heart. That was out of respect for his father. They left the kid's face clean so there could be an open casket at the funeral.

"Jimmy once killed his best friend, Remo, because he found out that Remo set up one of his cigarette loads for a pinch. They were so close. They went on vacations together with their wives. But when one of Remo's small loads got busted, he told the cops about a trailer truck-load Jimmy was putting together. Jimmy got suspicious when Remo invested only five thousand dollars in the two-hundred-thousand-dollar load. Remo usually took a third or fifty percent of the shipment. When Jimmy asked him why, he wasn't going in on this load, Remo said he didn't need that much. Of course, when the truck got stopped and Jimmy's whole shipment was confiscated, the fact that Remo had somehow not invested in that particular shipment got Jimmy curious enough to ask some of his friends in the Queens DA's office. They confirmed Jimmy's suspicion that Remo had ratted the load out in return for his freedom.

"Remo was dead within a week. He didn't have a clue what was coming to him. Jimmy could look at you and smile and you'd think you were sitting with your best friend in the world. Meanwhile he's got your grave dug. In fact, the very week Jimmy killed him, Remo had given Jimmy and Mickey a round-trip ticket to Florida as an anniversary present.

"I remember the night. We were all playing cards in Robert's when Jimmy said to Remo, 'Let's take a ride.' He motioned to Tommy and another guy to come along. Remo got in the front seat and Tommy and

Jimmy got in the rear. When they got to a quiet area, Tommy used a piano wire. Remo put up some fight. He kicked and swung and shit all over himself before he died. They buried him in the backyard at Robert's, under a layer of cement right next to the boccie court. From then on, every time they played, Jimmy and Tommy used to say, 'Hi, Remo, how ya doing?'

"It didn't take anything for these guys to kill you. They liked it. They would sit around drinking booze and talk about their favorite hits. They enjoyed talking about them. They liked to relive the moment while repeating how miserable the guy was. He was always the worst sonofabitch they knew. He was always a rat bastard, and most of the time it wasn't even business. Guys would get into arguments with each other and before you knew it one of them was dead. They were shooting each other all the time. Shooting people was a normal thing for them. It was no big deal. You didn't have to do anything. You just had to be there.

"One night, right after my arrest for assaulting the wrong guy, we were having a party in Robert's for Billy Batts. Billy had just gotten out of prison after six years. We usually gave a guy a party when he got out. Food. Booze. Hookers. It's a good time. Billy was a made guy. He was with Johnny Gotti from near Fulton Street and he was hooked up with the Gambinos. We're all bombed. Jimmy. Tommy. Me. Billy turned around and he saw Tommy, who he knew from before he went away. Tommy was only about twenty at the time, so the last time Billy saw him Tommy was just a kid. Billy started to kid around. He asked Tommy if he still shined shoes. It was just a snide remark, but you couldn't kid around with Tommy. He was wired very tight. One of Tommy's brothers had ratted people out years ago, and he was always living that down. He always had to show he was tougher than anyone around. He always had to be special. He was the only guy in the crew that used to drink Crown Royal. It was a Canadian whiskey that wasn't imported back when he was a kid. Tommy had it smuggled in. He was the kind of guy who was being so tough he managed to find a bootleg hooch to drink thirty years after Prohibition.

"I looked over at Tommy, and I could see he was fuming at the way Billy was talking. Tommy was going nuts, but he couldn't do or say anything. Billy was a made man. If Tommy so much as took a slap at Billy, Tommy was dead. Still, I knew he was pissed. We kept drinking and laughing, and just when I thought maybe it was all forgotten, Tommy leaned over to Jimmy and me and said, 'I'm gonna kill that fuck.' I joked back with him, but I saw he was serious.

"A couple of weeks later Billy was drinking in The Suite. It was late. I was praying he'd go home when Tommy walked in. It didn't take long. Tommy immediately sent his girlfriend home and he gave me and Jimmy a look. Right away Jimmy started getting real cozy with Billy Batts. He started buying Billy drinks. I could see he was setting Billy up for Tommy.

" 'Keep him here, I'm going for a bag,' Tommy whispered to me, and I knew he was going to kill Billy right in my own joint. He was going for a body bag—a plastic mattress cover—so Billy wouldn't bleed all over the place after he killed him. Tommy was back with the bag and a thirty-eight in twenty minutes. I was getting sick.

'By now Jimmy has Billy Batts in the corner of the bar near the wall. They were drinking and Jimmy was telling him stories. Billy was having a great time. As it got late almost everybody went home. Only Alex Corcione, who was seated in back with his girl, was left in the place. The bartender left. Jimmy had his arm hanging real loose around Billy's shoulder when Tommy came over. Billy didn't even look up. Why should he? He was with friends. Fellow wiseguys. He had no idea that Tommy was going to kill him.

"I was on the side of the bar when Tommy took the thirty-eight out of his pocket. Billy saw it in Tommy's hand. The second Billy saw what was happening, Jimmy tightened his arm around Billy's neck. 'Shine these fuckin' shoes,' Tommy yells and smashes the gun right into the side of Billy's head. Billy's eyes opened wide. Tommy smashed him again. Jimmy kept his grip. The blood began to come out of Billy's head. It looked black.

"By now Alex Corcione saw what was going on and he started to come over. Jimmy glared at him. 'You want some?' Jimmy said. Jimmy was ready to drop Billy and go after Alex. I got between them as though I was going to belt Alex. But I just grabbed Alex by the shoulders and steered him toward the door. 'Get out of here,' I said, real quiet, so Jimmy can't hear. 'They've got a beef.' I maneuvered Alex and his girl out the door and they were gone. Alex was with our own crew, but Jimmy and Tommy were so hot right then they would have whacked Alex and his girl right there if he gave them trouble. I locked the front door, and when I turned back I saw that Billy's body was spread out on the floor. His head was a bloody mess. Tommy had opened the mattress cover. Jimmy told me to bring the car around back.

"We had a problem. Billy Batts was untouchable. There has to be an okay before a made man can be killed. If the Gambino people ever found out that Tommy killed Billy, we were all dead. There was no place we could go. They could even have demanded that Paulie whack us himself. Tommy had done the worst possible thing he could have done, and we all knew it. Billy's body had to disappear. We couldn't leave it on the street. There would have been a war. With no body around, the Gotti crew would never know for sure.

"Jimmy said we had to bury the body where it couldn't be found. He had a friend upstate with a dog kennel, where nobody would ever look. We put Billy in the trunk of the car, and we drove by Tommy's house to pick up a shovel. His mother was already up and made us come in for coffee. She wouldn't let us leave. We have to have breakfast—with a body parked outside.

"Finally we left Tommy's and got on the Taconic. We'd been driving about an hour when I heard a funny noise. I'm in the back half asleep, with the shovel. Tommy was driving. Jimmy was asleep. I heard the noise again. It was like a thump. Jimmy woke up. The banging began again. It dawned on all of us at once. Billy Batts was alive. He was banging on the trunk. We were on our way to bury him and he wasn't even dead.

"Now Tommy really got mad. He slammed on the brakes. He leaned over the seat and grabbed the shovel. Nobody said a word. We got out of the car and waited until there were no more headlights coming up behind us. Then Jimmy got on one side and I got on the other and Tommy opened the trunk. The second it sprang open Tommy smashed the sack with the shovel. Jimmy grabbed a tire iron and he started banging away at the sack. It only took a few seconds, and we got back in the car. When we got to the spot where we were going to bury Billy, the ground was so frozen we had to dig for an hour to get him down deep enough. Then we covered him with lime and drove back to New York.

"But even then Billy was like a curse. About three months after we planted the guy, Jimmy came up to me at The Suite and said Tommy and I would have to dig up the body and bury it somewhere else. The guy who owned the kennel had just sold his property to a housing developer. He had been bragging to Jimmy about how much money he was going to make, but all Jimmy knew was that workmen might find the body. That night Tommy and I took my brand-new yellow Pontiac Catalina convertible and we dug Billy up. It was awful. We had put lime on the body to help it decompose, but it was only half gone. The smell was so bad I got sick. I started to throw up. All the time Tommy and I worked I was throwing up. We put the body in the trunk and took it to a junkyard we used in Jersey. Enough time had passed so nobody was going to think it was Billy.

"I stayed sick for a week. I couldn't get away from the smell. Everything smelled like the body. The restaurant grease. The kids' candy. I couldn't stop smelling it. I threw away the clothes, even the shoes I wore that night, thinking they were the problem. I couldn't get the smell of it out of the trunk of my car. I ripped out all the upholstery and threw it away. I gave the car a real scrubbing. I tossed a bottle of Karen's perfume inside and closed the lid. But I couldn't get rid of the smell. It never went away. I finally had to junk the car. Jimmy and Tommy thought I was nuts. Tommy said if he could have smelled it he would have kept the car just to remind him about how he took care of that miserable bastard Billy Batts.

"I don't know how many people Tommy killed. I don't even think

Jimmy knew. Tommy was out of control. He'd begun carrying two guns. One night Tommy shot a kid named Spider in the foot just because the kid didn't want to dance. It looked accidental, and Vinnie Asaro, who's with the Bonanno crew, took Spider to a neighborhood doctor to get the kid fixed up. We let Spider sleep in Robert's for a couple of weeks. He was walking around with his leg in bandages. But crazy Tommy kept making the kid dance. Tommy said he was using the kid for target practice.

"One night we're playing cards in the cellar—Tommy, Jimmy, me, Anthony Stabile, Angelo Sepe—when the Spider walks in. It's three o'clock in the morning and we're all smashed out of our minds. All of a sudden Tommy wants him to dance. 'Do a dance,' Tommy says. For some reason Spider tells Tommy to go fuck himself. Now we started getting on Tommy. Jimmy is joking and he says to Tommy, 'You take that shit from this punk?' We're all egging Tommy on, joking with him. He's getting mad, but he's still playing cards. Then, before anyone has any idea what he's going to do, he puts three shots into Spider's chest. I didn't even know where he had the gun, except for a second we're all deaf. I can smell burn. Nobody says a word, but now I'm convinced Tommy is a total psychopath.

"Finally Jimmy yelled at him, 'All right, you dumb fuck, if you're going to be a big fucking wise guy, you dig the hole.' That was it. Nothing else. Nobody said anything else. Jimmy just made Tommy dig the hole right there in the cellar, and all the while Tommy was grousing and pissed off that he had to dig the hole. He was like a kid who had been bad and had to clean the erasers after school.

"Every day was some kind of war. Every day was another sit-down. Every time we went out bouncing, somebody got bombed and there was a war. Everybody was getting very hot all the time. One night Paulie, who was usually calm, came into Robert's crazy mad. He wanted everybody. Call Jimmy. Call the cabstand. Get Brooksie from the junkyard. I thought it was a full-scale war. It turned out that he and Phyllis had gone to Don Pepe's Vesuvio Restaurant, on Lefferts Boulevard, just a few blocks south of Robert's. Don Pepe's was a great restaurant, but the owner was a real pain. There were no menus, and he wouldn't take reservations. Everybody waited on line, even Paulie.

"It turned out that Paulie and Phyllis had waited on line for half an hour while a new maître d' kept seating one doctor after another in front of Paulie. When Paulie complained, the guy finally gave him a table, but he was pissed at Paulie. When Paulie ordered some wine, the maître d' came to pour and, maybe by accident, spilled it all over Phyllis. By now Paulie's coming out of his skin. But when the maître d' pulled out a dirty rag and started putting his hands all over Phyllis' dress, Paulie turned over the table, and he started to slap the guy around. Paulie only managed to get one or two swings at the guy before he ran into the kitchen. When Paulie told him to come out, a half dozen waiters with heavy pans and knives blocked the kitchen door.

"I never saw Paulie so angry. He said if the waiters wanted to protect their friend, then they were all going to get their heads broken. Within an hour we had two carloads of guys with baseball bats and pipes waiting outside Don Pepe's. By eleven o'clock the waiters and kitchen help got off. The minute they saw us waiting for them they started to run. A few jumped in cars. We were chasing waiters and breaking heads all over Brooklyn that night.

"It was so easy. Lump them up. Whack them out. Nobody ever thought, Why? What for? Nobody thought about business. The truth was the violence began to damage the business. The hijackings, for instance, had been going beautifully, but all of a sudden everyone began getting very loose with their hands. 'Whack 'em!' 'Fuck 'em!' That's all they knew.

"I didn't usually go out on the actual hijackings. There was Tommy, Stanley, Joey Allegro, and other guys who enjoyed sticking a gun in a driver's face. I usually dealt with the distribution of the stuff. I had the buyers. I lined up some of the deals. Sometimes, however, if we got shorthanded I'd go on the heist myself. On this occasion we had a two-hundred-thousand-dollar cigarette load. It was going to be easy. It was half a 'give-up,' which meant one of the two drivers was in on the deal.

"We grabbed them right near their garage at the Elk Street warehouse. They were making the turn onto the Brooklyn-Queens Expressway when Tommy and Stanley jumped on the running boards, one on each side. They showed guns. Joey Allegro and I are in the backup car. Stanley made the driver who's with us give up the dashboard code. Big trucks with valuable loads usually had a keyboard under the dash with three buttons. You need to know the code to start the engine, or even open and close the doors, or the truck's burglar alarm would go off.

"Tommy put the drivers in the car and got in with Joey, and I got in the truck with Stanley, and we headed for the drop, which was a legitimate truck warehouse near the General Post Office on West Thirty-sixth Street. Jimmy was waiting there with five unloaders. He had long rollers, and we started running the cigarette cartons out of the trailer and into other trucks. There were other trucks being unloaded at the same time, and of course none of the workmen knew we were unloading a hot truck. We were in the middle of the job when this big burly guy comes over and wants to see our union cards. We don't have union cards, we've got guns.

"He was a big, chesty guy and he didn't know Jimmy and he didn't give a fuck. He started a beef that Jimmy's unloaders were not members of the union. He was going to close the whole place down. Jimmy tried to talk to him. No good. Jimmy tried to take care of him with a few bucks. No good. The guy wanted to see our union cards. He was a real pain, and Jimmy had another two hundred thousand dollars' worth of cigarettes lined up to be unloaded in the same place the next day.

"By now we've got the truck pretty well cleaned out, except for twenty cases of Laredo roll-your-own cigarettes we left in the track because nobody wanted them. Jimmy motioned to me and Stanley to move the truck out of there. Stanley, thank God, remembered the dashboard code to start the engine without the alarm going off, and within seconds we're heading down Ninth Avenue toward the Lincoln Tunnel and New Jersey to dump the truck.

"We hadn't gone a couple of blocks before I noticed that people were waving at us. They were screaming at us. They're pointing to the back of the truck. I stick my head out the window and I realize that Jimmy and the crew forgot to lock the back of the trailer and we've been dropping cartons of Laredo cigarettes along Ninth Avenue. It's unbelievable. People were screaming at us and we were pretending not to hear them, but when we got to the next corner, parked right in front of us was a police radio car. That was it. I looked at Stanley and said, 'Pull over and let's close it.' Stanley just looked at me, blank. I said, 'If I don't lock that rear door, we're going to get stopped.' But he looked really sad and said I couldn't lock the back door because I couldn't get out of the truck without triggering the alarm. He said he had been trying to remember the dashboard code for opening the doors, but he couldn't. If I got out of the truck in the middle of Ninth Avenue all the alarms would go off.

"I remember we just looked at each other for a minute, said 'Fuck it,' and wiggled out the truck windows. We must have looked pretty peculiar. As soon as we hit the pavement we took off. We made sure we weren't followed and went back to the drop, where Jimmy's really steaming because the union guy is still busting his chops. The guy was threatening Jimmy. He said there wouldn't be another truck unloaded unless the workers were union. The guy was hopeless.

"That night Jimmy sent Stanley Diamond and Tommy DeSimone to New Jersey, where the guy lived, to straighten him out. They were just going to rough him up a little bit. Just get him to mind his own business a little bit. Instead, Stanley and Tommy got so carried away with the ball buster that they killed the guy. They were so pissed that the guy wouldn't listen to Jimmy, that he lived in the boondocks of Jersey, and that they had to go all the way out there just to talk to him, they got themselves so worked up that they just couldn't keep from killing him."

from The Godfather
by Mario Puzo

Mario Puzo (1920–1999) is best remembered for his 1969 novel The Godfather, *as well as his Oscar-winning scripts for the first two* Godfather *movies. This passage from the book tells of Vito Corleone's rise from Sicilian peasant boy to "man of respect" in the immigrant slums of New York City.*

The Don was a real man at the age of twelve. Short, dark, slender, living in the strange Moorish-looking village of Corleone in Sicily, he had been born Vito Andolini, but when strange men came to kill the son of the man they had murdered, his mother sent the young boy to America to stay with friends. And in the new land he changed his name to Corleone to preserve some tie with his native village. It was one of the few gestures of sentiment he was ever to make.

In Sicily at the turn of the century the Mafia was the second government, far more powerful than the official one in Rome. Vito Corleone's father became involved in a feud with another villager who took his case to the Mafia. The father refused to knuckle under and in a public quarrel killed the local Mafia chief. A week later he himself was found dead, his body torn apart by *lupara* blasts. A month after the funeral Mafia gunmen came inquiring after the young boy, Vito. They had decided that he was too close to manhood, that he might try to avenge the death of his father in the years to come. The twelve-year-old Vito was hidden by relatives and shipped to America. There he was boarded with the Abbandandos, whose son Genco was later to become *Consigliori* to his Don.

Young Vito went to work in the Abbandando grocery store on Ninth Avenue in New York's Hell's Kitchen. At the age of eighteen Vito married an Italian girl freshly arrived from Sicily, a girl of only sixteen but a skilled cook, a good housewife. They settled down in a tenement on Tenth Avenue, near 35th Street, only a few blocks from where Vito worked, and two years later were blessed with their first child, Santino, called by all his friends Sonny because of his devotion to his father.

In the neighborhood lived a man called Fanucci. He was a heavy-set, fierce-looking Italian who wore expensive light-colored suits and a cream-colored fedora. This man was reputed to be of the "Black Hand," an offshoot of the Mafia which extorted money from families and storekeepers by threat of physical violence. However, since most of the inhabitants of the neighborhood were violent themselves, Fanucci's threats of bodily harm were effective only with elderly couples without male children to defend them. Some of the storekeepers paid him trifling sums as a matter of convenience. However, Fanucci was also a scavenger on fellow criminals, people who illegally sold Italian lottery or ran gambling games in their homes. The Abbandando grocery gave him a small tribute, this despite the protests of young Genco, who told his father he would settle the Fanucci hash. His father forbade him. Vito Corleone observed all this without feeling in any way involved.

One day Fanucci was set upon by three young men who cut his throat from ear to ear, not deeply enough to kill him, but enough to frighten him and make him bleed a great deal. Vito saw Fanucci fleeing from his punishers, the circular slash flowing red. What he never forgot was Fanucci holding the cream-colored fedora under his chin to catch the dripping blood as he ran. As if he did not want his suit soiled or did not want to leave a shameful trail of carmine.

But this attack proved a blessing in disguise for Fanucci. The three young men were not murderers, merely tough young boys determined to teach him a lesson and stop him from scavenging. Fanucci proved himself a murderer. A few weeks later the knife-wielder was shot to death and the families of the other two young men paid an indemnity to Fanucci to make him forswear his vengeance. After that the tributes became higher and Fanucci became a partner in the neighborhood gambling games. As for Vito Corleone, it was none of his affair. He forgot about it immediately.

During World War I, when imported olive oil became scarce, Fanucci acquired a part-interest in the Abbandando grocery store by supplying it not only with oil, but imported Italian salami, hams and cheeses. He then moved a nephew into the store and Vito Corleone found himself out of a job.

By this time, the second child, Frederico, had arrived and Vito Corleone had four mouths to feed. Up to this time he had been a quiet, very contained young man who kept his thoughts to himself. The son of the grocery store owner, young Genco Abbandando, was his closest friend, and to the surprise of both of them, Vito reproached his friend for his father's deed. Genco, flushed with shame, vowed to Vito that he would not have to worry about food. That he, Genco, would steal food from the grocery to supply his friend's needs. This offer though was sternly refused by Vito as too shameful, a son stealing from his father.

The young Vito, however, felt a cold anger for the dreaded Fanucci. He never showed this anger in any way but bided his time. He worked in the railroad for a few months and then, when the war ended, work became slow and he could earn only a few days' pay a month. Also, most of the foremen were Irish and American and abused the workmen in the foulest language, which Vito always bore stone-faced as if he did not comprehend, though he understood English very well despite his accent.

One evening as Vito was having supper with his family there was a knock on the window that led to the open air shaft that separated them from the next building. When Vito pulled aside the curtain he saw to his astonishment one of the young men in the neighborhood, Peter Clemenza, leaning out from a window on the other side of the air shaft. He was extending a white-sheeted bundle.

"Hey, *paisan*," Clemenza said. "Hold these for me until I ask for them. Hurry up." Automatically Vito reached over the empty space of the air shaft and took the bundle. Clemenza's face was strained and urgent. He was in some sort of trouble and Vito's helping action was instinctive. But when he untied the bundle in his kitchen, there were five oily guns staining the white cloth. He put them in his bedroom closet and waited. He learned that Clemenza had been taken away by the police. They must have been knocking on his door when he handed the guns over the air shaft.

Vito never said a word to anyone and of course his terrified wife dared not open her lips even in gossip for fear her own husband would be sent to prison. Two days later Peter Clemenza reappeared in the neighborhood and asked Vito casually, "Do you have my goods still?"

Vito nodded. He was in the habit of talking little. Clemenza came up to his tenement flat and was given a glass of wine while Vito dug the bundle out of his bedroom closet.

Clemenza drank his wine, his heavy good-natured face alertly watching Vito. "Did you look inside?"

Vito, his face impassive; shook his head. "I'm not interested in things that don't concern me," he said.

They drank wine together the rest of the evening. They found each other congenial. Clemenza was a storyteller; Vito Corleone was a listener to storytellers. They became casual friends.

A few days later Clemenza asked the wife of Vito Corleone if she would like a fine rug for her living room floor. He took Vito with him to help carry the rug.

Clemenza led Vito to an apartment house with two marble pillars and a white marble stoop. He used a key to open the door and they were inside a plush apartment. Clemenza grunted, "Go on the other side of the room and help me roll it up."

The rug was a rich red wool. Vito Corleone was astonished by

Clemenza's generosity. Together they rolled the rug into a pile and Clemenza took one end while Vito took the other. They lifted it and started carrying it toward the door.

At that moment the apartment bell rang. Clemenza immediately dropped the rug and strode to the window. He pulled the drape aside slightly and what he saw made him draw a gun from inside his jacket. It was only at that moment the astonished Vito Corleone realized that they were stealing the rug from some stranger's apartment.

The apartment bell rang again. Vito went up alongside Clemenza so that he too could see what was happening. At the door was a uniformed policeman. As they watched, the policeman gave the doorbell a final push, then shrugged and walked away down the marble steps and down the street.

Clemenza grunted in a satisfied way and said, "Come on, let's go." He picked up his end of the rug and Vito picked up the other end. The policeman had barely turned the corner before they were edging out the heavy oaken door and into the street with the rug between them. Thirty minutes later they were cutting the rug to fit the living room, of Vito Corleone's apartment. They had enough left over for the bedroom. Clemenza was an expert workman and from the pockets of his wide, ill-fitting jacket (even then he liked to wear loose clothes though he was not so fat), he had the necessary carpet-cutting tools.

Time went on, things did not improve. The Corleone family could not eat the beautiful rug. Very well, there was no work, his wife and children must starve. Vito took some parcels of food from his friend Genco while he thought things out. Finally he was approached by Clemenza and Tessio, another young tough of the neighborhood. They were men who thought well of him, the way he carried himself, and they knew he was desperate. They proposed to him that he become one of their gang which specialized in hijacking trucks of silk dresses after those trucks were loaded up at the factory on 31st Street. There was no risk. The truck drivers were sensible workingmen who at the sight of a gun flopped on the sidewalk like angels while the hijackers drove the truck away, to be unloaded at a friend's warehouse. Some of the merchandise would be sold to an Italian wholesaler, part of the loot would be sold door-to-door in the Italian neighborhoods—Arthur Avenue in the Bronx, Mulberry Street, and the Chelsea district in Manhattan—all to poor Italian families looking for a bargain, whose daughters could never be able to afford such fine apparel. Clemenza and Tessio needed Vito to drive since they knew he chauffeured the Abbandando grocery store delivery truck. In 1919, skilled automobile drivers were at a premium.

Against his better judgment, Vito Corleone accepted their offer. The clinching argument was that he would clear at least a thousand dollars for his share of the job. But his young companions struck him as rash, the planning of the job haphazard, the distribution of the loot foolhardy. Their whole approach was too careless for his taste. But he thought them of good, sound character. Peter Clemenza, already burly, inspired a certain trust and the lean saturnine Tessio inspired confidence.

The job itself went off without a hitch. Vito Corleone felt no fear, much to his astonishment, when his two comrades flashed guns and made the driver get out of the silk truck. He was also impressed with the coolness of Clemenza and Tessio. They didn't get excited but joked with the driver, told him if he was a good lad they'd send his wife a few dresses. Because Vito thought it stupid to peddle dresses himself and so gave his whole share of stock to the fence, he made only seven hundred dollars. But this was a considerable sum of money in 1919.

The next day on the street, Vito Corleone was stopped by the cream-suited, white-fedoraed Fanucci. Fanucci was a brutal-looking man and he had done nothing to disguise the circular scar that stretched in a white semicircle from ear to ear, looping under his chin. He had heavy black brows and coarse features which, when he smiled, were in some odd way amiable.

He spoke with a very thick Sicilian accent. "Ah, young fellow," he said to Vito. "People tell me you're rich. You and your two friends. But don't you think you've treated me a little shabbily? After all, this is my neighborhood and you should let me wet my beak." He used the Sicilian phrase of the Mafia, *"Fari vagnari a pizzu."* *Pizzu* means the beak of any small bird such as a canary. The phrase itself was a demand for part of the loot.

As was his habit, Vito Corleone did not answer. He understood the implication immediately and was waiting for a definite demand.

Fanucci smiled at him, showing gold teeth and stretching his noose-like scar tight around his face. He mopped his face with a handkerchief and unbuttoned his jacket for a moment as if to cool himself but really to show the gun he carried stuck in the waistband of his comfortably wide trousers. Then he sighed and said, "Give me five hundred dollars and I'll forget the insult. After all, young people don't know the courtesies due a man like myself."

Vito Corleone smiled at him and even as a young man still unblooded, there was something so chilling in his smile that Fanucci hesitated a moment before going on. "Otherwise the police will come to see you; your wife and children will be shamed and destitute. Of course if my information as to your gains is incorrect I'll dip my beak just a little. But no less than three hundred dollars. And don't try to deceive me."

For the first time Vito Corleone spoke. His voice was reasonable, showed no anger. It was courteous, as befitted a young man speaking to an older man of Fanucci's eminence. He said softly, "My two friends have my share of the money, I'll have to speak to them."

Fanucci was reassured. "You can tell your two friends that I expect them to let me wet my beak in the same manner. Don't be afraid to tell them," he added reassuringly. "Clemenza and I know each other well, he understands these things. Let yourself be guided by him. He has more experience in these matters."

Vito Corleone shrugged. He tried to look a little embarrassed. "Of course, he said. "You understand this is all new to me. Thank you for speaking to me as a godfather."

Fanucci was impressed. "You're a good fellow," he said. He took Vito's hand and clasped it in both of his hairy ones. "You have respect," he said. "A fine thing in the young. Next time speak to me first, eh? Perhaps I can help you in your plans."

In later years Vito Corleone understood that what had made him act in such a perfect, tactical way with Fanucci was the death of his own hot-tempered father who had been killed by the Mafia in Sicily. But at that time all he felt was an icy rage that this man planned to rob him of the money he had risked his life and freedom to earn. He had not been afraid. Indeed he thought, at that moment, that Fanucci was a crazy fool. From what he had seen of Clemenza, that burly Sicilian would sooner give up his life than a penny of his loot. After all, Clemenza had been ready to kill a policeman merely to steal a rug. And the slender Tessio had the deadly air of a viper.

But later that night, in Clemenza's tenement apartment across the air shaft, Vito Corleone received another lesson in the education he had just begun. Clemenza cursed, Tessio scowled, but then both men started talking about whether Fanucci would be satisfied with two hundred dollars. Tessio thought he might.

Clemenza was positive. "No, that scarface bastard must have found out what we made from the wholesaler who bought the dresses. Fanucci won't take a dime less than three hundred dollars. We'll have to pay."

Vito was astonished but was careful not to show his astonishment. "Why do we have to pay him? What can he do to the three of us? We're stronger than him. We have guns. Why do we have to hand over the money we earned?"

Clemenza explained patiently. "Fanucci has friends, real brutes. He has connections with the police. He'd like us to tell him our plans because he could set us up for the cops and earn their gratitude. Then they would owe him a favor. That's how he operates. And he has a license from Maranzalla himself to work this neighborhood." Maranzalla was a gangster often in the newspapers, reputed to be the leader of a criminal ring specializing in extortion, gambling and armed robbery.

Clemenza served wine that he had made himself. His wife, after putting a plate of salami, olives and a loaf of Italian bread on the table, went down to sit with her women cronies in front of the building, carrying her chair with her. She was a young Italian girl only a few years in the country and did not yet understand English.

Vito Corleone sat with his two friends and drank wine. He had never used his intelligence before as he was using it now. He was surprised at how clearly he could think. He recalled everything he knew about Fanucci. He remembered the day the man had had his throat cut and had run down the street holding his fedora under his chin to catch the dripping blood. He remembered the murder of the man who had wielded the knife and the other two having their sentences removed by paying an indemnity. And suddenly he was sure that Fanucci had no great connections, could not possibly have. Not a man who informed to the police. Not a man who allowed his vengeance to be bought off. A real *Mafioso* chief would have had the other two men killed also. No. Fanucci had got lucky and killed one man but had known he could not kill the other two after they were alerted. And so he had allowed himself to be paid. It was the personal brutal force of the man that allowed him to levy tribute on the shopkeepers, the gambling games that ran in the tenement apartments. But Vito Corleone knew of at least one gambling game that had never paid Fanucci tributes and nothing had ever happened to the man running it.

And so it was Fanucci alone. Or Fanucci with some gunmen hired for special jobs on a strictly cash basis. Which left Vito Corleone with another decision. The course his own life must take.

It was from this experience that came his oft-repeated belief that every man has but one destiny. On that night he could have paid Fanucci the tribute and have become again a grocery clerk with perhaps his own grocery store in the years to come. But destiny had decided that he was to become a Don and had brought Fanucci to him to set him on his destined path.

When they finished the bottle of wine, Vito said cautiously to Clemenza and Tessio, "If you like, why not give me two hundred dollars each to pay to Fanucci? I guarantee he will accept that amount from me. Then leave everything in my hands. I'll settle this problem to your satisfaction."

At once Clemenza's eyes gleamed with suspicion. Vito said to him coldly, "I never lie to people I have accepted as my friends. Speak to Fanucci yourself tomorrow. Let him ask you for the money. But don't pay him. And don't in any way quarrel with him. Tell him you have to get the money and will give it to me to give him. Let him understand that you are willing to pay what he asks. Don't bargain. I'll quarrel over the price with him. There's no point making him angry with us if he's as dangerous a man as you say he is."

They left it at that. The next day Clemenza spoke with Fanucci to make sure that Vito was not making up the story. Then Clemenza came to Vito's apartment and gave him the two hundred dollars. He peered at Vito Corleone and said, "Fanucci told me nothing below three hundred dollars, how will you make him take less?"

Vito Corleone said reasonably, "Surely that's no concern of yours. Just remember that I've done you a service."

Tessio came later. Tessio was more reserved than Clemenza, sharper, more clever but with less force. He sensed something amiss, something not quite right. He was a little worried. He said to Vito Corleone, "Watch yourself with that bastard of a Black Hand, he's tricky as a priest. Do you want me to be here when you hand him the money, as a witness?"

Vito Corleone shook his head. He didn't even bother to answer. He merely said to Tessio, "Tell Fanucci I'll pay him the money here in my house at nine o'clock tonight. I'll have to give him a glass of wine and talk, reason with him to take the lesser sum."

Tessio shook his head. "You won't have much luck. Fanucci never retreats."

"I'll reason with him," Vito Corleone said. It was to become a famous phrase in the years to come. It was to become the warning rattle before a deadly strike. When he became a Don and asked opponents to sit down and reason with him, they understood it was the last chance to resolve an affair without bloodshed and murder.

Vito Corleone told his wife to take the two children, Sonny and Fredo, down into the street after supper and on no account to let them come up to the house until he gave her permission. She was to sit on guard at the tenement door. He had some private business with Fanucci that could not be interrupted. He saw the look of fear on her face and was angry. He said to her quietly, "Do you think you've married a fool?" She didn't answer. She did not answer because she was frightened, not of Fanucci now, but of her husband. He was changing visibly before her eyes, hour by hour, into a man who radiated some dangerous force. He had always been quiet, speaking little, but always gentle, always reasonable, which was extraordinary in a young Sicilian male. What she was seeing was the shedding of his protective coloration of a harmless nobody now that he was ready to start on his destiny. He had started late, he was twenty-five years old, but he was to start with a flourish.

Vito Corleone had decided to murder Fanucci. By doing so he would have an extra seven hundred dollars in his bankroll. The three hundred dollars he himself would have to pay the Black Hand terrorist and the two hundred dollars from Tessio and the two hundred dollars from Clemenza. If he did not kill Fanucci, he would have to pay the man seven hundred dollars cold cash. Fanucci alive was not worth seven hundred dollars to him. He would not pay seven hundred dollars to keep Fanucci alive. If Fanucci needed seven hundred dollars for an operation to save his life, he would not give Fanucci seven hundred dollars for the surgeon. He owed Fanucci no personal debt of gratitude, they were not blood relatives, he did not love Fanucci. Whyfore, then, should he give Fanucci seven hundred dollars?

And it followed inevitably, that since Fanucci wished to take seven hundred dollars from him by force, why should he not kill Fanucci? Surely the world could do without such a person.

There were of course some practical reasons. Fanucci might indeed have powerful friends who would seek vengeance. Fanucci himself was a dangerous man, not so easily killed. There were the police and the electric chair, But Vito Corleone had lived under a sentence of death since the murder of his father. As a boy of twelve he had fled his executioners and crossed the ocean into a strange land, taking a strange name. And years of quiet observation had convinced him that he had more intelligence and more courage than other men, though he had never had the opportunity to use that intelligence and courage.

And yet he hesitated before taking the first step toward his destiny. He even packed the seven hundred dollars in a single fold of bills and put the money in a convenient side pocket of his trousers. But he put the money in the left side of his trousers. In the right-hand pocket he put the gun Clemenza had given him to use in the hijacking of the silk truck.

Fanucci came promptly at nine in the evening. Vito Corleone set out a jug of homemade wine that Clemenza had given him.

Fanucci put his white fedora on the table beside the jug of wine. He unloosened his broad multiflowered tie, its tomato stains camouflaged by the bright patterns. The summer night was hot, the gaslight feeble. It was very quiet in the apartment. But Vito Corleone was icy. To show his good faith he handed over the roll of bills and watched carefully as Fanucci, after counting it, took out a wide leather wallet and stuffed the money inside. Fanucci sipped his glass of wine and said, "You still owe me two hundred dollars." His heavy-browed face was expressionless.

Vito Corleone said in his cool reasonable voice, "I'm a little short, I've been out of work. Let me owe you the money for a few weeks."

This was a permissible gambit. Fanucci had the bulk of the money and would wait. He might even be persuaded to take nothing more or to wait a little longer. He chuckled over his wine and said, "Ah, you're a sharp young fellow. How is it I've never noticed you before? You're too quiet a chap for your own interest. I could find some work for you to do that would be very profitable."

Vito Corleone showed his interest with a polite nod and filled up the man's glass from the purple jug. But Fanucci thought better of what he was going to say and rose from his chair and shook Vito's hand. "Good night, young fellow," he said. "No hard feelings, eh? If I can ever do you a service let me know. You've done a good job for yourself tonight."

Vito let Fanucci go down the stairs and out of the building. The street was thronged with witnesses to show that he had left the Corleone home safely. Vito watched from the window. He saw Fanucci turn the corner toward 11th Avenue and knew he was headed toward his apartment, probably to put away his loot before coming out on the streets again. Perhaps to put away his gun. Vito Corleone left his apartment and ran up the stairs to the roof. He traveled over the square block of roofs and descended down the steps of an empty loft building fire escape that left him in the back yard. He kicked the back door open and went through the front door. Across the street was Fanucci's tenement apartment house.

The village of tenements extended only as far west as Tenth Avenue. Eleventh Avenue was mostly warehouses and lofts rented by firms who shipped by New York Central Railroad and wanted access to the freight yards that honeycombed the area from Eleventh Avenue to the Hudson River. Fanucci's apartment house was one of the few left standing in this wilderness and was occupied mostly by bachelor trainmen, yard workers, and the cheapest prostitutes. These people did not sit in the street and gossip like honest Italians, they sat in beer taverns guzzling their pay. So Vito Corleone found it an easy matter to slip across the deserted Eleventh Avenue and into the vestibule of Fanucci's apartment house. There he drew the gun he had never fired and waited for Fanucci.

He watched through the glass door of the vestibule, knowing Fanucci would come down from Tenth Avenue. Clemenza had showed him the safety on the gun and he had triggered it empty. But as a young boy in Sicily at the early age of nine, he had often gone hunting with his father, had often fired the heavy shotgun called the *lupara*. It was his skill with the *lupara* even as a small boy that had brought the sentence of death upon him by his father's murderers.

Now waiting in the darkened hallway, he saw the white blob of Fanucci crossing the street toward the doorway. Vito stepped back, shoulders pressed against the inner door that led to the stairs. He held his gun out to fire. His extended hand was only two paces from the outside door. The door swung in. Fanucci, white, broad, smelly, filled the square of light. Vito Corleone fired.

The opened door let some of the sound escape into the street, the rest of the gun's explosion shook the building. Fanucci was holding on to the sides of the door, trying to stand erect, trying to reach for his gun. The force of his struggle had torn the buttons off his jacket and made it swing loose. His gun was exposed but so was a spidery vein of red on the white shirtfront of his stomach. Very carefully, as if he were plunging a needle into a vein, Vito Corleone fired his second bullet into that red web.

Fanucci fell to his knees, propping the door open. He let out a terrible groan, the groan of a man in great physical distress that was almost comical. He kept giving these groans; Vito remembered hearing at least three of them before he put the gun against Fanucci's sweaty, suety cheek and fired into his brain. No more than five seconds had passed when Fanucci slumped into death, jamming the door open with his body.

Very carefully Vito took the wide wallet out of the dead man's jacket pocket and put it inside his shirt. Then he walked across the street into the loft building, through that into the yard and climbed the fire escape to the roof. From there he surveyed the street. Fanucci's body was still lying in the doorway but there was no sign of any other person. Two windows had gone up in the tenement and he could see dark heads poked out but since he could not see their features they had certainly not seem his. And such men would not give information to the police. Fanucci might lie there until dawn or until a patrolman making the rounds stumbled on his body. No person in that house would deliberately expose himself to police suspicion or questioning. They would lock their doors and pretend they had heard nothing.

He could take his time. He traveled over the rooftops to his own roof door and down to his own flat. He unlocked the door, went inside and then locked the door behind him. He rifled the dead man's wallet. Besides the seven hundred dollars he had given Fanucci there were only some singles and a five-dollar note.

Tucked inside the flap was an old five-dollar gold piece, probably a luck token. If Fanucci was a rich gangster, he certainly did not carry his wealth with him. This confirmed some of Vito's suspicions.

He knew he had to get rid of the wallet and the gun (knowing enough even then that he must leave the gold piece in the wallet). He went up on the roof again and traveled over a few ledges. He threw the wallet down one air shaft and then he emptied the gun of bullets and smashed its barrel against the roof ledge. The barrel wouldn't break. He reversed it in his hand and smashed the butt against the side of a chimney. The butt split into two halves. He smashed it again and the pistol broke into barrel, and handle, two separate pieces. He used a separate air shaft for each. They made no sound when they struck the earth five stories below, but sank into the soft hill of garbage that had accumulated there. In the morning more garbage would be thrown out of the windows and, with luck, would cover everything. Vito returned to his apartment.

He was trembling a little but was absolutely under control. He changed his clothes and fearful that some blood might have splattered on them, he threw them into a metal tub his wife used for washing. He took lye and heavy brown laundry soap to soak the clothes and scrubbed them with the metal wash board beneath the sink. Then he scoured tub and sink with lye and soap. He found a bundle of newly washed clothes in the corner of the bedroom and mingled his own clothes with these. Then he put on a fresh shirt and trousers and went down to join his wife and children and neighbors in front of the tenement.

All these precautions proved to be unnecessary. The police, after discovering the dead body at dawn, never questioned Vito Corleone. Indeed he was astonished that they never learned about Fanucci's visit to his home on the night he was shot to death. He had counted on that for an alibi, Fanucci leaving the tenement alive. He only learned later that the police had been delighted with the murder of Fanucci and not too anxious to pursue his killers. They had assumed it was another gang execution, and had questioned hoodlums with records in the rackets and a history of strong-arm. Since Vito had never been in trouble he never came into the picture.

But if he had outwitted the police, his partners were another matter. Pete Clemenza and Tessio avoided him for the next week, for the next two weeks, then they came to call on him one evening. They came with obvious respect. Vito Corleone greeted them with impassive courtesy and served them wine.

Clemenza spoke first. He said softly, "Nobody is collecting from the store owners on Ninth Avenue. Nobody is collecting from the card games and gambling in the neighborhood."

Vito Corleone gazed at both men steadily but did not reply. Tessio spoke. "We could take over Fanucci's customers. They would pay us."

Vito Corleone shrugged. "Why come to me? I have no interest in such things."

Clemenza laughed. Even in his youth, before growing his enormous belly, he had a fat man's laugh. He said now to Vito Corleone, "How about that gun I gave you for the truck job? Since you won't need it anymore you can give it back to me."

Very slowly and deliberately Vito Corleone took a wad of bills out of his side pocket and peeled off five tens. "Here, I'll pay you. I threw the gun away after the truck job." He smiled at the two men.

At that time Vito Corleone did not know the effect of this smile. It was chilling because it attempted no menace. He smiled as if it was some private joke only he himself could appreciate. But since he smiled in that fashion only in affairs that were lethal, and since the joke was not really private and since his eyes did not smile, and since his outward character was usually so reasonable and quiet, the sudden unmasking of his true self was frightening.

Clemenza shook his head. "I don't want the money," he said. Vito pocketed the bills. He waited. They all understood each other. They knew he had killed Fanucci and though they never spoke about it to anyone, the whole neighborhood, within a few weeks, also knew. Vito Corleone was treated as a "man of respect" by everyone. But he made no attempt to take over the Fanucci rackets and tributes.

What followed then was inevitable. One night Vito's wife brought a neighbor, a widow, to the flat. The woman was Italian and of unimpeachable character. She worked hard to keep a home for her fatherless children. Her sixteen-year-old son brought home his pay envelope sealed, to hand over to her in the old-country style; her seventeen-year-old daughter, a dressmaker, did the same. The whole family sewed buttons on cards at night at slave labor piece rates. The woman's name was Signora Colombo.

Vito Corleone's wife said, "The Signora has a favor to ask of you. She is having some trouble."

Vito Corleone expected to be asked for money, which he was ready to give. But it seemed that Mrs. Colombo owned a dog which her youngest son adored. The landlord had received complaints on the dog barking at night and had told Mrs. Colombo to get rid of it. She had pretended to do so. The landlord had found out that she had deceived him and had ordered her to vacate her apartment. She had promised this time to truly get rid of the dog and she had done so. But the landlord was so angry that he would not revoke his order. She had to get out or the police would be summoned to put her out. And her poor little boy had cried so when they had given the dog away to relatives who lived in Long Island. All for nothing, they would lose their home.

Vito Corleone asked her gently, "Why do you ask me to help you?"

Mrs. Colombo nodded toward his wife. "She told me to ask you."

He was surprised. His wife had never questioned him about the clothes he had washed the night he had murdered Fanucci. Had never asked him where all the money came from when he was not working. Even now her face was impassive. Vito said to Mrs Colombo, "I can give you some money to help you move, is that what you want?"

The woman shook her head, she was in tears. "All my friends are here, all the girls I grew up with in Italy. How can I move to another neighborhood with strangers? I want you to speak to the landlord to let me stay."

Vito nodded: "It's done then. You won't have to move. I'll speak to him tomorrow morning."

His wife gave him a smile which he did not acknowledge, but he felt pleased. Mrs. Colombo looked a little uncertain. "You're sure he'll say yes, the landlord?" she asked.

"Signor Roberto?" Vito said in a surprised voice. "Of course he will. He's a good-hearted fellow. Once I explain how things are with you he'll take pity on your misfortunes. Now don't let it trouble you anymore. Don't get so upset. Guard your health, for the sake of your children."

The landlord, Mr. Roberto, came to the neighborhood every day to check on the row of five tenements that he owned. He was a *padrone*, a man who sold Italian laborers just off the boat to the big corporations. With his profits he had bought the tenements one by one. An educated man from the North of Italy, he felt only contempt for these illiterate Southerners from Sicily and Naples, who swarmed like vermin through his buildings, who threw garbage down the air shafts, who let cockroaches and rats eat away his walls without lifting a hand to preserve his property. He was not a bad man, he was a good husband and father, but constant worry about his investments, about the money he earned, about the inevitable expenses that came with being a man of property had worn his nerves to a frazzle so that he was in a constant state of irritation. When Vito Corleone stopped him on the street to ask for a word, Mr. Roberto was brusque. Not rude, since any one of these Southerners might stick a knife into you if rubbed the wrong way, though this young man looked like a quiet fellow.

"Signor Roberto," said Vito Corleone, "the friend of my wife, a poor widow with no man to protect her, tells me that for some reason she has been ordered to move from her apartment in your building. She is in despair. She has no money, she has no friends except those that live here. I told her that I would speak to you, that you are a reasonable man who acted out of some misunderstanding. She has gotten rid off the animal that caused all the trouble and so why shouldn't she stay? As one Italian to another, I ask you the favor."

Signor Roberto studied the young man in front of him. He saw a man of medium stature but strongly built, a peasant but not a bandit, though he so laughably dared to call himself an Italian. Roberto shrugged. "I have already rented the apartment to another family for higher rent," he said. "I cannot disappoint them for the sake of your friend."

Vito Corleone nodded in agreeable understanding. "How much more a month?" he asked.

"Five dollars," Mr. Roberto said. This was a lie. The railway flat, four dark rooms, rented for twelve dollars a month to the widow and he had not been able to get more than that from the new tenant.

Vito Corleone took a roll of bills out of his pocket and peeled off three tens. "Here is the six months' increace in advance. You needn't speak to her about it, she's a proud woman. See me again in another six months. But of course you'll let her keep her dog."

"Like hell," Mr. Roberto said. "And who the hell are you to give me orders. Watch your manners or you'll be out on your Sicilian ass in the street there."

Vito Corleone raised his hands in surprise. "I'm asking you a favor, only that. One never knows when one might need a friend, isn't that true? Here, take this money as a sign of my goodwill and make your own decision. I wouldn't dare to quarrel with it." He thrust the money into Mr. Roberto's hand. "Do me this little favor, just take the money and think things over. Tomorrow morning if you want to give me the money back by all means do so. If you want the woman out of your house, how can I stop you? It's your property, after all. If you don't want the dog in there, I can understand. I dislike animals myself." He patted Mr. Roberto on the shoulder. "Do me this service, eh? I won't forget it. Ask your friends in the neighborhood about me, they'll tell you, I'm a man who believes in showing his gratitude."

But of course Mr. Roberto had already begun to understand. That evening he made inquiries about Vito Corleone. He did not wait until the next morning. He knocked on the Corleone door that very night, apologizing for the lateness of the hour and accepted a glass of wine from Signora Corleone. He assured Vito Corleone that it had all been a dreadful misunderstanding, that of course Signora Colombo could remain in the flat, of course she could keep her dog. Who were those miserable tenants to complain about noise from a poor animal when they paid such a low rent? At the finish he threw the thirty dollars Vito Corleone had given him on the table and said in the most sincere fashion, "Your good heart in helping this poor widow has shamed me and I wish to show that I, too, have some Christian charity. Her rent will remain what it was."

All concerned played this comedy prettily. Vito poured wine, called for cakes, wrung Mr. Roberto's hand and praised his warm heart. Mr. Roberto sighed and said that having made the acquaintance of such a man as Vito Corleone restored his faith in human nature. Finally they tore themselves away from each other. Mr. Roberto, his bones turned to jelly with fear at his narrow escape, caught the streetcar to his home in the Bronx and took to his bed. He did not reappear in his tenements for three days.

Vito Corleone was now a "man of respect" in the neighborhood.

The Black Hand
from The Business of Crime
by Humbert S. Nelli

*Humbert S. Nelli's (born 1930) account of extortion in the
American immigant community before Prohibition offers
insight into the roots of organized crime in this country.*

B y 1891 criminal bands were at work in any American cities that
contained sizable Southern Italian immigrant populations. As
early as 1878 a gang composed of expatriate Sicilian bandits carried on a flourishing extortion business among successful residents in Southern Italian communities in San Francisco and
surrounding towns. To ensure maximum publicity and to capitalize
on the prestige of the Sicilian society, the San Francisco brigands called
themselves "La Maffia." The San Francisco *Examiner* described the
gang as "a neat little tea party of Sicilian brigands" who were
"attempting to bulldoze such of their countrymen who would stand
their blackmailing tricks." The "villainous gang" had for its objective
"the extortion of money from their countrymen by a system of blackmail, which includes attacks on character and threats to kill." This
gang disintegrated when the corpse of a Sicilian immigrant named

Catalani was found near Sausalito. When evidence pointed to Rosario Meli, Iganzio Trapani, Salvatore Messing, and Giuseppe Bianchi, they were arrested and eventually convicted—not of murder, which authorities were unable to prove—of robbing Catalani prior to his death.

Giuseppe Esposito, who shortly after he arrived in New Orleans in 1880 apparently organized a "band of seventy-five cut-throats" specializing in kidnapping, was not the first to practice extortion in Italian New Orleans. After Esposito's arrest in July 1881, prominent Southern Italian residents confided to American newsmen that for years prior to his arrival affluent residents of the community had been forced to submit to extortion. These activities were not organized, and were not the deeds of "idle men who spend their ill-gotten gold in riotous living," but rather those of "thrifty, industrious people who work hard but grumble at fate because some of their countrymen are more wealthy than they." Usually the extortionists were common laborers who needed money for one reason or another. They were not, however, ordinary members of the laboring class: because of a criminal record in Italy or a reputation for violence and viciousness, they elicited fear and acquiescence from compatriots. Extortion was apparently conducted on a personal basis at this time in New Orleans. Thus Gaetano Arditto, who was convicted of the murder of Tony Labousse in late 1881, sent a note to a prominent Italian citizen demanding $4,000 on pain of death. Arditto signed his name and (as the New Orleans *Times* reported the event) "the victim well knowing the character of the man was forced to submit to the demand."

Blackmail activities continued through the 1880s. During the course of the decade, however, they became more impersonal and the extortionists more circumspect. Vincent Provenza received an unsigned note dated September 24, 1886, advising him to deposit $1,000 at a designated location while wearing a white handkerchief in his hat for identification purposes, and to comply with the demand within three days. Other Italians, including the Matranga brothers, indicated that for years they had submitted to extortion demands from unknown blackmailers.

Immigration from Southern Italy increased rapidly during the 1890s and after the turn of the century, and 90 per cent of the newcomers settled in cities, particularly those of the East and Middle West. As more and more Southern Italians flocked into urban America, they provided an increasingly tempting source of money, readily intimidated as they were because of the evil reputation of secret societies in the homeland.

In 1908, amid a flurry of Black Hand *(Mano Nera)* activity, American and Italian-American writers sought to determine the origin of the term "Black Hand." Alessandro Mastro-Valerio, publisher and editor of Chicago's *La Tribuna Italiana Transatlantica,* claimed that Carlo Barsotti, editor of *Il Progresso Italo-Americano* (New York), had coined the term in order to avoid using the word *"mafia,"* and in the hope that the offenses thus identified would be viewed as responses to American conditions. For his part, Gaetano D'Amato, former President of the United Italian Societies of New York and friend of Police Lieutenant Joseph Petrosino of that city's Italian detective squad, held that the name had first been used in Spain in the 1880s by a society of thieves and murderers who styled themselves protectors and guardians of the downtrodden against persons of wealth. The term was first used in the United States "about ten years ago," according to D'Amato, and "probably by some Italian desperado who had heard of the exploits of the Spanish society, and considered the combination of words to be high-sounding and terror-inspiring." After a few successful ventures, "the newspapers finally applied it to all crimes committed by Italian banditti in the United States."

American journalist Lindsay Denison believed also that the name was of Spanish origin, but that it was first used during the Inquisition by "a secret society which fought the government and the church." When it ceased to exist in Spain, "the secret societies of Southern Italy were its heirs." Then during the 1870s and 1880s, continued Denison, "a false report was raised in Spain" that it had been revived. The story, he said, "lingered in the brain of a [New York] *Herald* reporter, and one fine day he attempted to rejuvenate waning interest in a puzzling

Italian murder case by speculating as to the coming to life of the Black Hand among Latin immigrants in America. The other newspapers seized on the idea eagerly, and kept it going."

All the writers seemed certain that the term *Mano Nera* first appeared in the United States around 1898. They were mistaken. Its initial appearance in relation to Italian-American crime was in September 1903, in the aftermath of the gruesome "Barrel Murder Case" in New York.

Extortion and blackmail gangs had apparently begun to operate on a large scale in the Italian colonies in Manhattan and Brooklyn in 1901. During the subsequent two years, when groups operated under such names as "La Società Camorrista," "La Mala Vita," and "Mafia," police estimated that they "reaped a harvest from hundreds of wealthy Italians." In September 1902, Charles Bacigalupo, so-called "Mayor of Mulberry Bend" (the Lower Manhattan Italian district), told a New York *Herald* reporter that the extortionists were "bad people to deal with, and are, I believe, working, in all cities in this country where there are Italian colonies." In New York, Bacigalupo continued, "a great many doctors, bankers and others have received blackmailing letters in the last few months, and, from what I hear, most of the recipients sent the money asked. Bacigalupo himself had never paid a cent in tribute or even received a blackmail letter—"but if I did receive one I hardly think I would ignore it."

On rare occasions during this early period police were successful in capturing blackmailers. In January 1902 Detective Petrosino managed to persuade Stephen Carmenciti, a prosperous wholsesale tailor living on East 103rd Street in the East Harlem Italian neighborhood, to agree to a rendezvous to pay $150 to an extortion society calling itself "Holy House." Two Holy House members were arrested—Joseph Mascarello of East 107th Street and Carmine Mursuneso of East 106th Street—but the men were found innocent when the merchant refused to testify, fearing for the safety of his family.

There was grave concern among residents of the Italian colony over this situation and the dozens if not hundreds of crimes that never came to official attention during 1901, 1902, and 1903. The event that focused the American public's attention on the blackmail activities taking place in the city's Italian neighborhoods was the Barrel Murder, which, ironically, had no connection with extortion. On April 14, 1903, the corpse of a man with seventeen stab wounds and the head nearly severed from the body was found stuffed in a barrel in a vacant lot at East 11th Street and Avenue D on Manhattan's Lower East Side. There was no identification on the corpse, and the case appeared to be unsolvable. Detective Petrosino remembered having seen the victim, but for a time could not recall when or where. Finally he "placed" the dead man at the trial of a counterfeiter, Giuseppe De Priemo, at the Federal Court in New York a year or so earlier. Since at the time of the Barrel Murder De Priemo was at Sing Sing, the detective traveled up the river to interview him there. As soon as De Priemo saw a photograph of the dead man, he cried, "That's my brother-in-law, Benedetto Madonia," and added that the victim had recently visited him in the company of a man named Tomasso Petto, who was known as "Petto the Ox."

The few existing scraps of evidence pointed to Petto, either as the murderer or as one who knew a great deal about the events surrounding Madonia's death. A pair of gloves found in the barrel bore the label of a Buffalo store—and Petto had recently lived in that city. Furthermore, according to De Priemo, his brother-in-law always carried a watch with certain distinctive markings "on the neck." A watch chain, but no watch, was found on the body. Pawn shops were checked, and Madonia's watch was found in one of them. Petto was identified as the man who had pawned the watch (for a dollar), and when he was arrested the pawn ticket was found in his possession. Petto did not deny pawning the watch but did deny that he had obtained it from Madonia: an Italian named "John," whom he had known for three years but whose last name he did not know, had given it to him. Not wanting or needing it, Petto said, he had simply pawned it.

Madonia was apparently an agent for a counterfeiting ring. His job was to distribute bogus bills to dealers throughout the country. As Secret Service agents conjectured, either he could not account for counterfeit bills that were to have been put into circulation, or he had held out proceeds from the sales in the course of his travels; then when fellow gang members learned of his double dealing, they murdered him. The manner in which Madonia was killed and the decision to leave his corpse where it could be found quickly (the body was still warm when it was discovered) indicated that the murder was intended as a warning.

Leaders of the gang were Ignazio Saietta ("Lupo the Wolf") and his brother-in-law, Giuseppe Morello, who were to play a part in New York's crime until the mid-1930s. Another member was Madonia's brother-in-law. Petto was a known member of the gang; his work usually consisted of strong-arm assignments. Physically powerful but unintelligent, he apparently could not resist the temptation to steal the only valuable (and traceable) possession on the body—the watch. It seems certain that he participated in the murder, but probably not as the sole knife wielder. The state's case against Petto was insufficiently strong to convict him, particularly after Madonia's wife, son, and brother-in-law refused to help. Petto the Ox went free.

Although the Barrel Murder was an internal gang matter, probably not even connected with the blackmail wave then sweeping the city's Italian district, it became a major factor not only in riveting Italian-Americans' concern on these activities but especially in focusing the attention of America at large on immigrant community crime. Thus, in the midst of the Madonia investigation an article appeared in the *Herald* headlined "Scores of New York Business Men Pay Blackmail to *Mafia*," and recounting that prominent Italian bankers, merchants, and physicians had "corroborated the accounts of blackmailing schemes perpetrated by the same class of men who are charged with the murder of Benedetto Madonia." As these men were generally successful in collecting thousands of dollars from their victims, apparently with little risk of punishment (according to the story), the Barrel Murder and its resultant publicity doubtless encouraged still more crooks to turn to this line of business. In the following months crimes of extortion increased in New York's "Little Italies." Finally, on September 13, 1903, a fear-inspiring name was given to this form of criminal activity, when "Black Hand" (*Mano Nera*) appeared for the first time in the American press—in a *Herald* article captioned " 'Black Hand' Band in Extortion Plot," an account of how one Nicola Cappiello, a wealthy Brooklyn contractor and dock builder, had been the target of blackmail efforts for more than a month.

On August 3, 1903, Cappiello received the following note embellished with three black crosses surmounted by a skull and crossbones (in translation):

> Nicola Cappiello
>
> If you don't meet us at Seventy-second Street and Thirteenth Avenue, Brooklyn, to-morrow afternoon, your house will be dynamited and you and your family killed. The same fate awaits you in the event of your betraying our purposes to the police.
> *Mano Nera*

Cappiello decided to ignore the demand. Two days later he received another letter.

> You did not meet us as ordered in our first letter. If you still refuse to accede to our terms, but wish to preserve the lives of your family, you can do so by sacrificing your own life. Walk in Sixteenth Street, near Seventh Avenue between the hours of four and five tonite [August 5].
> Beware of *Mano Nera*

Because of his stubbornness and unwillingness to listen to reason, the Black Hand next demanded $10,000. A few days later, three of his oldest friends and a fourth man whom he did not know called on him and offered to intercede in his behalf with the blackmail band, promising that if he could provide $1,000 they would do their best to persuade the blackmailers to spare his life. Cappiello delivered the money on August 26, but within days the four men were back for an additional $3,000. Convinced now that the gang intended systematically to drain him of his fortune (estimated to be in excess of $100,000), Cappiello reported the threats to the Brooklyn police. As a result, the original four Black Handers—Mariano Esposito, Fortunato Castellano, Annunziato Lingria, and Biaggio Giordano (three of them the contractor's "best friends" who had proffered their intercession), along with a fifth man, Antonio Giordano, who had not been with the helpful quartet—were arrested, brought to trial, and found guilty.

Although this first case ended more favorably for the victim than did hundreds of others that were to follow, the pattern was set at the very beginning of Black Hand history. The extortion campaign usually began with the delivery of a note demanding payment and threatening dire consequences if the victim ignored it. If the recipient did not comply at once, additional notes were sent, to be followed by the appearance of a delegation, usually including trusted friends, who offered to deal with the blackmailers. The "friends" returned with a demand for a sum of money often beyond the victim's ability to pay. A series of bargaining sessions followed, and a compromise figure was reached; the victim usually paid this negotiated sum. Sooner or later, however, the extortionists demanded still more money, and the process continued until the victim was drained of his resources (or gave a believable appearance of being penniless), turned to the authorities, was killed, or left the city. All this while, the Black Handers worked diligently to create a pervasive atmosphere of terror among the potential victims. This feeling of impending evil was reflected by Mrs. Cappiello, who lamented to a *Herald* reporter that "For more than a month we have been living in constant expectation of death. We know not whom to trust."

With the Cappiello case the *Herald* began applying the term "Black Hand" to all Italian-colony blackmail cases. This policy was soon followed by the other city papers. The *Times*, which did not report its original use by the Cappiello criminals, first mentioned *Mano Nera* on January 17, 1904, noting that the term had been in use "for some time." Newspapers in other cities soon recognized the possibilities in such an attention-getting name. It had a sinister quality. When applied to Italian criminals in the United States it caught the public's fancy in a sensational manner and gained wide currency. The extent of its use varied from city to city, however. In Chicago and New York, for example, "Black Hand" became the preferred term and *mafia* fell into disuse, although in New Orleans the two terms were used interchangeably.

After September 1903, and continuing into the 1920s, "Black Hand" came into general (although not exclusive) use to indicate extortion and blackmail among Italians. Such crimes were usually the work of individuals or small groups who came together only briefly to carry out a single job or a limited number of jobs. There were organized gangs specializing in typical Black Hand projects, and these followed set procedures. "Specialists" were also employed for certain functions.

The usual consequences of ignoring the demands of a Black Hand note (often delivered through the U.S. mail) were the kidnapping of a loved one (especially a child), the bombing of property, the wounding or slaying of the victim, or the murder of a member of the family. Such activities were not limited to any one economic class; no one living in an Italian district was exempt. Bankers, barbers, and beggars were potential victims of extortion; people of differing means were asked to pay according to their known or suspected resources. Criminals, some as prominent as James ("Big Jim") Colosimo, who dominated prostitution and gambling in Chicago's Near South Side Italian district for two decades, received Black Hand notes. Colosimo decided in 1909 to import outside help against Black Hand threats, and brought his wife's nephew, John Torrio, from New York. Torrio had a reputation for dealing successfully with New York's Black Handers, and fulfilled his uncle's expectations in Chicago. He eventually succeeded Colosimo and became the dominant figure in Chicago syndicate crime in the early 1920s.

Black Handers, unless dealt with efficiently and severely (in the Torrio fashion) fattened off the financial resources of prominent criminals in every American city. Ignazio Saietta ("Lupo the Wolf" to associates, the police, and newspaper readers) was the chief of one of the most successful counterfeiting gangs in New York and thus one of the city's most notorious Italian criminals. In 1909 Lupo filed a petition of bankruptcy. During the proceedings it was divulged that he had received numerous Black Hand threats over the years. Although he ignored most of these threats, he had turned over $10,000 to various extortionists. "He made the announcement . . . as a thing to be taken for granted," noted a newspaper reporter, and seemed surprised "at the interest his announcement received. Like most Black Hand victims, Lupo had received threatening letters, and like many other Italian residents fearing for the lives of their loved ones, he had paid.

Giosue Galluci, another New York crime leader, dubbed "King" of the East Harlem Italian colony, was known to have been "the prey of Black Handers." When he was murdered in April 1915, police immediately theorized that he was the victim of a Black Hand gang, though it is more likely that he was the casualty in a war between East Harlem Sicilian gangs (the killer was never caught). Nevertheless, events connected with this confrontation—which culminated even more violently two years later in Brooklyn—suggest that Italian gangs of this era used the Black Hand reputation and known techniques as covers, eliminating rivals in such a manner as to suggest Black Hand operations to the police and to the public.

Although Black Handers worked on all levels of immigrant societies, they limited themselves geographically to Italians living or working in the colonies. Non-Italians also attempted to use the notoriety of the name in order to obtain easy money. Evidence suggests that every instance of non-Italian Black Hand activity took place during a flurry of newspaper interest and publicity focusing on Italian Black Hand activities, or during and after sensational and well-publicized cases. It is important to note that the Italian population in American cities was not static; a great deal of residential mobility occurred constantly. In the decades of *Mano Nera* activity, immigrants and second-generation Italians who could manage to do so moved out of Italian districts, at the first opportunity shifting to less crowded and more pleasant environments. Those who moved away from Italian districts also left the Black Hand behind. A computer-assisted study of 141 Black Hand cases that took place during 1908 in New York, Boston, Philadelphia, Baltimore, Chicago, Pittsburgh, Cleveland, New Orleans, Kansas City, and San Francisco, uncovered the fact that not one Black Hand case reported in the press took place outside an immigrant district. Those who had left the colony were unmolested, and for good reasons: they usually comprised the immigrants who were adjusting to American customs and standards, they might seek police protection, and in general they were far less pliable than the newcomers to the various "Little Italies." The Black Handers themselves remained in the immigrant community, where there was an almost limitless supply of compliant, hard-working victims; the territory was familiar, and the Black Hander blended in with other residents. In a non-ethnic neighborhood he would be a conspicuous alien if he delivered a note at the home of an intended victim or attempted to observe the reaction to demands sent through the mail. He would find it more difficult to apply pressure on the victim or to punish him for non-compliance.

Blackmail letters were straightforward, explicit, and often crude:

[New York City]
This is the second tine that I have warned you. Sunday at ten o'clock in the morning, at the corner of Second Street and Third Avenue, bring three hundred dollars without fail. Otherwise we will set fire to you and blow you up with a bomb. Consider this matter well, for this is the last warning I will give you.
I sign the Black Hand.

St. Louis, Mo., Aug. 9
Dear Friend,
This is your second letter. You did not answer or come. What have you in your head? You know what you did in

Brooklyn and that you went to Italy and then returned to Dago Hill [St. Louis' Italian colony] to hide yourself. You can go to hell to hide but we will find you. It will be very bad for you and your family if you do not come to an understanding. So come Thursday night at 10 o'clock. If you do not come we will cut you up in pieces. How will that be, you dirty false face. So we will wait for you. With best regards, good-by. [Beneath the words were two pictures, one a skull and crossbones, and one a man in a coffin. There was also a postscript.]

So this will be your presentment if you do not do as we tell you. The way the blood flows in my veins is the way the blood will flow from your veins.

New York, May 24, 1911
Mr. Tano Sferrazzo
307 East 45th Street
City

Various men of my society as you know well will demand some money because we need it in our urgent business and you finally have never consented to satisfy us to fulfill your duty. Therefore today finishes your case. In a few words I will explain the matter. You must know that in cases of this kind as your own when they are handled by useless persons the matter can be easily dropped or in other words neglected, but in your case we are men of high society and of great importance, and therefore the matter cannot be dropped, or in other words we cannot neglect this matter because the society will inflict a severe penalty. Therefore today talking with the chief I have decided that you must do your duty otherwise death will take you and you must not worry over it because these are our rules, so you are warned which road do you wish to choose, do what you please, it is immaterial to us. Money or death. If you want to save your life tomorrow

May 25th at 10 p.m. take the Third avenue train, go to 129th street, walk toward Second avenue. Walk as far as the First avenue bridge that leads you to the Bronx, walk up and down the bridge for a while; two men will then present themselves and will ask you, where are you going? to them you will give not less than $200.

Signed Black Hand

Pittsburgh, Pa.
May 27, 1908
Mr. G. Satarano:

You please you know the company of Black Hands. I want you to send $2,000, all gold money. You find some friend to tell you about it. Send it to head man, Johnstown. We don't want you to tell no person that talks too much. If you report about this letter we will kill you. We will kill you with a steel knife. You and your family. Give me money right away, for I want to use it. And remember, keep it quiet.

Black Hand

Phila., Pa.

You will never see Italy again if you do not give $1,000 to the person that pinches you after he salutes you.

(I say one thousand.)

Carry it with you always and remember that I am more powerful than the police and your God.

Black Hand.

Financial success aroused the envy of less successful Italian immigrants and alerted those who made a career of extortion. Black Hand letters could come from envious neighbors or professional criminals, or both. As a case in point, Carmello Cannatella, who owned a fruit stand at 322 West Camden Street in Baltimore, bought a house on South Paca Street in 1906, and this sign of prosperity brought forth a Black Hand letter. Cannatella took it to the police. With detectives following him, he brought the required amount of money to the designated place, but no one appeared to take it. Subsequently he received other letters, and on November 10, 1908, his fruit stand was burned. The police never discovered who had set the fire, but they speculated that Cannatella's prosperity had aroused local envy, fanned undoubtedly by the ostentatious manner in which his son Lawrence displayed the family's wealth—dressing expensively, exhibiting jewelry, and attending the theater regularly. Cannatella's wife was in favor of buying additional property, but he feared that this would only arouse more jealousy; so instead they kept their money in the bank.

While Cannatella's problems were probably caused by envious neighbors, those of New York's Domenico Gumina were the work of an organized and highly professional extortion gang. Gumina operated a small grocery store at 305 East 71st Street, where he and his, family (a wife and five children) also lived. At about one o'clock on the afternoon of April 28, 1914, his five-year-old son Giuseppe disappeared while playing in front of the store. At six or seven o'clock that evening Gumina received a Special Delivery letter stating that if he wanted his son returned he must raise $2,000, then go to his "influential and confidential friends," who would help him. Gumina immediately talked to the police, who advised him to do as directed in the letter. Officers were assigned to the case. Gumina then went to his "friends" and reported the kidnapping.

A few days later, a friend of eight years, Benedetto Randazzo, and his brother-in-law Matteo Pallazzolo offered to contact "people." In a second meeting a few days later, Pallazzolo dickered with the grocer over the price necessary to get Giuseppe back. Gumina complained that he was a poor man, that business was bad, and that although he wanted his son back he could never raise $2,000. Pallazzolo offered to negotiate. Talks drifted on for two weeks, and finally it was agreed that Gumina should pay $125. Since the grocer could not scrape together even that much, the police assigned to the case contributed $45. The money was handed to Randazzo and Pallazzolo at Gumina's house. Police followed the two men when they left, and shortly thereafter rounded up five men and a woman comprising a Black Hand gang that specialized in kidnapping children.

The pattern was typical of Black Hand techniques. At the trial the prosecution proved that each stage of the operation, from taking the child to the arrangements made for his return to his parents, had been carefully planned. As Assistant District Attorney Royal H. Weller stated, "Each one of these people played his or her own particular part, each one doing a particular thing which none other did, and each one filled the entire circuit." This gang was unusually well organized and professional, and prior to its abduction of Giuseppe Gumina, unusually successful. The grocer by his action proved that not all Sicilians were afraid to turn to the authorities for aid. In this instance the machinery of justice also functioned effectively, finding all the accused guilty and sentencing them to jail terms of from ten to thirty years.

Sometimes Black Hand gangs or techniques became the means by which Italian-colony businessmen reduced the effectiveness of business rivals, or eliminated them entirely. Shortly after midnight on December 10, 1907, the rear of Joseph Di Giorgio's home in Baltimore was wrecked by a dynamite explosion. A native of Sicily, Di Giorgio had become, through hard work, one of the leading Italian fruit dealers on the East Coast. He was president of the Atlantic Fruit Company, the Di Giorgio Fruit Company, the Baltimore Fruit Exchange, and the Mediterranean Fruit Importing Company of New York, and vice-president of the Connolly Auction Company of New York, and through these companies controlled the importation and sales in the Baltimore area of fruit from California and Italy, and of bananas from Central America.

During the month before his home was bombed, Di Giorgio had received three blackmail letters, all bearing Pittsburgh postmarks, and demanding $10,000—but none indicated where or how the money was to be delivered. In January 1908 eight men—among them Di Giorgio's old business rival Antonio Lanasa—were arrested and charged with attempted murder and conspiracy to extort money. Prior to Di Giorgio's arrival in Baltimore ten years before, Lanasa had been the leading fruit merchant in the city. Within the decade the positions were reversed: Di Giorgio, who had started his career penniless, was rich, and Lanasa was deep in debt. In addition to his financial problems (and apparently at least partly responsible for them), Lanasa had been victimized several times by Black Hand extortion gangs. The obvious objective of the operation was to eliminate Lanasa's rival, using the Black Hand as a cover. Extortion as a major factor seemed to be ruled out by the fact that none of the letters named a place or date to hand over the money demanded. According to a police authority, some prominent Italians in Baltimore regularly employed Black Hand gangs within their businesses to extort money from rivals.

The State's case was based primarily on the testimony of two of Lanasa's co-defendants, Salvatore Lupo and Joseph Tamburo. In the trial, which began on March 8, 1908, Lupo disclosed that Lanasa had traveled to Pittsburgh the previous November to arrange with Philip Rei, an alleged Black Hander, to have extortion letters sent to Di Giorgio, and had at the same time hired Lupo to bomb Di Giorgio's house. Lupo had attended a meeting held on December 8 to plan the bombing, and Lanasa and the other accused participated also. As Lupo testified, he then departed for Pittsburgh, intending to return to Baltimore on the tenth, but was delayed and appeared only after the explosion. Thus he claimed to be an accessory to, but not guilty of, attempted murder. Tamburo, another of the accused, agreed with Lupo's testimony. On April 28, 1908, the jury found Lanasa guilty and he was sentenced to ten years in prison. Lupo received a 15-month term.

Two members of the dynamite group hired to blow up Di Giorgio's home were hired outside Baltimore—Lupo in Pittsburgh, and John Scarletta in Cleveland—comprising only one of many instances in which Black Handers traveled to different cities to practice their trade. "Diamond Jim" Colosimo's problems with *Mano Nera* extortion letters in Chicago were solved by John Torrio, who tracked down three Pittsburgh residents who, believing that Chicago would be their city of opportunity, tried to blackmail Colosimo. They discovered that they had chosen the wrong victim. Torrio ordered the trio murdered and saw to it that the news of their fate was publicized. Unlike many victims, Colosimo had no further trouble from Black Handers.

Most Black Hand threats and payments went unreported. New York Italian-American police officers, quoted in a June 1909 *Cosmopolitan Magazine* article, estimated that for every extortion case reported to police in the New York area there were "probably two hundred and fifty of which nothing is said." If this assessment is accurate, the extent of Black Hand activity in the city was staggering, for police department records disclosed that 424 Black Hand offenses were reported during 1908. Yet only a small proportion of these crimes found their way into the pages of the city's newspapers. A careful reading of every issue for 1908 of the New York *Times, Il Progresso Italo-Americano,* and *L'Araldo Italiano* (the last-named being two of the country's leading Italian-language journals) discloses that only 33 Black Hand offenses were reported in one or another of the papers during the year.

Although the situation in other cities was less serious than that of New York, with its huge population from Southern Italy, it is clear that countless extortion letters were sent in every city containing Italian colonies. Some victims paid quietly without the knowledge of neighbors or friends; there is much evidence to indicate, however, that many recipients simply ignored threatening letters and were not bothered further. The cases reaching the papers tended to include violence or arrests, and hence might be more sensational than the vast numbers of unreported incidents; yet these newspaper stories formed the lurid picture that the general public, both Italian and American, had of the Black Hand.

Although both contemporaneous and more recent writers have provided ample literature on the Black Hand, none has attempted to examine systematically the Black Handers' activities, either over a period of time or in a number of cities. Thus the extent of Black Hand operations remains unknown, and variations in patterns of operation remain isolated. Since the period from the turn of the century to the end of World War I formed the era of *Mano Nera* activities, a single year, 1908, was selected for intensive examination, as being the mid-point in the development and functioning of the Black Hand as well as in the efforts of law-enforcement agencies and concerned citizens to subdue it. Seventeen newspapers published in ten major cities containing a sizable Italian immigrant population and located in different parts of the country—New York, Boston, Philadelphia, Baltimore, New Orleans, Pittsburgh, Cleveland, Chicago, Kansas City, and San Francisco—were read to determine the nationality of senders and recipients of *Mano Nera* threats, methods used (oral, written, pictorial), number of threats made, type of threat (e.g., death, bombing, abduction, robbery, physical violence), demands made and the amount of money involved, and the result (e.g., arrest or other police action, action taken by Black Handers against the recipient).

A total of 141 Black Hand cases appeared in the seventeen newspapers. (Several cases were reported in more than one paper, and some papers—notably the New York *Times* and *Il Progresso*—reported not only offenses that occurred in their own area but also those of other sections of the country.) Examination of these cases indicated that Black Handers operated in the "Little Italy" of every city examined, although the greater part of the action was localized on the East Coast, since most of the new immigrants, who provided the most malleable victims for extortionists, landed there. Of the hundred cases involving Italians reported during 1908 in the seventeen newspapers, exactly half were committed in the three eastern Italian nuclei (New York, Philadelphia, Boston); 33 per cent occurred in New York alone. The smallest amount of Black Hand activity was in the settled and predominantly Northern Italian community of San Francisco, where only one offense was reported during the year—and that the work of a recent arrival from New York who needed money and decided (as he told police after his capture) to take it from a San Franciscan Italian who "had plenty." A wealthy Berkeley merchant of Italian background received a blackmail note in May 1908, but the extortionist turned out to be a non-Italian, Harry Tiesel.

Perhaps the best publicized Black Hand case in San Francisco involved Antonio, Antonio Jr., and Joseph Pedone. The Pedones operated successfully in the Bay Area from 1914 until their involvement in a shoot-out with Gaetano Ingrassio on November 30, 1916. Late in 1915 Ingrassio received the first of several Black Hand threats. The letter, postmarked San Mateo, read:

> Dear Friend:
>   Some of our friends in our society wish you to carry $2,000 in gold. Then we want you to go from San Francisco by the electric car to San Mateo on a Saturday afternoon. When you get there, walk back on the railroad track and some good friend is going to approach you. He is our friend, and you give him the money. Otherwise it will be very bad for you.

Subsequent letters threatened bodily injury to Ingrassio's family; yet he refused to submit to the threats. On November 30, 1916, he encountered the Pedones (who were, as he believed, responsible for the letters) on Columbia Avenue between Filbert and Greenwich streets. In an exchange of gunfire, Ingrassio wounded both Pedone brothers, Joseph and Antonio, and was in turn killed by Antonio, Jr. The Pedones were indicted for the killing and found guilty, and the Bay Area's most notorious Black Hand gang was destroyed.

While Black Hand threats were sent every month of the year reviewed, the highest incidence was during the mid-winter months of December (when 15 were sent), January (14), and February (14), representing 43 per cent of the total for the year. As Lieutenant Joseph Petrosino of New York's Italian squad explained, "The winter is the hard time of the year with all Italians, and naturally the collections come harder." Consequently, "men who have given up a few dollars now and then for months suddenly decide that, come what may, they will pay no more. According to the laws of the 'trade,' this means punishment, and there you have your outrages." It is likely that this is an accurate analysis; it is also possible that the high winter incidence was due in part to the fact that many Italian immigrants were engaged in seasonal labor—especially on the railroads, on construction sites, or in maintenance work. Such men either returned to Italy for the winter months or holed up in a tenement in the Italian section of an American city until the following spring. By December or January the money saved during the preceding season had been used up. Many borrowed (often at exorbitant rates) from a padrone or labor agent, and then worked on his railroad or construction gang the following season to pay off the winter's debts. Others among the unemployed resorted to sending *Mano Nera* letters to obtain enough money to tide them over.

The hundred cases reported in 1908 in the press were distributed as follows:

BLACK HAND CASES INVOLVING ITALIANS
REPORTED IN THE PRESS IN 1908

CITY	NO. OF CASES AND % OF TOTAL
New York	33
Chicago	12
Boston	9
Baltimore	5
Cleveland	4
Pittsburgh	6
Philadelphia	9
Kansas City	5
New Orleans	9
San Francisco	1
Others*	7

Total 100

*Pottsville, Pa.: 2 Export, Pa.: 1; Richmond, Va.: 1; Elkins, W. Va.: 1; Punxsutawney, Pa.: 1; Berkeley, Calif.:1.

All but eight of the one hundred reported cases involved use of the mails. In two of the exceptions, Black Handers pinned the note to the victim's apartment door, and in the other cases made the demands orally. In nearly all the cases reported in the press, the victim received more than one threatening letter.

The most frequent demand was for money: $500 in twelve instances, $1,000 in seventeen; in thirteen cases, the letters simply made a general demand for money. The most frequent threat was that of death—in 35 per cent of the cases, that of the victim, and 29 per cent, some form of bodily harm to the recipient's family, generally his children.

Apparently the newspapers tended to publicize the more violent and sensational cases, for in one-fourth of the cases involving Italians reported by the press, bombs damaged the victim's house, business, or other property. Bombings had the effect not only of intimidating the entire colony but also of attracting the attention of reporters and leading to the public's demands that the police take action. This public pressure resulted in greater police effort to find the bombers, although such effort did not necessarily have positive results. Only seven of the bombings ended in arrest; only twenty-one cases in all culminated in arrest.

Eight of the bombing cases occurred in New York. The most sensational and frightening concerned Francesco Spinella, a successful interior decorator, who owned two tenement houses and leased a third on East 11th Street in Manhattan's Lower East Side Italian district. On May 7, 1908, Spinella received a Black Hand letter demanding $7,000, with the alternative that his "entire property" would be destroyed. Spinella had immigrated twenty years before, had worked hard to earn his prosperity, and meant to keep for himself and his family the money he had accumulated. The Black Handers were just as determined to take it from him, or to ruin him in the attempt. On May 19 a bomb explosion damaged the front of the two buildings, 314 and 316 East 11th, though no one was injured. Spinella still refused to give in. Over the following ten weeks he received twenty blackmail notes, and during the same period ten explosions destroyed his and surrounding buildings and drove away all his tenants.

As Frank Marshall White reported five years later in *Outlook Magazine*, Spinella was a ruined man. "He has not paid anything to the Black Hand, but his decorating business has failed, his houses are mortgaged up to nearly their full value, and he and his wife and children are working out by the day to pay the interest on the mortgages." The unfortunate man, White noted, had "almost given up hope of being able to pull through financially." Although the publicity given this case should have provided an object lesson for other victims on the futility of trying to withstand the Black Hand, yet, as court records show, many Italians in New York and other cities successfully opposed the Black Hand.

In Chicago, Black Handers sent extortion letters not only to individuals but also to schools. On April 24, 1908, the Jenner School, an elementary school in Chicago's (predominantly Italian) Near North Side, received a note which, translated, read: "The Jenner school and two other schools will be blown to pieces at 2 o'clock today." At the foot was the picture of a black hand and a dagger. Similar notes were delivered to two nearby schools, Adams and Two Sisters, a Protestant institution. Staff workers at nearby Eli Bates settlement house advised parents that the letters were probably written by "hoodlums merely to frighten the residents of the Italian neighborhood," a theory supported by the fact that the note made no monetary demands. Nevertheless, parents and pupils panicked. The results apparently so satisfied the writers that they sent notes to other schools. Fortunately, this form of terrorizing lasted only a short time. With the exception of a letter sent on April 8 to the largely Italian Seventh Avenue public school in Newark, New Jersey, these Chicago letters were the only Black Hand notes directed to institutions rather than individuals.

Violence and alleged Black Hand activities were not limited to the urban areas. The 1908 trial and conviction of a reputed Black Hand leader, Rocco Racco, for the murder of Seeley Houk two years before in rural western Pennsylvania received considerable publicity in the

American and Italian-language press. It was a widely held belief that western Pennsylvania's Mahoning Valley was "a hotbed for the society." In the years after 1900 violence prevailed among Italians in the limestone quarry towns stretching from New Castle, Pennsylvania, to Youngstown, Ohio, and the numerous beatings, knifings, and murders were attributed to the Black Hand. The violent situation reached its climax on April 24, 1906, when the body of Seeley Houk, a fish and game warden, was discovered weighted down with stones in the Mahoning River a short distance east of Hillsville, in Lawrence County. Houk's watch, money and other valuables remained on the body—an indication that robbery had not been a motive for the killing. Suspicion turned at once to Rocco Racco, allegedly the Black Hand Society leader in Hillsville. Seven months earlier, the warden had killed a dog belonging to Racco, and the owner reportedly vowed that "just as my dog died in the woods, so shall this man die." Although it was never proved in court that Racco had identified Houk as his dog's killer, nonetheless, since an American official had apparently been the victim of a foreigner's vengeance, authorities swung into action. Local police and inspectors from the State Board of Game Commissioners called in the Pinkerton Detective Agency to help.

At William Pinkerton's direction, Frank Dimaio, superintendent of the Pittsburgh office, had in 1905 formed a group of agents of Italian birth or extraction in anticipation of his Agency's inevitable involvement in Black Hand cases. Following Houk's murder, operatives traveled to New York to pose as newly arrived immigrants; they were to manage to be transported to the Mahoning Valley. Early in 1907 they descended on Hillsville, New Castle, and other mining towns; where they set about making friends, infiltrating local organizations, and collecting evidence that would lead to the arrest of Racco later that year. The trial in 1908 rested on this evidence, and Racco was found guilty. After an appeal failed, the Italian was executed.

More significant than the evidence collected against Racco was the light shed on secret societies in the mining towns. Thus, although these groups were called Black Hand societies by outsiders and by many Italian residents of the towns, they did not operate like the groups in New York, Baltimore, Chicago, and other large cities. As Agent No. 89, who centered his activities in Hillsville (called "Helltown" by residents), reported to the Agency on May 22, 1907, "I have not heard of any threats being made by the members of the Society or any other Italians in the shape of a letter." Individual members might engage in blackmail "unknown to the head man," but "if they are found doing this by the head man, they are likely to be severely punished by him." Two days later No. 89 stated that "the so-called black hand letters are not the work of the Society." Further, data collected by the Pinkerton agent revealed that an autonomous organization existed in each of the towns; members consisted entirely of Calabrians; and each member referred to his group as "the Society." Moreover, residents of the town believed the organization to be *mafia*-like, although the various leaders with whom he had talked could not agree "as to the formation of the Society and the reasons for its existence." The agent's letters pinpointed extortion as a general group motive; such extortion victimized the organization's weaker and more vulnerable members for the profit of the stronger.

Many concerned people within the Italian community and in American officialdom wrestled with the problem of crime among the newcomers—a problem increasing over the years in importance and impact, according to newspaper accounts as well as official reports. "Sooner or later, if the Black Hand is not checked," commented Lindsay Denison, "it will be a menace not only to Italian-born Americans but to all of us." In fact, non-Italians did receive Black Hand threats, but in every case the senders as well as the recipients were non-Italians. Some would-be extortionists attempted to profit from the fear fostered by publicity accorded Black Hand violence. Thus, George Boljer, a prosperous butcher and owner of several tenements who resided at 412 Henry Street in Brooklyn, received a Black Hand letter threatening death if he did not deliver $700 to a designated place. When the police set a trap for the expected Italian brigands, the aspiring extortionist turned out to be one Mrs. Mary Peters, a tenant of

Boljer's who believed that he should share some of the wealth that he displayed so ostentatiously. In a similar situation, W. J. Snow, owner of a tenement on Vivian Place in Lynn, Massachusetts, received a Black Hand letter on February 14, 1908, demanding that rents not be raised; his death would be the price of non-compliance. Not surprisingly, the police conjectured that tenants had sent the letter.

In March 1908 Harry Reik, a farmer's son who hoped to capitalize on Black Hand notoriety, sent dairyman Albert Snedeger, who lived just outside Wheeling, West Virginia, a Black Hand letter demanding $1,000 on pain of death. When caught by the police, Reik stated that he had heard of other people's obtaining money in this way, and he wanted his share. Others sent perverse or callous letters. In the wake of the Di Giorgio bombing in Baltimore, George Savage of 115 Park Avenue, Baltimore, received a letter demanding $500 and threatening to kidnap his daughter. According to the police, the threat, dated December 12, 1907, was the work of "some youths with rather a peculiar sense of humor." Miss Henrietta Trippe of the same city received a note on January 19, 1908, demanding $25. The perpetrator turned out to be a "mischievous boy."

Non-Italian as well as Italian-Americans applauded the formation in early 1904 (shortly after the press had identified and publicized the Black Hand) of the 8-man Italian squad in New York City's Detective Bureau under the leadership of Sergeant (soon to be Lieutenant) Joseph Petrosino. Similar units were formed in other cities. Non-Italians also approved of measures taken by the "better elements" within the Italian communities to fight the Black Hand. In one such undertaking, Italian leaders in Chicago joined together and on November 11, 1907, organized the White Hand Society, amid much fanfare and the full support of the city's leading Italian-language newspapers, *L'Italia* and *La Tribuna Italiana Transatlantica*, as well as of the Italian Ambassador in Washington and the Italian Minister of Foreign Affairs in Rome. Organizers expressed the hope that a glorious new era would begin with this "war without truce, war without quarter" against the Black Hand, and looked forward to the day when there would be White Hand (*Mano Bianca*) groups "in all the cities which contain large Italian colonies, which suspect the existence of *Mafiosi* or *Camorristi* in their midst. By the end of the month *Mano Bianca* units existed in Pittsburgh, New Orleans, Baltimore, and other cities, but the early hopes were not fulfilled. White Hand groups, however, realized some successes: Giuseppe Sunseri and E. Bisi, rich Pittsburgh merchants and members of that city's White Hand, and friends of Baltimore Black Hand victim Joseph Di Giorgio, fought a battle with Black Handers in the Pennsylvania Railroad yards on December 9, 1907. In the exchange of gunfire Sunseri was wounded, but he killed one of his assailants, Philip Rei.

Despite good publicity and some support in other cities, the *Mano Bianca* remained primarily a Chicago operation, and clearly its success or failure would be determined in that city. By January 1908 it claimed to have driven ten of Chicago's most dangerous Italian criminals out of the city, and in February it announced additional successes. During the same month, however, the *Mano Nera* counterattacked. On February 28, Dr. Carlo Volini, president of Chicago's White Hand Society, received a letter informing him that

> the supreme council of the Black Hand has voted that you must die. You have not heeded our warnings in the past, but you must heed this. Your killing has been assigned and the man waits for you.

Volini professed to reporters that he was unafraid, and that he and his organization intended to continue the fight. "They may kill me," the reporters quoted him, "but the cause for which I live will go on."

Dr. Volini was not killed, but the fortunes of the White Hand declined rapidly after that—not so much because of Black Hand pressures as of lack of Italian immigrant support for the White Hand. The instinct of self-preservation, rather than apathy or indifference, lay behind this lack of support. Immigrants knew that crime pervaded their community; they knew also that authorities could or would do little to eliminate it. They believed that the White Hand was powerless in the face of official corruption or tolerance of corruption, and they had no desire to get involved in a lost cause.

The murder of Lieutenant Petrosino in Palermo on March 12, 1909, sent tremors of terror through the Italian communities and the American community as well. Joseph Petrosino seemed to epitomize the American success story for many within and outside the Italian colony. The son of a tailor, Petrosino migrated to New York with his parents from Padula, province of Salerno, when he was nine. He supplemented the family income first as a newsboy and later as a boot-black, while he attended school. Before entering the police department in 1883 (when he was 23), he worked as a tailor, a clerk in a bank, and a "white wing" (Sanitation Department employee). Dependable, hard-working, loyal, and physically brave, the short, husky Petrosino formed a model police officer—though his rise through the ranks was slow, in part because of prejudice against Italians, in part because he was not noted for an incisive or probing mind.

His greatest opportunity came in 1904 when, in the midst of the city's first Black Hand scare, he assumed command of the newly formed Italian squad, and shortly thereafter received promotion to lieutenant. On February 19, 1909, less than a month before his trip to Italy, he was named head of the new secret service branch of the police department, a high-powered super-secret agency whose function was to crush anarchists and the Black Hand. (In the public view, and apparently also that of Police Commissioner Theodore Bingham, the two were intertwined.) As head of this powerful unit, Petrosino was in line for a captaincy.

With the approval of the Italian government and the Italian police, Bingham sent Petrosino to Italy to gain information on several of the (estimated) five thousand Italians in New York who—Petrosino believed—had Old World criminal records. During his 26-year career with the police, Petrosino was credited with returning more than five hundred criminals to Italy to serve jail sentences they had eluded by emigrating. He was to gain further information in Italy so that even more criminals could be returned to Italian jail cells.

Petrosino's murder, like that of Hennessy in New Orleans nineteen years before, inflated the reputation of *mafia* power in Sicily and Black Hand power in America, and confirmed the widespread belief that if the *mafia* decided to "get" someone, sooner or later that person would die violently, despite any precautions he might take. This belief presupposed, of course, that Petrosino's trip to Italy was a tightly guarded secret, and since it was a secret (the public reasoned), that the *mafia* found it out and killed him meant that the *mafia* had informers within the Italian government and the police force, probably in both Palermo and Rome. But Petrosino's trip was common knowledge before he left America. Thus, on February 5, 1909, New York's *L'Araldo Italiano* carried an announcement of Petrosino's departure for Italy on the 9th; the announcement outlined his itinerary. The purpose of his trip was described, and the writer wished him well in his information-gathering mission. Any person with access to the Italian-language press of New York knew of Petrosino's plans and itinerary. English-language newspapers also discussed Petrosino's forthcoming trip. A *Herald* editor on February 20, 1909, told of his presence in Italy to "procure important information about Italian criminals who have come to this country." New York police sought this information, explained the writer, because they knew of "many criminals in the city whom they would like to deport, . . . [but] lack definite information about their records in Europe necessary to prove their case." Hence, anyone who could read—particularly one with money and contacts—could travel to Italy, or send the information to friends or relatives there. Petrosino's death could easily have been arranged.

So great was the prestige attendant upon accomplishing the murder of a law enforcement officer of the status of Petrosino that criminals in both Italy and the United States competed for responsibility. Don Vito Cascio Ferro, the dominant *mafia* leader in Sicily from the turn of the century to the 1920s (when the Fascists broke his power), allegedly admitted publicly of only one murder, that of Petrosino. After arranging an alibi at the home of a friend who was a member of the Chamber of Deputies, Don Vito drove to the center of Palermo—in his friend's carriage—and waited for Petrosino. According to Michele Pantaleone, he, then "killed him with one deadly shot" and returned to the deputy's house. When he was charged with the murder, Don Vito "easily got away with his crime through the testimony of his authoritative friend who swore that his guest had never left his home."

Michael Fiaschetti, an associate of Petrosino on the Italian squad and his successor as its head, later claimed that on an undercover trip to Italy in 1921 he learned the identity of the murderer. Friends he made among the Neapolitan *Camorra* openly discussed the activities of their Sicilian counterparts. According to Fiaschetti, the killer had emigrated to the United States several years after Petrosino's death. "The man who killed Petrosino is still somewhere in the United States," Fiaschetti wrote in 1930, although he never learned the assassin's name. This man could not have been Don Vito, who at that time resided in a Fascist prison. Reporter Ed Reid maintained that "the murderer of Joseph Petrosino, or rather the man who plotted that infamous crime," was New Orleans crime figure Paul Di Cristina. *L'Araldo Italiano* claimed the dubious honor for those New York criminals who were potential targets of Petrosino's fact-finding trip. Regardless of who pulled the trigger, Petrosino's death was an important victory for the underworld. Information leakages to the press made the assassination attempt possible. Petrosino made the murderer's task easier by traveling alone, although he knew that he was in enemy territory and had made many enemies by virtue of his effective (if rough) handling of Black Hand and other Italian-descended criminals in New York.

The New York Italian squad continued to function after Petrosino's death. Anti-crime groups (like the White Hand) and Italian squads organized to battle the extortion gangs contributed to the decline of the Black Hand during the late 1910s and the virtual disappearance of the gangs in the 1920s, but neither citizen committees nor police squads were primarily responsible for the end of the Black Hand era. At least three factors contributed to its demise. First, the supply of vulnerable victims dwindled with the termination of immigration after

1914 and the onset of hostilities in Europe. Second, there existed the potential for effective federal action, as pointed out in June 1915 in the Chicago *Herald*:

> The fact that the "Black Hand" criminal can hardly operate without sending his letters through the mail—as personal delivery of any sort would leave dangerous clues behind— gives the Government practical jurisdiction of the greater part of these offenses.

In 1915 federal officials enforced the laws prohibiting the use of the mails to defraud, and Black Handers did indeed have to resort to personal delivery of notes. Since the risk of being recognized rose drastically, many would-be extortionists were undoubtedly discouraged from taking this approach. As journalist Frank Marshall White accurately predicted in 1918, "There is every reason to believe that the words black and hand in conjunction will soon cease to have a sinister connotation in this country."

These two factors limited the opportunities for criminals in the ethnic colony. The third factor involved a vast new field of endeavor that presented itself when federal laws (enacted originally as a wartime measure) prohibited the manufacture and sale of alcoholic beverages. American tastes and habits did not adjust to the new regulations, and enterprising young men found themselves in a position to reap immense profits. Many well-qualified Black Handers like Frank Uale (Yale) of Brooklyn, "Scarface" Di Giovanni of Kansas City, Vincenzo Cosmanno and the Genna brothers of Chicago left the less profitable extortion rackets of the Italian quarter in order to move into the more lucrative work of producing and distributing illicit alcohol. Indicative of this shift, and also one consequence of it, was the decision of the New York City Police Department in 1924 to disband the Italian squad, then headed by Mike Fiaschetti. The reason, wrote Edward Dean Sullivan in 1930, was that "the top calibre blackhanders were all in the booze game. No work—slight risk—vast remuneration."

Although some Black Hand bands continued to operate in the 1920s, especially in New York, which continued to receive a trickle of new immigrants even after the restrictive immigration laws of 1921 and 1924 were passed, prohibition marked the end of the Black Hand era.

from The Mafia in America
by Howard Abadinsky

Some interesting work on organized crime comes from scholars fascinated by its role in society. Howard Abadinsky (born 1941) recorded a New Jersey mafioso's matter-of-fact account of various scams and their outcomes.

The Big Con

In the early 1960s I decided that I was going into the disposal end of the garbage business. Environmental controls were becoming more stringent, and the public was becoming aware of the pollution that getting rid of garbage was causing. The politicians started to enact legislation to control this situation, and landfill laws, which had been on the books for a long time, were now being enforced. A landfill is essentially a garbage dump, except that at the end of each day's work you have to cover the garbage with earth fill; you have to make a cell out of the garbage brought in each day. Upon completion of the landfill, which might have a longevity of anywhere from 1 year to 20 years, the entire area has to be covered with two feet of cover material. There were other things that had to be done: prepare proper drainage, provide ventilation for the methane gas that the garbage produces as it deteriorates, and apply other engineering techniques. If you did not conform to the rules, you lost your permit to operate the landfill in a given municipality. In all of this I saw an opportunity. I had always been well-read in the technology of refuse collection and disposal, and I was a member of several professional organizations: the American Public Works Association, the Institute for Solid Wastes, and the Association of Mechanical Engineers, although I was obviously not an engineer.

At that point in time, there were really only two acceptable ways to get rid of solid waste: landfill and, the more expensive, incineration. In looking at the situation as it applied to North Jersey, more refuse disposal outlets were needed, and the situation was on its way to being critical. I approached some municipalities on a very informal basis in efforts to acquire the necessary permits to operate a landfill. The responses were totally negative. Because of public animosity, there was no way that I could beg, borrow, steal, or lease a piece of land and get the permits that were necessary to operate a landfill. This left incineration.

If you could convince a group of politicians that you would operate an environmentally clean incinerator facility, you might stand a chance. In researching the environmental law and the pollution control law, I came across a New Jersey statute that allowed a municipality, under home rule, to grant a franchise for a period not to exceed 20 years for the construction and operation of an incinerator facility within the confines of a municipality. All you had to do was find a municipality that would allow you to do this. I started to speak, informally, to municipal officials. I put together a presentation package using engineers. The response was negative until I reached (we will call it) Viceroy. They were desperate for a "ratable," a taxable piece of property, a building that they could assess a tax against. An incinerator is a very expensive building; we were talking about several million dollars. This small town had an astronomically high property tax and a piece of industrial-zoned land perfect for the incinerator. I designed a very attractive presentation and made some "presentations" (bribes), and the officials agreed to issue the permit.

The next step was to get money. I had put some of my own money in the preliminaries and a deposit of $7,500 for the parcel of land. I also discussed this venture with Joe Paterno who thought the idea was great; he could see all kinds of dollar signs, and I felt that he could bring me all the business I needed once the project was completed. In addition, I felt that if anything went wrong, I could rely on his financial and political power.

I formed a corporation (we will call)—the North Jersey Incinerator Authority, Inc. I got some static from the New Jersey attorney general because the word *authority* designates some kind of governmental agency. However, there were no legal prohibitions against the private use of the term, although since that time this has been corrected by legislation. I established two classifications of stock, class A, voting, and class B, nonvoting. The stock was going to sell for $50 a share in blocks of 100 shares. For a $5,000 investment you would get 95 shares of nonvoting stock and 5 shares of voting stock. For me it would be the reverse. This was legit because I founded the corporation, and I could acquire this type of stock for services that I rendered and would continue to render. Several business associates were approached, legitimate people, and I invited them and their friends to an expensive restaurant for dinner and a presentation of the advantages of investing in the corporation. At first things went poorly, but several dinners and presentations later the money began to roll in.

To set prospective investors at ease, I had them send the check to the office of the attorney for the corporation. In a matter of several months, I raised in actual cash about $125,000, still considerably short of what it was going to take to really put this package together. However, during 1965 and 1966 I was drawing $300 a week in salary as administrator of the Incinerator Authority, Inc. In addition, I had several garbage accounts that I had kept even after deciding to get into the disposal end of the business.

If the project was to reach fruition, however, more money would be needed. At the same time I began to get some static from indignant stockholders: "When are we going to get this show on the road. You know you've had my money tied up for one, two years, and I'm not getting any return. When are we going to start making money?" I called a stockholder's meeting, a dinner meeting—steaks, always the best, it wasn't my money—to discuss a financial commitment from the Small Business Investment Corporation (SBIC), which gets its money from the Small Business Administration, a federal agency. The commitment was for $1.5 million and I had been using it as a way to get the stockholders off my back. However, in order to qualify for the loan, it was necessary to produce the financial records of the corporation for an audit. This I did not want to do—not because of my salary, which was legit, but because of some payments that had been made. There had been payoffs to officials in Viceroy, to officials of the New Jersey Environmental Pollution Control Agency, or whatever it was called, and so on. Most of the stockholders were not aware of these payoffs, which amounted to about $25,000. There were also other questionable items. In an attempt to get officials to issue me a permit, I had taken them to the Playboy Club in New York and other such places. I showed them all a good time and, in plain English, a lot of guys got laid. These payments were covered by checks made out to cash in small amounts, $100 to $300, adding up to about $6,000. These items would be difficult to explain to a legitimate lending organization like the SBIC. It would taint the project and keep them from getting involved.

My reluctance to move for the loan resulted in several stockholders suing for the return of their money. I fought the suit and there was not much to worry about; at that time it took about three years for a civil action to get into court—that's how crowded the calendars were. I felt like discarding the whole project, turning it into one big rip-off—it didn't really take me long to get this feeling. I just figured that this lawsuit would make it impossible to get any more money from any legitimate lending institution. It's one thing if the incinerator were already built, but a lawsuit in the embryo stage just knocks you out of the ballgame.

I raised my salary from $15,000 to $30,000 a year and started to drain off the money. I had my attorney give me some inflated bills for legal services rendered to the corporation. In six months I extracted all of the remaining assets, about $100,000; and for all intents and purposes, the corporation was bankrupt. The stockholders started to use funny terms like *fraud*, *criminal fraud*, things like that, but it didn't faze me in the least. They were hollow threats, and no such action was ever commenced. The lawsuit did not even come before the courts until, would you believe, 1972, at which time I was in the Witness Protection Program. The Justice Department did advise me that I would have to defend against the suit, and they even went to the expense of bringing me back to New Jersey, giving me all kinds of security protection. The court session was held *in camera*, no one was allowed into the courtroom except direct participants, and the courtroom doors were locked with U.S. marshals all over the place. I lost the case, and a judgment was rendered against me. I guess it remains rendered against me, and the stockholders are still trying to collect.[*]

The Uncertainties Of Loan Sharking

While this was going on, I accepted an "assignment" from Joe Paterno. There was this street guy by the name of Carmine Sassone. Carmine had been given some money by Paterno to lend on the street. Carmine was a trusted street soldier, and Paterno did not want anything to do directly with Shylocking anymore. To insulate himself he would give sums of money to trusted people to loan out. The guy that was lending it would get half of the profit; Joe would get the other half. Carmine went to jail for about 18 months, and he had a couple of his guys

---

[*] The Witness Protection Program was provided for in the Organized Crime Control Act of 1970. It authorized the attorney general to provide for the security of witnesses, potential witnesses, and their families in legal proceedings against any person alleged to have participated in an organized criminal activity. The legislation, which was amended in 1977 (with the passage of the Criminal Code Reform Act), authorizes the attorney general to relocate witnesses and their families, providing transportation and housing, "suitable official documents to enable the person to establish a new identity," and assist the person relocated in obtaining employment. The statute permits the attorney general to refuse to disclose any and all information about the identity of the person relocated, etcetera. However, the statute does require that the attorney general make reasonable efforts to ensure witness compliance in civil cases.

handle Paterno's money on the street. When he got out of prison, Carmine found some discrepancies, but he became very ill with cancer. Carmine had married a woman by the name of Katherine—"Kathy the Jew" was her nickname for the obvious reason that she was Jewish. This was a very bad broad. When I say "bad," I mean that she had her own criminal record: abortions and paperhanging—all kinds of stuff.

In any event, Carmine dies and Kathy wants to continue in the Shylock business. She has her husband's book that says who owes how much, but she is experiencing difficulty getting her money. She was using very low-echelon street people who were ripping her off as they would collect the money. At the same time, Paterno was not getting his share of the money. He told me about it in passing; it wasn't something that he told me to do specifically: "See if you can get close to the broad and find out what she is doing with my money before I have to get involved directly." So I worked out an introduction to Kathy and started spending time at her house. She was in dire financial straits, and I helped her refinance the mortgage on her house and gave her some pocket money to carry her over during this period of time. At the same time I was able to get hold of the book and find out what was happening to Joe's money. But this crazy broad falls in love with me; it was a question of being there at the right time and befriending her during a difficult period. Her husband had a wristwatch that had 48 diamonds around the face; it had a retail value of about $20,000. How he acquired it I don't know, although I could guess. Besides the dollar value, the watch also had sentimental value to Kathy. Because of our relationship, she gave the wristwatch to me as a gift.

Now I had done my job, and I was no longer interested in continuing my relationship with Kathy. Being aware of the danger of a "woman scorned," I commenced the breakaway process a little at a time. I concocted some stories about how my wife was getting suspicious, and so on. During this time one of her acquaintances, an auto thief, asked her for permission to store a stolen Cadillac in her garage—he was going to store the car until it cooled off and he could sell it. Somebody, I don't know who, and I tell you it wasn't me, "dropped a dime"—called up anonymously and told the police that this woman had a stolen automobile in her garage. The police came and they checked out the serial number, found out it was stolen, and arrested Kathy. She accused me of "ratting her out" on the basis that I had been trying to get rid of her and this was a quick way to do it. I didn't deny the fact that I wanted to get rid of her, but I denied ratting on her because I hadn't.

In any event, to and behold I get charged with having stolen the car on her word only. This is a hell of a weak case because it's only her word against mine; there is no corroborating evidence. But, the district attorney figures he's got a case. I am charged and indicted and go to trial. Before a jury in Essex County Superior Court Kathy is placed on the stand, and my lawyer tore her to pieces. She got me off as much as she got me indicted. My lawyer dragged out her criminal background, and she lost all credibility. In addition, it was also brought out that I was her lover and that she was a woman seeking vengeance. The jury was out only about 15 minutes when they brought back a verdict of not guilty. Of course, I refused to give back the watch.

As I noted, the watch was quite expensive, and Kathy demanded that it be returned, threatening dire consequences if it was not. The only trouble that I feared was that my wife would find out about the situation, but this was not the kind of trouble Kathy was offering. Instead, she got a fellow whose last name I never knew, but we called him "Jerry the Jew." Jerry was a tall, young man who had a reputation for serious violent activity: assault, assault with attempt to kill, assault with attempt to maim. Jerry was a very vicious guy with a bad reputation. He called me at home and wanted to set up a meeting, and I said, Sure, "Sure, we'll meet at Howard Johnson's in Bloomfield, New Jersey." At the restaurant Jerry told me right out in front that he wanted the watch returned to Kathy—or I was going to get my legs broken or worse. I am not a violent person, but I asked him if he knew who he was talking to: "I don't give a crap who you are. I want the watch." I told my menacing companion that he was not going to get it and advised him to take back what he had said—"Because I don't want to see you get hurt." I informed Jerry that he was being disrespectful to the people I am with, and if I take it back to them, there is going to be a lot of trouble. I tried to impress upon him just how important "respect" was to the people I was with. He didn't care.

I called Paterno from the Howard Johnson's and he says, "We'll take care of it." Three days later I get a call from Joe: "Meet me at the Mai Kai." This is a Chinese restaurant on Bloomfield Avenue where Italian street people would meet, and Joe used to go there all the time. I arrived at the Mai Kai and walked into the small back room. Joe was there as well as Jerry. One of Joe's men was outside and another guy was in the room we called the "Count": he was involved in numbers gambling. Jerry was apparently associated with him. The meeting only lasted a few short minutes. I sat down and Joe began: "Look," he said, pointing to me, "Vito has something that was given to him and you want it. You want it for yourself or you want it because somebody asked you to get it for them. Now it ain't going back; it is staying right where it is. Do you understand that? Vito is with me—leave him alone. One more phone call, one more meeting, one more threat, and *it's all over for you.*" Now he is pointing at Jerry. Jerry is not saying a word, but he looks over to the Count and shakes his head up and down in agreement. Thank you, goodbye, it was all over. I never heard another thing about it. As it turned out, I lost the friggin' watch in a crap game about three months later.

The Big Rip-Off

I was at home reading the newspaper when I saw an advertisement for a warehouseman in a nearby community. As a lark, a total lark, I went down and applied for the job. I knew nothing about warehousing, inventory controls, and all that. From a three-minute interview with the warehouse manager, I realized that he knew less about running a warehouse than I did—and I knew nothing. Ben Moss not his real name had gotten the job through the efforts of his brother Joe, who was president of the corporation that owned the warehouse. Ben was the epitome of the "Peter principle"; he had been elevated to a position that was far above his capabilities. The firm (we will call), the Neuman Corporation, was listed on the American Stock Exchange, and it manufactured expensive ceramic tiles. It had plants in Boston and Alabama, and the warehouse was going to provide a centralized receiving area from which the finished product would be shipped to distributors throughout the New York–New Jersey metropolitan area. The facility was very large, over 10,000 square feet of floor space, and I ran it completely. I filled the orders as they came in over the phone or off the street. Ben spent the entire day in the front office, doing what I don't know. We had one other employee, Judy, a young girl who Ben had hired to take care of the paper work. Judy and I became very good friends—we are sleeping together and I am promoting her, getting her salary raises. This is all necessary to milk the company for everything that it is worth.

After being there for about two months, and by pure coincidence, who should walk into the showroom but Joe's brother, Nick Paterno. You must remember that Nick, as well as Joe Paterno, had absolutely nothing to do with his time. The guy was totally and completely unemployed except on paper. Because of his brother's affiliations, Nick was listed as a consultant for a major construction company in northern New Jersey. He was drawing $500 or $600 a week for a no-show job. With so much time on his hands he would often go window-shopping or look at new automobiles. Apparently he saw that this warehouse had opened up, that they had a showroom where they displayed their wares, and he came in to look. I bumped into him and took the opportunity to outline my plan for ripping off this company, and he suggested that I talk to Joe about it.

It is an unwritten rule that if you are with these *mafia* people, and you have done each other favors, you must share some of the fruits of successful activities. Joe said, "If you are going to eat, you don't eat alone." You pay tribute; in return for paying this tribute, you hope that if anything goes wrong, that somehow or someway they will be able to help you. Joe, for example, had heavy connections in the Essex County government; the prosecutor's office was one agency that he had influence with. I learned this rule from Joe: "If you eat alone, you're going to die alone." This, of course, could mean a lot of things. It could mean that you wouldn't have any friends, that no one is going to help you. It could, obviously, also be viewed as a threat. However, if you are involved with somebody that is important in organized crime, that person may have some activity in the geographic area that he is in control of that you do not know anything about.

If you are going to become involved in some additional criminal activity in that same area, you may be doing something detrimental to his interests. For example, let's suppose that I was a professional bank robber and I planned to rob the bank on the corner. Now Paterno may be sponsoring another group of thieves, providing financing and giving his approval, who plan to rip off the savings and loan only two blocks away from here. That will bring heat into the area and will be detrimental to his plans and his investment. A professional, whether or not he is directly in organized crime, will often touch bases with the *capo* in an area he is planning to work. You do this, and you also let him "wet his beak"—give him a small portion of the proceeds. This is insurance money. If trouble would have come in a big way, with law enforcement authorities, for example, Joe Paterno could help. It might be nothing more than getting your indictment put to the bottom of the pile. Delay is always the friend of the defendant. Joe always said that time was your friend: "People forget, they move away, and," he meant this from a violent point of view, "people could take vacations and never come back."

My plan was really simple. I was the receiver of all goods that entered the warehouse. I received the incoming slips for trailer loads of material. These slips would, in turn, go to the front office where Ben would conceivably check them out and give them to Judy who would make the entries in the inventory control book. Because of my relationship with Judy, she made false entries. Instead of putting down 1,000 boxes of number 235 tile, for example, she would make an entry that there were only 500 boxes of number 235, leaving 500 boxes for me to dispose of privately. If you go to the house that Nick Paterno lived in, you will find his kitchen, his bathroom, part of his game room, and his garage walls lined with Neuman tiles that were stolen from the corporation warehouse. Ceramic tiles are very expensive, and I eventually built up a tremendous inventory of my own: I knew what was the company's and what was "mine," so to speak. The next problem, and it wasn't any problem, was finding an outlet for my inventory. There were countless contractors who came into the warehouse to make purchases. They were often big guys who employed a number of people and had a lot of jobs going simultaneously. They would make large purchases of tile. My approach was direct: "Can you use some good colors"—not every color in tile was necessarily popular—"at a reduced cost? You've got to pay me in cash." "Are you kidding, I'll take all you can give me," was the usual reply. Customers were no problem, and these were otherwise legitimate businessmen.

I did so much business with these people in cash that in the basement of my home there were three 20 gallon garbage cans, the regular kind that you use to put out for the garbageman to pick up. Only these garbage cans were stuffed full of cash—so much cash that I had to get in the cans and stomp down on them to make room for more. In addition, I was giving a small portion of this cash flow to my attorney in a trust for me in his name. Theoretically, the money could then not be traced to me. I could hardly put it in the bank; here I am drawing $300 a week from the incinerator and getting $90 a week from Neuman; they were exploiting me; how can you have a bank account with $50,000 in it?

I was also paying tribute to Paterno, insurance that in the event the bubble burst I would get the benefit of Paterno's connections. I paid him 10 percent of whatever I took in and he accepted my word. He said, "I want ten percent of whatever you take in." I didn't have to furnish him with an accounting; if at the end of the week I gave him $200, that meant that I had taken in $2,000 for myself. He didn't ever question my word; I was beating him and he probably knew it, but as long as he was getting something for doing absolutely nothing, there were no complaints.

At the end of the year, in December, we had to take an inventory of the entire warehouse. Naturally, I helped Judy do the inventory and I felt very safe. At the same time Ben was placing more and more responsibility on my shoulders owing to his inability to run the operation. We were building a big business, and the operation was getting to be too much for me to handle. I told Ben that we had to hire someone to help me. He says, "I've got just the guy, and he's out of work. His name is (we will call him) Jim Benson, and he used to work for me in my little tile business. I'll bring him in to talk with you." Jim was younger than me and as naive and dumb as they come. I even made him an officer in the North Jersey Incinerator Authority, Inc.

I wasn't about to take Jimmy into my confidence because I didn't know him. One day we got an order, a big order of what in the trade is called bathroom fixtures: soap dishes, toothbrush holders, towel racks, and so on. They came in a box called a five-piece bathroom fixture set. It was in a very popular color, fawn brown, and I went through my usual procedure of shorting the load. All of a sudden I realized that a lot of these boxes were disappearing without benefit of having been written down on a sales ticket. So one day a tile contractor came in whom I had never done any illegitimate business with. I told Jimmy to take care of his order, and I went off into another part of the warehouse and watched very closely. I saw Jimmy fill the order, and I saw him go to the cash register and make out the sales slip. The customer got one copy and the other copy would go into a box under the counter. The slips would eventually go to the front office. After the guy left, I sent Jimmy to get coffee and pulled the slip from the box. I noticed that there were items that the contractor had received but that Jimmy had not written down.

Jimmy came back with the coffee and I sat him down: "Jimmy, you gave that guy 15 boxes of tile that are not on the slip. Did you forget about it, or do you have something going for yourself here?" Well the kid—when I say *kid*, I'm talking about a married man in his late twenties—broke down and cried. "Yes," he confessed, "I had done business with that guy when I worked for Ben before, and the guy paid me in cash." Much to Jimmy's surprise I said, "If you're going to rip off the company, you're going to do it with me, not alone. I'm taking a little bit, too, Jimmy, but you're not doing anything to cover it up. We are both going to get hurt unless you do what I tell you."

Jimmy thought this was the greatest thing since the invention of toilet paper; I probably increased his take by 50 percent. I insisted that I didn't want to see any new cars being bought; you have got to live exactly like you have been doing. Live within your means I told him. And to help drain off some of the money—or to have an explanation for having it—I told him that we were going on a holiday to Las Vegas. I made all of the arrangements. I took $32,000 in cash with me, and Jimmy took about $5,000; and we went off to Vegas. I started to win a great deal of money, but then you lose perspective of what the money really is. In your mind you get the thought: "Oh hell, I'm not playing with my money. Now I'm playing with the house's money." You even lose the idea of what the value of money is because you are not playing with real money—you play with chips, a piece of plastic. Well, I got so hot at the blackjack table that I wasn't even counting the money anymore, not counting the chips. I was just pushing a stack of chips forward, and the dealer would just be matching the height of my chips with chips of the same color. In the matter of about an hour at the Silver Dollar, I won about $16,000 and Jimmy was going wild: "Send it home," he advised, "they will take it all away from you again; don't play with it, wire it home to your wife." This was good advice from a guy who I said was not too bright. I lost complete control of myself: "They can't beat me." But they did, and the Sands across the street took it away from me in about the same length of time. I came back broke, but I had enjoyed myself immensely.

The bilking continued at an even more hectic pace because the business was booming and the material was really flowing in from the factories. I even got a raise: I was actually making $125 by the time I left the job. Suddenly, disaster; Judy finds out that I am married—not only married but I have kids. Now this was a very straight girl. What she was doing was wrong, but she was doing it for me because she was in love with me. I was unquestionably taking advantage of her, using her. She found out that I was married and was heartbroken. I had told her that I was a widower living with my brother and his wife. One day my wife called and the two got into a conversation: "This is Vito's wife," she said, and that burst the bubble. Now this was disastrous. I didn't know what to expect from Judy. She went into the usual hysterics, and we had a meeting after work. She was still crying, threatening suicide, but at least not threatening to blow the whistle on my operation. I was able to calm her down by telling her that it was my intention to ulti-mately leave my wife, the usual bullshit guys give women in these sit-uations. She calmed down sufficiently in the next two days and said that it would be best for all concerned if she just left the company and discontinued any further contact with me. Afterward we communi-cated on a few occasions on a friendly basis. It was initiated by me because I wanted to satisfy myself that she was not going to take vengeance on me.

Judy's leaving presented a big problem for me. I now had nobody to make the false entries, and Ben was taking her place until a replace-ment could be hired. He advertised in the newspapers and finally hired a young woman (we will call), Laura. Laura was there a few weeks, and I was trying to feel her out, trying to figure out an approach. She was single and I took her to lunch a few times and decided to level with her. I explained the operation and said that there would be money in it for her. She was engaged to be married and wanted to sock some extra money away; the deal was made.

Now they say that truth is stranger than fiction, and this will blow your mind. I got into the habit of taking Laura out a couple of times a week for lunch and sometimes to supper as well. During one of our conversations, she says "I've had a wish for a long time, a desire." "To do what?" I asked. "Oh, you're going to laugh at me." "No, I'm not going to laugh. Tell me what it is." "I'd love to be a—prostitute." I was taken aback and couldn't tell if she was serious or pulling my leg. There was nothing in her background that would indicate this type of activity. She was about 20, tall, blonde, with a pretty face and a good figure. I told her that a lot of money could be earned in this area if she were really interested. She insisted that she was. I told her that she would have to learn the ropes—the kinkiness of sex that some people might expect. She was quite a willing pupil. After a few days of "education," I decided to call her bluff. I told her that I would set something up, and I did. I told Jimmy and a couple of tile guys—I asked them if they wanted to get laid. It was even easier than finding customers for the stolen tiles.

Laura's first exposure to prostitution was six men on the Neuman showroom couch. I collected the money, 20 bucks a shot, but I never kept any of it, I turned it all over to her. Now this has got to sound ridiculous, but it went against my grain to be a pimp. While this activity allowed me to have great control over her, I did not want *this* kind of money and gave it all to her. I didn't take any cut. I continued to pimp her on a weekly basis with countless people. What amazed me was the demand for this type of service. It is apparently a way of life for a lot of guys. I never kept a tally, but this broad must have easily made $7,000 for herself during the brief time that I was associated with her.

At the end of the year, inventory time rolls around again. Apparently a large shortage surfaced, and all of a sudden I see strange faces coming into the warehouse from the main office. They are tearing the figures apart, and when they can't find the shortage, they bring in an independent inventory company to make the physical count and check it against the records. For obvious reasons, I am not allowed to participate. Everybody starts asking questions, examining the procedures, and looking at the system that was used, and they find gaping holes in the management of the operation. They probably know that Ben is not a totally competent individual, but the thing is blatant. A guy from the main office is brought in to run the warehouse. He starts imposing rules and regulations on me for running the warehouse. They are not impossible to live with if you are running a legitimate operation. For me it's impossible to work under these conditions—for a lousy $125 a week. At the same time management was suspicious of me. The massive shortages pointed to me, although they could not prove it. One afternoon the manager calls me into the front office and tells me that he is letting me go. He doesn't pull any punches; he tells me out in front that a lot of bullshit has been going on and accuses me of being involved with it. Jimmy is to be fired also. "To be fair," he says, "I am going to give you two weeks pay, but I want you off the property *immediately.*"

I'm pissed off now. I'm hot because not only is the son-of-a-bitch taking away my bread, he is also being arrogant to me. "Look Bob," I say to him, "I'm a card-carrying member of the Teamsters Union (which was a lie). Every goddamn delivery that comes in here comes with team-ster drivers. Even though this is not a union shop and the normal rules do not apply, you are firing me without benefit of any cause. You are firing me on the basis that you have a suspicion. If you do this, I'm going to see to it that there's a picket line in front of this joint, because I'm a union member. You ain't gonna get any shipments." He laughed, and I was infuriated. "I am shutting this place down," I shouted to him. "Here's your money," he replied. "Now get out."*

I was so hot that when I left the warehouse, I went directly to see Joe Paterno. I told him what had happened. "I'll get you a union card, and you be down at Neuman's at 8:00 in the morning. There'll be three other guys there. Get some placards made up: 'On Strike,' 'Unfair to Labor,' the usual shit. We'll close 'em down." The next morning Jimmy and I, along with three of Paterno's goons, started picketing. Sure as hell, at about 10:00 in the morning a tractor trailer arrived. There ain't no way he is going to cross the picket line: "Hi Vito," he says, "what the hell is going on?" "These bastards fired us. They had no cause, and I'm a teamster card man." "Shit," he responds, "there ain't no way I'm gonna bring this load in." And he goes down to the corner store and calls up his shop, telling them that he is not going to cross the picket

---

* I have discussed this incident with several colleagues. All agreed that were they in a similar situation, they would have been only too glad to leave Neuman without being prosecuted. After all, Vito had systematically embez-zled thousands of dollars from the company, so why the "righteous indigna-tion"? Psychopath or sociopath were the frequent conclusions.

line. This went on for a week the warehouse got no shipments. I thought this was fantastic; here's a nobody like me tying up a massive corporation.

One afternoon Bob comes trotting out and says he wants to talk to me. "We are going to start all kinds of legal actions, the labor relations board, the courts, the whole thing. This is unfair to management. We are not a union shop; we do not want to go through all this expense, and I don't think that you want to go through it either because there may be other revelations." He didn't elaborate on what these revelations might be, but he added: "Can't we compromise this situation?" "I want to be compensated," I replied. I said that I'm not talking about compensation in the form of a reference or some other job—I want to be compensated in the form of dollars. He could have gotten us tossed away anyhow because he was legally in the right. What good would it do to continue to harass the company? The whole picket thing was just my way of blowing off steam, vengeance. "Will another couple of weeks severance pay make you happy until you can find something else?" "A couple of weeks," I answered, "I want a couple of months." We settled on an additional $600 and the picket line was disbanded. Again, it wasn't a matter of money; it was a strange streak of pride.

For a 19-month period they came up with a shortage of $350,000; it looks like they got ripped off by their inventory firm also—I had stolen a lot more than that. I had secreted more than $150,000 in cash in my garbage cans. I had also purchased, through my lawyer, a three-acre parcel of land for $15,000. I built my house with the proceeds of the Neuman rip-off; it cost me $150,000. I also owned two Jaguar automobiles and showered my family with gifts: diamond rings, fur coats, and so on.

Mafia House

I built my house in (we will call it) Mason, New Jersey, and, although it did not start out that way, it became the most pretentious house in the neighborhood. While it was under construction, the money kept rolling in. So, instead of the asphalt shingle roof that the plans called for, I used ceramic tiles, and this required a change in the structure so that the roof could hold the weight of the tiles. Instead of a wooden exterior, I used stone and stone veneer. I made a connection through Paterno and had a 90-foot hall running the whole length of the house covered with marble. There were solid walnut cabinets, a slate floor in the kitchen, and quarry tiles in the dining room. I put in a sodded lawn—instant lawn, because in the morning there was nothing but topsoil all nicely raked and graded and by afternoon there was a whole brand new lawn of Kentucky blue grass. It cost me $4,000.

The house became known in the neighborhood as the *mafioso's* house. I learned that the neighbors used that term for the first time from my kids: "They think that we are *mafia*, daddy." Remember, we rode around in Jaguar automobiles and I kept irregular hours. I was an Italian who was in a business, garbage, known to be mob-infiltrated or mob connected. Another thing that tended to lend credence to the *Mafioso* image was Nick Paterno, who often came to visit. Nick drove a big, black Cadillac, and if there is anything to the stereotype of a *Mafioso*-type person, Nick would fall into that category. He dressed like one, and he acted like one. He wore black Italian silk suits and expensive jewelry, diamond pinky rings. He looked like a Mediterranean, an Italian, and he spoke like a street person, not too much culture. I never tried to change people's impressions of me, and certainly no one ever asked me directly if I was in the *mafia*. If they had, I don't know what I would have answered, but nobody ever did. It is not a question that you ask somebody.*

---

* "For those present, many sources of information become accessible and many carriers (or 'sign-vehicles') become available for conveying this information. If unacquainted with the individual, observers can glean clues from his conduct and appearance which allow them to apply their previous experience with individuals roughly similar to the one before them or, more important, to apply untested stereotypes to him. They can assume from past experience that only individuals of a particular kind are likely to be found in a given social setting. They can rely on what the individual says about himself or on documentary evidence he provides as to who and what he is. If they know, or know of, the individual by virtue of experience prior to the interaction, they can rely on assumptions as to the persistence and generality of psychological traits as a means of predicting his present and future behavior" (Goffman, 1973, p. 1).

An incident occurred that added to the *mafia* image. This little "Mickey Mouse" community of Mason had a garbage contract with a small refuse firm. He provided rear yard collection: he walked behind your house with his barrel, dumped your barrels into his barrel, and carried his barrel out to the truck. At the expiration of his contract, he wanted to change to a curbside service, meaning that the residents of this club community would have to take their garbage out to the curbline. This did not please the board of directors. Because I had been in the garbage business, these directors came to me for advice. I told them not to worry about it, that I would take care of everything. I also did not like having to take the refuse out to the curbline. The dogs are always knocking it over, and it would make the neighborhood look trashy. I told them I would get it all straightened out.

I called the contractor, who knew of me from the association, and asked him to do me a favor: continue his current service for another year. I told him that at that time I would try to help him shift to a curbside service. I intimated that I was acting as his friend, that the directors would not accept the change he proposed at this time. He was reluctant, but he agreed. "I'll go along with it for another year." A week later he completely reneged; he sent a letter to the directors telling them that effective on a certain date the refuse would have to be put out on the curbline or it would not be serviced. Needless to say, this made me look like a fool.* I had told my neighbors that I would take care of it. We

---

* "Given the fact that the individual effectively projects a definition of the situation when he enters the presence of others, we can assume that events may occur within the interaction which contradict, discredit, or otherwise throw doubt upon this projection. When these disruptive events occur, the interaction itself may come to a confused and embarrassed halt. Some of the assumptions upon which the responses of the participants had been predicated become untenable, and the participants find themselves lodged in interaction for which the situation has been wrongly defined and is now no longer defined. At such moments the individual whose presentation had been discredited may feel ashamed while others present may feel hostile, and all the participants may come to feel ill at ease, nonplussed, out of countenance, embarrassed, experiencing the kind of anomy that is generated when the minute social system of face-to-face interaction breaks down" (Goffman, 1973, p. 12).

were all socially close: we had backyard gatherings, we went to each other's homes, and we went out socially. One afternoon a neighbor from across the street came over and told me that the board had received this letter from the contractor, and they were going to have a meeting—would I attend and was there anything I could do about it?[*]

It was a matter of pride: this was going to be straightened out one way or another. At that instant, in front of my neighbor, I picked up the telephone and called the contractor. In no uncertain terms I told him that I was holding him to his word; there would be very serious repercussions: "I will personally see to it that not only will you not have any work in Mason, you won't have any work—*period*."

On the effective date that the householders were supposed to put their garbage out on the curbline, I told the board of directors that it would not be necessary. There had merely been a "misunderstanding." And as sure as God made little red apples, the contractor came around on his regularly scheduled day and went behind each and every household to pick up the refuse. He also entered into another contract for continued rear-yard service. He apparently believed me when I threatened him over the phone. He knew of my former contractor's association and my connection to Paterno; whichever it was, he was in no position to test me. I saw him on a couple of occasions after that, and he was always quite pleasant to the point of being apologetic.[**]

Stocks, Bonds, And Checks

(During the latter part of the 1960s and early 1970s, there was substantial growth in the securities industry. Record sales resulted in hasty expansion on the part of trading companies. The physical security and

---

[*] "An individual who implicitly signifies that he has certain social characteristics ought in fact to be what he claims he is." He exerts a "moral demand" that requires fulfillment (Goffman, 1973, p. 13).

[**] "Insofar as the others act *as if* the individual had conveyed a particular impression, we may take a functional or pragmatic view and say that the individual has 'effectively' projected a given definition of the situation and 'effectively' fostered the understanding that a given state of affairs obtains" (Goffman, 1973, p. 6).

controls that should normally accompany such expansion were neglected, as companies rushed to capitalize on the sales boom. The result was inevitable: large-scale thefts of bonds, stocks, and negotiable securities.

Prior to the 1960s, stolen "paper"—checks, stocks, and bonds—was not usually recognized as having any value to most criminals. They were accustomed to dealing with cash, jewels, and other such tangible items. Organized crime figures, however, had ready access to this type of paper. Carmine Lombardozi, [*] for example, is reputed to have had several securities employees under his control as a result of gambling and Shylock indebtedness. These organized crime figures, however, did not have the necessary expertise to convert the paper into cash. They needed the assistance of experts, the paperman.)

One day Paterno asks if I could convert some stocks and bonds into cash: "See what you can work out and I'll give you a percentage. I'm getting involved with other things and I won't have much time for this activity. You work with my brother Nickie." At this point in time Joe was heavily involved in real estate. [**] He had formed an association with a legitimate Jewish guy whose first name was Howard, but I can't remember his last name. [***] This guy had a lot of smarts and knew real estate investment.

---

[*] Carmine Lombardozi was a *caporegime* in the Gambino family.

[**] Sullivan (1972) reported that New Jersey officials were investigating real estate transactions in the Hackensack Meadowlands on which a football stadium for the New York Giants was built. It was reported that Joseph Paterno owned 21.4 acres of the sports complex site valued (in 1972) at about $90,000 an acre. Paterno was also identified as being partners with his brother-in-law in two realty concerns that owned another 9.2 acres on the edge of the Meadowlands district slated to be developed for business, recreation, and housing. The report identified Paterno as Carlo Gambino's manager in New Jersey and stated that he is believed to be involved in gambling, loan sharking, and hijacking (p. 41).

[***] "Howard" is apparently Howard N. Garfinkle who was reputed to be an associate of Meyer Lansky, not a "legitimate Jewish guy." It was reported (Seigel, 1976) that Garfinkle had been indicted for, among other offenses, paying $92,000 in kickbacks for loans from a New Jersey union welfare fund that amounted to an outright embezzlement of more than $1 million.

I had made a connection with a banker at the Lakewood Trust Company in Lakewood, New Jersey, during the incinerator job. I met him in the bank and we went out to lunch. I asked him, probably in more complex terms than I am using here, what would happen if a loan with stocks or bonds as collateral is not paid back. He responded that the bank would sell the collateral and probably realize a profit; they usually only loan 65 to 75 percent on the face value of a blue chip stock. I asked what kind of trouble he would get in personally for making a number of "bad" loans. He explained that it was like in baseball; a Babe Ruth or Mickey Mantle would strike out so many times, but their overall record is good. It's the same way in the bank. I came right to the point: Would he consider a fee for granting a loan? And, if I recall correctly, he hedged a bit, but the bottom line was that he would.

The plan was very simple. Periodically, I would send persons, besides myself, into the bank with stock certificates and phony identification. He would make loans to these individuals using the stock as collateral to justify the loan. If the loan defaulted, the bank was not going to get hurt. If it just so happened that the stocks were stolen and ultimately turned up on the "hot sheet," the bank was still not going to get hurt because they had insurance to protect them against such fraud. Nobody was going to get hurt, and the only one who could go to prison was the guy who went into the bank with the stock certificates and happened to get caught red-handed with it. There was no way to trace the individual who had put up the stock as collateral because he was using phony identification. The banker does not have any obligation beyond the normal identification documents to determine who you are. You come in with a driver's license, Social Security card, credit cards, and the like, and say that you are John Jones and have just moved into the area. You want to establish a relationship with the bank because you are planning to open a business and you need some cash. You provide good collateral.

My deal with the banker was that he got 5 percent of any loan that he granted, and I would get 25 percent. Paterno would be given the balance, which he would have to share with whoever secured and whoever cashed the stock certificates. The first stock certificates that were given to me by Nick Paterno were bearer certificates; if I remember correctly, they were IBM. I went to the banker and told him I wanted to borrow against the stock. For a blue chip you get about 65 percent, considerably less on something more speculative. I walked out with $60,000. The banker was eventually indicted and convicted for his activities.

Everybody was happy; we were all eating well off this thing. However, you reach a saturation point with one bank. You cannot continually go back to the same guy and make these deals on a weekly basis. He can usually absorb only about six deals because they are ultimately going to blow up. There are going to be no repayments; it's going to be defaulted, and eventually the stock is going to turn up on a hot sheet as being stolen. This often took a long time because the security houses were totally and completely lacking any kind of security. You could walk into a broker's office in New York City, and on a clerk's desk would be sitting thousands, sometimes even millions, of dollars worth of stocks that hadn't been recorded. Eventually, there were investigations and some tightening up. Anyway, new banking contacts had to be located.

At the same time I developed a technique for bilking banks with checks. Paterno, Nick, and Joe, because of underworld connections, had access to all kinds of things—from the proceeds of a guy breaking and entering a household to guys who performed bigger operations such as commercial and industrial burglaries. I asked Nick Paterno: "You got these guys who break and enter. Do they ever steal checks?"[*] "Sure," he says, "all the time. But they throw them away because that's how you get caught." I told him, to give me the checks, that I knew a way to cash them. Nick threw up his hands: "That's all bullshit, Vito. You've got to have identification and you've got to show your face." I tell him that's true but to get the checks anyway. "Don't throw them

---

[*] According to law enforcement officials, Joe Paterno sponsored a burglary ring that specialized in business and industrial firms.

away anymore." Besides breaking and entering as a source for checks, there was the United States mails. They had a guy who had expertise in robbing the mails. Mike Mariani (not his real name) had made criminal activities a lifetime career. He also made a lifetime career of getting caught at it. It was my association with Mariani that resulted in my one and only conviction. We'll talk about that later. Anyway, Mike had a long criminal record.

The method that I devised was really quite simple. If I have a check that's written out to you that has been stolen from you either in a burglary or from the mails, to cash that check at the bank I have to have some form of identification. For example, if you write a check out to me, I can take it to the supermarket and possibly cash it if they know me; I can deposit it in my account, and it will clear your bank in three or four days; or I can endorse it on the back and go to your bank where the check is written. There I can say that Howard gave me this check and I want to cash it. The teller will ask for some form of identification, which she will note on the back of the check. When you are dealing with legitimate checks, that's okay; but, when you're dealing with stolen checks, you need a different approach. Since it would normally require a constant flow of new identification, and identifications were getting tighter (photographs on driver's licenses, for example), I worked out something else. I devised a scheme for circumventing the need for identification.

If I have your check and a couple of other checks, I also have your checking account number because it is printed on the bottom of the check. Now suppose I had three other checks besides yours. I go to your bank and ask for a deposit slip: "Gee, I forgot my deposit slip. Could you give me a blank one?" Many times that is not necessary because the banks have deposit slips right on the counter. Now I have a deposit slip, and I put down Howard's name and bank checking account number. I endorse the other three checks over to Howard by signing the appropriate name. I then walk up to a teller with two of those checks and the deposit slip and indicate that I want to make this deposit. I am putting money *into* your account, and the teller nicely takes the deposit. At the same time the third check that I have, which I am not depositing, which may be for any amount of money, $150, $200, or $300, whatever: "Would you mind cashing this for me?" I never had single refusal. They would cash it and not ask for any identification for the simple reason that I am making a deposit in Howard's account, and she thinks that I am Howard. I have already deposited $500, $600, or $700, whatever the checks are worth, in your checking account, and I'm only asking her to cash a check in the amount of $300 or $400.

Well, the first few times I tried this personally with legit checks it was 100 percent successful. Of course, it was necessary to size up the tellers and pick the one who would not be prone to ask any questions. Sometimes, of course, the person whose checking account I was using was well-known in the bank. "You're not Howard," or "How is Howard today?" or "Where is Howard? "Oh, he's my brother-in-law and is on a trip. He asked me to make this deposit for him." Accepted every time, no questions asked. Another technique was to use the drive-up window that some banks have, and this would require a confederate. He would be inside the bank looking busy at one of the counters, and I would drive up to the window. If the teller walked away, if she went to ask the manager or otherwise check the situation out, the confederate would be watching. He would signal, brush his hair back, and that meant to drive away. This happened on a few occasions; once I left $20,000 on the counter.

The flow of stolen checks was astronomical, and I was getting more than I could personally handle. I decided to develop an organization in order to continue pursuing this activity on a larger scale. The organization was nothing more than people who were known to Joe Paterno or people who knew Paterno who knew other people who wanted to make a fast, dishonest buck. Paterno would introduce them to me and I would explain the procedures that were to be followed. I would set it all up and prepare the packages of stolen checks. Paterno introduced me to all kinds of criminals—people who participated in illegal activities as their primary source of income. He would say, "This guy's a street guy," meaning he makes his money illegally. A lot of the time I would get a sympathetic comment: "He's down on hard times, having a bad run of luck, and he needs a favor." The faces were forever changing because I did not want the same people all of the time. This scheme required the services of a guy like Paterno who had all these criminal contacts, even with very low types.

I was with Nick Paterno one day when he said: "Vito, I want you to meet somebody who can do us some good," meaning another source of checks. Nick took me to a house in West Caldwell, New Jersey, and introduced me to a fellow by the name of Mike Mariani. Nick told me that Mike had been in and out of trouble and was essentially a loser; that is a guy who is constantly getting into trouble by being caught at what he was doing. Mike had just gotten out of jail for break and entry; it had been reduced from a felony to a misdemeanor and he did his time in the county penitentiary as opposed to the state prison. I felt that with good guidance and good control I could make money with this guy. Believe it or not, Mike was a family type with six or seven kids and a hell of a nice wife. That's one thing that has always amazed me about the criminal element—they always have nice wives. When I say *nice*, I mean real ladies, nice looking, but not the flashy, show-girl type.

Mike's thing was essentially break and entry, but on occasion he would participate in more violent activities. He was perfectly capable of picking up a gun and using it in an armed robbery. As a matter of fact, during the course of time that I knew him, he did in fact participate in armed robbery. I had nothing to do with that; the use of a weapon to me is a dumb move, a stupid turnoff. You don't need a weapon, other than a pen, to make lots of illegitimate money. I got to know Mike very well, and he had been throwing away all of the checks that he had taken in a robbery or burglary. Like many other thieves, he did not know how to handle paper. Some of these guys would run out right away and try to pass one or two checks. They would often get caught because the person who had been robbed puts the check on their sheet: "My checks were stolen." Right away the bank is alerted.

But, as discussed earlier, there are ways to get rid of these checks profitably, and Mike was a good source of checks.

One night he called me up as I was about to go to bed; it was about 11:00. "Come on down to my house. I've got something to show you." I tried to put it off for the following day, but Mike was insistent. I went to West Caldwell to see why he was all excited. Now Mike was a guy who would discuss criminal activity right in front of his family, in front of his wife and kids. You and I would try to keep this kind of thing away from the kids, but not him. He would talk about stolen goods at the kitchen table with the kids around. When I walked in, I saw an array of mail on his kitchen table. He had just ripped off the post office in Orange, New Jersey. A mail bag was just lying on the platform ready to be shipped out and Mike had lifted it. You would be amazed at the amount of cash that people send through the mail. I mean anywhere from $5 in a birthday card to hundreds of dollars for the payment of some bill. Everybody says not to send cash through the mails, but people do it all the time. In addition to the cash, there were also a great number of checks, and that's what I was interested in. And there were a lot of checks on the table. He was very proud of himself, because when you rob a mail bag, it's like a grab bag you don't know what's in it until you open it up. It could be anything from third-class advertising to who knows what. This happened to be a good bag, which is why he wanted to show it to me that same night. "Terrific," I told him, "put all the checks aside and we'll try to make some packages out of them with deposit slips and what have you. We'll turn some paper."

Mike also introduced me to some full-fledged criminals—I mean people who devote all of their time and energy to criminal pursuits. One guy was called "Biggie." The reason for his name was the fact that he was very big, naturally, weighing about 300 pounds. Biggie had done eight years in Rahway State Prison for armed robbery. He had attempted to rob a messenger making a bank deposit, but he had bungled the job and received something like a 10-to-15 year sentence and did 8 of it. As soon as he got out, he went right back to various sundry criminal activities. Now Biggie was a psycho. There were really some screws loose in his head. He could kill without thinking twice about it; he was prone to violence and loved guns. But Biggie was down on his luck at this time, and Mike suggested we use him to hang some paper.

I would always try to avoid hanging paper directly. I may very well participate in such activities by being the watcher, the guy who would give the signal if something was going wrong, but that was it. I would usually avoid going up to a bank teller and handling the transaction personally. Not because I was afraid, but by doing this you were exposing yourself so often that they are going to nail you. The police and the banks will put together a composite sketch rather quickly. Up until this time I was clean; I had avoided trouble and I wanted to keep it that way. The way to do this was to avoid any direct involvement, to insulate yourself as best as possible.

Mike Mariani had stolen a safe from the Wayne Construction Company in Montclair, New Jersey, and borrowed my pickup truck to bring it home and peel it. I had no qualms about this, because my excuse, if Mike got caught, was: "Sure I lent him the truck. He called and asked to borrow it; I didn't ask him what he was going to use it for, and he didn't say." Inside the safe was about $1,500 in cash, of which I got a piece because he used my truck. However, there were also some checks, in particular, one from the Wayne Construction Company—a $35,000 check from the Glen Ridge Board of Education, almost as good as cash. It was written to the Wayne Construction Company for work that had been done refurbishing one of their school buildings.

Usually you have between three to five business days in which to convert a stolen check before it pops up on a computerized sheet used by banks in a particular area. First, it usually pops up on a hot sheet at the immediate bank that it's drawn on, and then the bank in turn feeds the information out to its branches. From there it may or may not go out to other banks in a broader geographic area, but it takes time, usually three to five working days. I know all this because I made it my business to learn banking procedures. A great deal of information came from a couple of tellers I befriended, two girls, in a bank that I did legitimate business with for my refuse firm—I literally picked their brains. At the same time I went to the public library and took out books on banking procedures, particularly procedures used by bank clearinghouses. I needed to know how long it takes for checks to clear from geographic area to area. Today, with high-speed computers, it takes about two days.

I had this big check from Wayne for $35,000, and a few smaller ones, and I sent Biggie to the National Bank in Caldwell to open up a bank account in the name of the Wayne Construction Company. Biggie, following my instructions, told the bank officer that he expected to be doing a big job in the area and needed a local bank in Caldwell on which to draw his payroll checks and so on. He opened that account with an initial deposit of about $40,000, using the board of education check and a few smaller ones, all duly endorsed. Now the bank is going to kiss your feet: you are opening an account with $40,000, and the main check is almost like cash, a government board of education check. Biggie opens up the account on Monday, and I have until Wednesday, possibly Friday, but I'm taking no chances. When you open up a checking account, they give you starter checks, about half a dozen, on which to draw upon until your checkbook is printed up. I sent Biggie to the bank with a $20,000 check drawn against the account Wayne Construction Company made out to payroll. With the check was a piece of paper informing the teller that so much of the $20,000 payroll was to be in fifties, so much in twenties, so much in tens, and so on. This is a payroll check; I am paying my employees in cash, not at all unusual in the construction trades. My total payroll is $20,000, and this is the way I want it broken down.

Biggie is prone to violence, and there is always the risk that some cutie-pie teller is going to start asking questions and call somebody else over for consultation. Instead of having the ability to talk his way out of it, Biggie might pull out a gun and drop someone. You do that and there are obviously big problems, especially since Biggie is not the hardest person in the world to describe. I tell Biggie that no matter what happens, you must remain cool. To further assure him, I stand behind him in the bank, right on the same line "Unless I pat you on the ass, you ain't got nothing to worry about, okay? I'll show you which teller to go to." And I picked out a very young girl. Biggie went up and gave her the check, she punched it into the computer that's hooked up to the bookkeeping department to make sure that there are adequate funds to cover it in the account. Because of the nature of the check for $35,000, it went in as cash. The computer now indicates more than sufficient funds to cover this payroll check. The teller starts to count out the money but runs short of some denominations in her drawer. She leans over to the other teller and asks her to borrow some money from her drawer. The other teller is a sharp woman who must have been there since the bank opened umpteen years ago. "You know you are cashing a big check, let me see it." I get a surge of panic—something's wrong. I can't see Biggie's face, but I feel his huge body in a bit of a tremble: "Oh shit, he's getting excited." I keep watching his hands. "Please don't pull that fuckin' gun" is all that is going through my head. The older teller asks a few questions, normal and routine, and Biggie fields them easily. We walk out with $20,0000 never to return. There's no way to draw out any more, from that account. By Friday it's going to be all over the world that the check is stolen and the account is a phony. I never read about this caper in the newspapers, but banks don't like to advertise their mistakes—it's bad for their image. We split the $20,000 three ways: I got half, and Biggie and Mike split the other 50 percent. Paterno did not get anything out of this particular job; it wasn't a question of each score being broken down in percentages with Joe getting so much from each one. The tribute was a generalized thing, unless Paterno was directly involved in setting up the situation or had some other direct involvement.

One thing that I found strange was that Paterno kept the stolen checks in his house until I picked them up. This struck me as being quite unusual because Joe was always security conscious. He always felt that he was being watched, and I believe that he was actually paranoid about it. Joe would avoid using the telephone and would never talk about any business whatsoever on the phone. "Meet me at the diner," was all he would say, and I would meet him at the Andover Diner on Route 10 in Hanover. There we would go in either his car or mine and ride with the radio turned up loud, just in case there was some kind of listening device planted in the car. If it came down to serious business, we would park the car, take a walk through a park, and converse while walking. Joe would often talk in Italian—he used to say: "Talk in Italian so that nobody will understand." This was absolutely stupid. Don't you think the FBI has people that understand this language? If somebody were monitoring the conversation, they would understand Italian better than we understand Italian.[*] Despite these precautions though, Joe kept stolen checks in his house.

The problem with the check scheme is that you would saturate an area very quickly, and banks communicate with each other. They soon find out that frauds are being perpetuated in their area. Then you have to move to another area, and this requires contacts with people who are operating, stealing checks, in that area. If you are planning to work Essex County, you want checks from banks in Essex County. It was an amazing thing that no one ever got caught. I got 25 percent, the guy who was doing the work got 50 percent, and Paterno got 25 percent from which he would have to pay for the checks. I would get up in the morning and it would not be at all unusual for me to have 10 or 12 deposits ready to go in 10 or 12 different banks with a bottom line for

---

[*] Actually, Vito may be underestimating Paterno's strategy in this instance. Statutes governing electronic eavesdropping (assuming the eavesdropping is legal and could thus be used in court) are quite strict. There must be constant monitoring of the equipment to ensure that whatever is recorded is relevant to the court order and not personal or privileged—e.g., between husband and wife, lawyer and client. Under 1968 federal statutes, two recordings must be made simultaneously. One is continuous and at the end of the order must be sealed and turned over to the court. The second is monitored and must be turned off whenever nonauthorized conversation is being conducted. The monitoring agent must take off his/her headphones and place them in a soundproof box. An agent's falling asleep can result in weeks of recordings being suppressed by the court.

Thus, communicating in Italian would severely limit the number of agents available for monitoring and would make (lawful) eavesdropping very difficult.

the day of about $8,500. After I had saturated the six or seven counties in North Jersey, there was no place for me to go unless I wanted to continue to move south or across the river to New York. This I was afraid of doing; the banks in New York were much more sophisticated than those at the time in suburban New Jersey. It's a city thing; they are sharp in New York and you're not going to get away with the same stuff there that you will in the Jersey suburbs. So, the scheme just burned itself out after about a year.

It was my association with Mike Mariani that brought my first and only criminal conviction. It happened quite stupidly; I should have known better, but I didn't—boy, have I heard that before. One day Mike and I went to Newark Airport where he had previously worked as a baggage handler, freight handler; he knew the airport inside out. I went there with him for the purpose of looking over some new refuse containers that had been purchased by the airport. I thought that they might be of use in my garbage collection business. Mike, without alerting me, went there to steal mail. When I told Mike about the containers and said that they were at the food-processing area, he said he knew how to get me into that parking lot so that I would be right on top of the containers. I would not have to get lost in the shuffle and hubbub of the airport. However, after I parked the car, Mike said he was going over to get a mail bag. "Let's not screw around, Mike. Let me get a look at the garbage containers and then let's just go." He just looked at me in a puzzled kind of way: "Vito, it's as easy as taking candy from a baby. There's nothing to it. These people don't have nobody around. I can hop the fence and go faster than I'm talking to you." With that he ran out and scaled the fence. When he got to the mail platform, the receiving area for mail coming in on airplanes, he grabbed a bag at random and reapproached the fence; we're talking about 75 to 100 feet away. He threw the bag over the fence and yelled to me: "Get it off the ground. Put it in the car." I was hesitant; this was stupid and I was scared to death. The dummy that I was, I got out of the car, picked up the bag, and threw it into the car.

We both got back into the car and as I was pulling out of the parking lot, I looked into the rear-view mirror. "Oh shit, there's a police car behind us." It was unmarked, but there were two guys in it, and it was the heat. I glanced around. "Mike, somebody's on our butt." He tells me to turn down the next aisle like we are looking for a parking spot, but the car is still behind us. For a few more minutes we maneuver in and out of parking aisles. Suddenly, two Port of New York Authority marked police cars with their lights on converge on us. "Get rid of that fuckin' bag," I screamed at Mike. "Throw it under another car, but get it out of here." It was too late and they were on us. I pulled over, but they did not know whether we were armed. They yanked us out of the car, pulled us by the back of the collar, and threw us up against the car: "Spread your legs. Put your hands on the roof of the car." And then the body search. We were roughed up, handcuffed, and thrown into the back of one police car. We were driven to a federal building and turned over to the postal inspectors; it was a federal rap. We spent the night in a holding cell that the city of Newark apparently leases to the federal government.

I called my brother and told him what had happened. He was shocked but didn't argue about the role he would have to play. He would be there for the arraignment the next morning and would make sure that there was a bail bondsman there as well as an attorney. I was released on personal recognizance because I was a homeowner who had no previous record. Mike Mariani, who had a long record, was held in lieu of $2,500 bail. For some reason, and I never did understand why, the newspapers picked up on this situation: "Local Contractor Arrested in Alleged Mail Theft." They didn't blast it on page one, but they did not bury it either. It stood out: name, address, refuse contractor, and so on. It wasn't that kind of crime, so I still don't know why they picked up on it. Anyway, it hurt my family; it hurt my kids most of all. They were poked fun of at school: "You know your *mafia* father got caught; he's nothing but a thief"—that kind of crap. I could take it, but when your family has to be hurt, that's rough. It's embarrassing, let's face it.

My lawyer separated my case from Mike Mariani's since he pled guilty and got a reduced sentence. He could have picked up five and, instead, got two years in Danbury (Correctional Facility in Connecticut). I had in fact thrown the bag into my car at the request of Mike, but it was not my intent to go to Newark Airport to steal anything. I felt that I had a chance to walk. I attempted to reach Mike through his wife and have him appear in my defense at the trial. He would do it—for a price. The price was $10,000. His family was destitute, on welfare and really down. He saw $10,000 as giving them $100 a week while he was away for two years. I could understand this, but when I told my attorney he would not go for it. But, I kept trying. I was not on Mike's visitor list, and I didn't want to be. I told his wife that I would give her $1,000 down and that after he makes his statement, she would be given the balance. In the meantime, I will give the balance to my lawyer to hold. Mike wouldn't go for it, and I went on trial. The jury did not buy my story. After being out about six hours, they returned a verdict of guilty. I was hoping for at least a hung jury, but I didn't even get that. The judge wanted a pre-sentence report from the probation department before he would hand down a sentence. We asked for a continuance of bail, based on the fact that we wanted to file an appeal. During the appeal process the pre-sentence report was completed, and I received a six-month sentence and a $2,500 fine. I never did the six months, nor did I ever pay the fine. I also continued to work the check scheme.

However, things had changed. I was agonizing mentally over my plight. I was most concerned about the shame I had brought on my family. There's just no way you can make up for that kind of situation. I began to reflect on my situation and my past activities: Was I really benefiting by all of this? Was my family benefiting? A beautiful home and a nice surrounding, but . . . I was asking myself questions like: Couldn't I have gotten this without dirtying myself? At the same time trouble was coming from Uncle Sam—the criminal division of the

Internal Revenue Service (IRS). They had subpoenaed my books and my financial records and were tearing my returns to pieces. They had assigned this Italian guy to my case, and he was thorough as he was vindictive; I was in trouble. There was no way in hell that I could cover up or justify the tax on my income for too many years. I was going to get hurt; they were making a criminal investigation, not a civil. Civil I could handle. "It's money, okay. You want money, fine me and you will get the money." If they had taken that route, maybe my thinking would have changed, but they didn't. Quite frankly, of all enforcement agencies, the IRS frightened me more than any other. I remembered how they audited my father's books; and he was legit. The horrors they put him through, and they were approaching him from a routine normal audit. They were not approaching me that way.

All this stuff was running through my head, and it all boiled down to two choices. I could either cop out to the whole situation and take what was coming, come out of jail, or maybe not even go to jail except for the six months, and start anew. Maybe we would move to another area where I was not known, where my family would not have to be embarrassed. I could use my connections to go back into business. This would be the "man's" way out; this would be the way that a supposed macho man would take—a stand-up guy. You take the blows and you keep your mouth shut. That's one of the rules. I started to search my mind for alternatives.

I went to the FBI office in Morristown, New Jersey. In return for helping them, I wanted my legal problems to be taken care of. It could not be revealed that I had informed—this would save my face and my life. "I know you guys can't make any promises," I said, "and I am willing to do the six months on the mail theft rap. But, I want the IRS off my back, and I don't want any other problems. When it's all over, I just want to drift away. I will sell my business and drift away, put down roots someplace else. I can't do that if it becomes known that I was an informant."

(Vito provided a great deal of information to the Justice Department, Some of this information resulted in several indictments, including that of a hit man. However, it turned out that the Justice Department also needed his testimony to ensure a conviction.)

Witness Protection Program

When I arrived at the Strike Force office,[*] I was told that there was no way to protect my anonymity. I was going to have to testify, and I was offered two choices: take it on the run, on my own, or let us relocate you and give you a new identity. This was the first time that I had heard of the Witness Protection Program. The word *relocation* hit me like a sledge hammer. I had not even considered this alternative; I believed that my identity would be protected. But, the bottom line was that they wanted a conviction more than they wanted to protect my role. I was naive.

Late that afternoon, I came home with a half-dozen U.S. marshals. They concocted a story for the benefit of my family that I had been actively engaged in undercover work for various enforcement agencies in the federal government for a long period of time. This helped me save face with my family. It also masked the mail theft situation, because my involvement in the mail theft was supposedly to get me in better with mobsters, and that I really was not a thief. My family totally and completely believed what was said—because they wanted to believe it. They wanted to believe that their husband and father was not a criminal, not a thief or "wise guy." Deep down inside I felt that they were not believing this tale, but it offered an excuse. To firm it up I had the FBI agents come to the house and talk to my family. I told my wife that I had been involved in a great deal of undercover activity on a patriotic basis and that there would be a couple of guys who would be coming pretty soon to explain the whole situation. "Let's wait for them," I suggested, because I did not want to start telling stories that might conflict with the

---

[*] The Strike Force was developed under Robert Kennedy when he was attorney general. It is designed to coordinate and integrate federal (and sometimes local) efforts to combat organized crime. Strike Force units were set up in all major cities where the type of organized crime being discussed in this study is known to exist.

stories the agents were going to tell. I called my brother and asked him to come over to the house, because it had been explained to me that we were going to leave, disappear.

We could not be moved out overnight as the marshals had indicated. They had a personnel problem; there were some civil disorders or something in Washington and thousands of people had been arrested. Many of the marshals were assigned to deal with the situation and were not available to help move us out. Because of the delay, we had an advantage that many other relocated witnesses apparently do not have. They are simply picked up and taken away overnight, which doesn't allow them any time whatsoever to plan for what is being left behind. In my situation there was a lot being left behind. I had a business, real estate, and a house. Since they would not allow the kids to go to school anymore, they yanked the school records. There were little things like providing for the care of several cats and a dog. I was able to sit down with my attorney and transferred everything to him to dispose of by power of attorney.

After about two weeks under guard in our own house, we were moved to Washington, D.C., by airplane. I was using a fictitious name. After one night in a Washington motel, we were driven to a place in Maryland just outside of Annapolis and housed in a motel for almost nine weeks. There were six people in two rooms, and this left a lot to be desired. We looked upon it as a temporary inconvenience, and it was very expensive for the government. We ate out three meals every day. Whenever any of us ventured out to buy a newspaper or toilet articles, marshals accompanied us. At this time the government was picking up the tab for everything. The marshals told us that they would help me to get a job, change our names, and provide us new identification, in addition to finding us new housing. However, to get these things was like pulling teeth from a hen, which, as you are aware, has no teeth.

After almost nine weeks we were relocated to Columbia, South Carolina, where we lived in garden apartment complex. The 24-hour protection ceased, and we were devoid of all identification except for our original documents, which, of course, would be too dangerous to use. They had given us a name out of the air, a cover name, a code name, which was "Domino." So we put that name on our mailbox and became known as the Domino family. They continued to pay the rent, but we were reduced to $75 a week for our table and personal use. I picked this up in cash every week from the U.S. marshal in Columbia. At the same time I was in touch almost daily with Bob Richardson (the U.S. attorney) in Newark. I was asking, in fact begging, for the process to unfold and reach its ultimate conclusion.

Although I kept asking, I was not told how they would get me a job, and I found out that the United States Marshals Service is very ineffective when it comes to helping a witness. The simple truth is that as a street person, as a guy who was into criminal activity, I can produce identification ten times faster than the marshals, and mine will stand up. I'm talking about birth certificates, school records, and Social Security cards. It took the marshals weeks to produce that type of documentation. And what are you supposed to do until then? You are, in effect, a nonperson. If you use your real name, then everybody and his brother knows who you are and where you're from. You are opening the door for being found, and the one thing that they made clear is that they do not want you to be found.

You have to completely sever every single relationship or association that you had, other than with the immediate members of your family. Even then, you communicate through a third party, through the marshals' office, which supplies a mail drop. In my situation they failed to even provide that. When dealing with your relatives, you have to be very careful; you cannot tell them where you are. You say that you are "down South" instead of saying Columbia. It's not that you are afraid that they are going to tell the wrong people, but information often gets dropped innocently. It's particularly hard on the kids because they have school friends they would like to write to or telephone, and you cannot let them. They just have to forget it, wipe the slate clear. We did that very well, I believe. The only people I communicated with were my mother and brother (Vito's father was deceased) and my attorney. My wife did the same. We wanted to protect ourselves. Yet, if someone were really looking for us very hard, we could have been found. This is because the government did not have funds for us to deal with such items as transportation. In a suburban or rural area, a car is must; yet we had no car, and there was no public transportation. The stores were too far to walk to, but when we asked the marshals what to do, they just shrugged their shoulders. "What the hell am I supposed to do? You told me to sell my car." The answer turned out, to my way of thinking, to be an invitation: "I don't know. You'll have to find a way." They way I found was simple.

I had gone in and out of the federal building in Columbia many times, often with marshals. I found out that there was a motor pool for agents, marshals, and other government officials. Very nonchalantly, I just walked into the basement of the federal building, into the parking lot, and drove out with a motor pool car. I went right past the guard who knew my face and assumed that I was a federal agent since I was often with the marshals. I just waved to him and drove out. I figured that the worst they could do was what they did—nothing. After about a week of using the government's car, which also included the credit card attached to the key chain to buy gasoline, one of the marshals asked me: "Vito, how did you get here today." They had been sending somebody to pick me up whenever I came to get my allowance. "Oh, I drove in—in one of your cars," I answered nonchalantly. "Oh what? One of our cars? What do you mean?" I told him the simple truth: "I went downstairs and took a car from the motor pool. I've been using it since last week." After the look of astonishment: "You're kidding, right?" I said: "I'm using your friggin' car, and I'm going to continue using it." "Oh no," he said, "you can't do that. You're not a government employee. If you had an accident, there would be a lot of red tape, complications." I conned him into allowing me to use the car for a few more days. Realizing that they would eventually take the car away from me, I turned it in and went over to an alternate plan. Using my own credit card in the name of Palermo, I rented an automobile. Of course I was never going to be known by that name anymore, and I had no intention of paying for the rental—how could they find me? I used the car for about five months; as far as I know, Uncle Sam never paid for it either. Of course, this was a dangerous move, using my real name—but what can you do?

Employment

The government also failed to provide me with a background that I could use to find a job, so I designed one. I fabricated a résumé with education and work background and submitted it to Bob Richardson and Gerald Shur, who I believe was the alleged liason between the criminal division of the Justice Department and the United States Marshals Service. I say "alleged" because at that time it seemed that he really ran the whole show with respect to the protection program. I wrote: "Since you have failed to provide me with the promised background, in order to get a job I have manufactured the attached résumé." I asked if he agreed with it and would he support it? I received no reply, which to me meant implied consent. I began to apply for jobs.

The résumé that I prepared stated that I had been employed in a family-owned and -operated business, a large northern New Jersey waste collection company. After many years, it stated, I went into business on my own, and I used my attorney and my brother as references. The résumé said that I eventually sold this business and took a job with the Bureau of Solid Wastes, a federal agency. I started out as the person who established guidelines for disposal facilities. These guidelines, I wrote, were ultimately adopted by the Environmental Protection Agency. The résumé continued that over the next few years I received promotions to—I forget the title that I gave myself—administrative director or something like that (it sounded good). I gave myself a line of progression leading up to this position. I also noted that during the last few years that I was with the Bureau of Solid Waste, when it was incorporated into the Office of Solid Waste Management, I was "loaned," and I put quotation marks around the word *loaned*, to the U.S. Department of Justice. The Department of Justice, I said, was making a probe of possible infiltration of mob elements into the private sector of solid waste management. Now this gave it an air of mystery, and the bottom line was that due to the sensitive nature of my employment, I am unable to elaborate beyond this point. I concluded by stating that I was seeking employment on a stationary basis, that I was tired of traveling around, tired of uprooting my family. I was looking for a stable position. I also listed as my references several federal agents and my brother.

My résumé also indicated that I had a Bachelor of Science degree in business management from the Wharton School of Business (University of Pennsylvania)—why not the best? Some employers were looking for a person with an engineering degree, but there was no way I could fake that. I did not have the knowledge in math and related areas to get away with that. In addition, to be a "P.E.," a professional engineer, tests had to be passed. I felt that I was qualified in the management of solid waste systems, particularly in the public sector, where I had experience and knowledge in the operation of municipalities in northern New Jersey. I knew the bureaucracy in solid waste management. Using leads from trade publications, I began sending out the résumé. The government paid for transportation costs, and a marshal always accompanied me when I traveled for a job interview.

(Vito was quite successful in securing important and well-paying positions both in the private and public sector. However, during his last job he had been "uncovered" and was now in North Carolina very bitter about the lack of help he was getting from the government.)

Life of Crime

by Richard Stratton

Screenwriter and producer Richard Stratton spent three years in a cell next to Joe Stassi at the federal prison in Petersburg, Virginia. Stassi, born in 1906, fired his first gun at age 14 and divided the rest of his long life between working for the mafia and serving 30 years' worth of jail time. He was 95 when he told his story—some of it—to Stratton.

Joe says he can't talk about the killings. Not yet. There is no statute of limitations for murder; the government won't give him immunity, and he doesn't want to go back to prison, not at his age. He's done enough time already—more than thirty years, counting the strict Special Parole and the year he did when they locked him back up, at 88, for associating with known organized-crime figures.

Now 95, Joe Stassi, also known as Hoboken Joe and Joe Rogers during his forty-year criminal career, may well lay claim to the title Oldest Living Mafioso. The crimes Stassi has agreed to talk about include some of the most infamous events in gangland history. And Stassi was there. Stassi's life spanned the heyday of organized crime and intersected with all the major players. Though he was accorded what the Justice Department called ambassadorial rank and classified

as a Top Hoodlum by the FBI, few outside law enforcement know anything about Joe Stassi. Now, after nearly a century, of dedication to
thee rigors of omerta, Srassi has agreed to go beyond the thousands of
pages of government documents chronicling his life of crime and tell
his story.

"I'm only talkin' about what I know," he says, and reaches for a
sparerib. We are at Christine Lee's, a Chinese place in North Miami.
Joe's voice is a raspy whisper, sibilant echoes of Marlon Brando's in *The
Godfather.* "What I seen with my own eyes," he says. "And what I done.
Not what they write in books or what you see in movies. That's all bullshit. That's rats and agents talking." At the mention of rats, he looks at
me with a fierce glint in his eye, and I see the throttled rage and intense
criminal passion that earned Stassi an underworld reputation as the
most dangerous man in La Cosa Nostra.

Joe falls silent, gnaws on the sparerib using the upper set of his den-
tures and his lower gum. His false teeth, the ones that were made for
him while he was locked up in the federal penitentiary at Marion, Illinois, are the best he's ever had. The trouble is, he has only the uppers
because his dogs keep stealing the lower set and burying them in the
garden out behind the house.

"You can't believe these fuckin' stool pigeons." He practically spits the
words. "They're only saying what the agents and prosecutors want them
to say." I have to lean in close to hear him. "What I'm saying is the truth.
I'll take a lie-detector test, I'll swear an affidavit, I don't care. What I'm
telling you is the way it really happened."

The check comes, and Joe nabs it, pays with a crisp $100 bill, leaves
a hefty tip. As we get up to leave, I help him stand and steady himself
on his cane. Scoliosis has curved his spine into the shape of a question mark.

In the parking lot, I ease him into the low-slung rental, and we
drive off into the soft Florida night. Joe hunkers down over the console; the lights from the dashboard glow red and green on his wiz-
ened, white-bearded face as he looks up at me and allows the intimacy
of the car to relax a lifetime habit of secrecy. "We never talked about

what we did," he says. "Not even to each other. They killed you if you talked." He licks his flinty lips several times. "I've never told anyone what I'm telling you. No one."

But the killings are off-limits, at least for now. Except to say that there were five. Five that stand out.

When I met Joe Stassi at the federal prison in Petersburg, Virginia, he had already served more than two decades in some of America's toughest penitentiaries. For three years, I lived in the cell next to Joe's. I saw him every day, many times a day, in the forced proximity that is prison. I found out who Joe was by chance. Someone loaned me a book, *Gangster #2: Longy Zwillman, the Man Who Invented Organized Crime,* by Mark A. Stuart. Leafing through the photos of gangland legends such as Charles "Lucky" Luciano, Frank Costello, Meyer Lansky, Benjamin "Bugsy" Siegel and Joe Adonis, I came upon a group shot taken at the wedding reception for one of Longy's people. Seated at a table were Longy, New Jersey Mafia boss Gerry Catena, Longy's close associate Joseph "Doc" Stacher and a, well-dressed, good-looking man identified as "Joe Rogers, who ran the numbers for Zwillman in Union County." Joe Rogers looked an awful lot like a young Joe Srassi.

"Yeah, that's me," Joe admitted when I asked him. But he wouldn't tell me any more than that. By that time, I had become a jailhouse lawyer of some repute. It was only when he asked me to look into his case after he was refused parole—this after twenty years of good behavior—that I began to get a sense of just how important an organized-crime figure Joe was. Much of what I know about Stassi and his various cases I learned while digging into his paperwork for the elusive loophole. Eventually, I found a mistake: Joe had been denied fourteen months of "meritorious good time" that when added to his time served would spring him from prison. I was in another prison when I heard through the grapevine that Joe had been set free and that he sent me his gratitude and regards.

In 1990 I was released after serving eight years for smuggling marijuana. I settled in Brooklyn and began working for a criminal lawyer in Manhattan. One day while riding the subway to work, I looked over and saw an old man accompanied by two large characters who looked like muscle. On second glance, we recognized each other. "Richie!" Joe exclaimed, and hugged me. I asked him what he was doing riding the subway; he said, "Gotta keep a low profile, FBI's all over me."

A couple of weeks later, Joe and I risked violating our respective paroles when he took me to lunch. He asked what I was doing, and I told him that in addition to writing legal briefs, I had written a novel and was publishing a magazine, *Prison Life.* Joe invited me to his home in Brooklyn to examine the dozen cartons of legal papers he had accumulated and stored in his basement. "There's a story in there," he said. "A hell of a story. I'm not saying a goddamn word. Your story is in the documents."

But before I could take him up on the offer, the Feds grabbed Joe yet again. He was caught having breakfast with another organized-crime figure. Joe's parole officer photographed the get-together, and quicker than you can say "Two over easy," Joe's parole was revoked and he was locked up again for "association."

During that stint at the Metropolitan Detention Center in Brooklyn, Joe began to reassess his life of crime. Frances Paxton, his wife of more than sixty years, a former Miss California who waited for Joe while he was locked up, died of throat cancer just a month after his release after the parole violation. Joe sold his home in Brooklyn and moved to Florida. Soon after settling in the land where paroled gangsters go to die, Joe urged me to come down to Miami, pick up where we'd left off.

Talking to Joe, listening to his life story, is like setting out on an archaeological dig. Newly released FBI documents, obtained under my repeated Freedom of Information Act requests, prove Stassi is a bona fide gangster and stimulate more digging.

"The Jews made the Mafia," he states resolutely as we cruise along Collins Avenue beside the huge hotels lining the beach. "Without the Jews, the Italians wouldn't have gotten anywhere. The Jews were the ones that done the work." Joe says he means the series of hits carried out in the early '30s by the mostly Jewish killers of Murder, Inc., that opened the way for the modern Mob to take control of the rackets under the planning and leadership of the affiliated East Coast bosses known as the Big Six: Meyer Lansky, Abe Zwillman, Ben Siegel, Frank Costello, Joe Adonis and Charlie Luciano. Stassi knew them all.

Joe was born on New York's Lower East Side in the early 1900s, when hoards of tough immigrant Jewish and Italian kids took over the streets from the Irish gangs. He graduated from being a street urchin stealing quarters from tenement gas heaters to heisting craps games and sticking up payroll deliveries. Arrested for robbery, possession of a weapon and other petty charges while still a kid, he says it was the connections he made with older criminals in jail that gave him entrée to the beer barons and bootleggers of Prohibition. Though Sicilian, Joe forged a series of close bonds with top Jewish gangsters who trusted him and served as his criminal mentors. The most influential of these men was the undisputed boss of the New Jersey rackets, Abner "Longy" Zwillman.

Just two years older than Joe when they met in the early 20s, Zwillman was already well established as the smartest, if not the wealthiest and toughest, of the brash Jersey bootleggers. Abe was born and raised in Newark's predominantly Jewish Third Ward. His father died when he was 14, and Abe took it upon himself to become the breadwinner; he quit school and went to work selling fruits and vegetables from a pushcart. When the Irish kids would roam into the Third Ward to harass the peddlers, the cry would go out in Yiddish: *"Reef der Langer!"* Go get the Tall One, the Defender. Longy would come running and chase off the outsiders.

With Prohibition, Zwillman went to work for Joseph Reinfeld, owner of Reinfeld's Tavern. Reinfeld bought whiskey from the Bronfman brothers' Seagram Distillery in Montreal and began shipping directly to the Jersey shore, where Zwillman would oversee the off-loading and distribution to speakeasies all over the East Coast. By 1922 Newark had become the bootleg capital of the country, and

Zwillman, though just 19, presented Reinfeld with an offer he couldn't refuse: fifty-fifty partnership or Longy would go out on his own. Reinfeld knew that to spurn Zwillman would mean war, and Longy had the gunmen. Reinfeld swallowed his pride; they shook hands. Before Prohibition ended, the Zwillman-Reinfeld partnership made them both millions in tax-free cash.

"Right around this time, there was a war going on," Joe says. "There was always wars, but this one I remember was the war between the Jews and the Italians to control Newark. Newark, Elizabeth, Union City was where we had all the big breweries. Tugboats would bring barges up the river with tens of thousands of gallons of molasses and pump it into the stills. We owned everybody in Jersey—judges, police, politicians. Nobody bothered us. Except other mobs."

We pull in to the driveway of a house that is a low-end version of the anonymous suburban Miami home Lee Strasberg, as Hyman Roth (a character based on Meyer Lansky) in *The Godfather II*, was living in when he was visited by Michael Corleone. Joe says it was through Zwillman and his partner, Gerry Catena, that he became friendly with the men who conceived and ran the national crime syndicate. Both loyal soldier and downrange thinker, Stassi learned early on to follow Lansky's first law: Retreat to the background and turn over the high-visibility street activities to others. Joe became a master of the low profile. He never used his real name; he moved from place to place. "All the mobs knew I was connected," he explains, "but no one knew exactly how or why. I was the only one who was free to go wherever I wanted, meet whoever I wanted, without having to report. Because I was with Abe and Meyer."

Joe remembers that around this time, Lansky and Ben Siegel had their headquarters in a building on the Lower East Side. They were at war with the four Fabrizzo brothers from Brooklyn. One of the brothers, a killer known as Tough Tony, climbed onto the roof of the building where Siegel and Lansky had their office and dropped a bomb down the chimney. One man was killed, and Siegel was injured; Tough Tony was seen fleeing over the rooftops. A few weeks later, as Tough

Tony was having dinner at his parents' home, a couple of Siegel and Lansky's men showed up dressed as cops and demanded to talk to Tony. When he got up from the table and went to the door, the men barged in and shot him to death right in front of his parents.

In the '40s, Stassi was one of the first men invited to invest when Siegel began to explore the possibilities of founding a gambling empire in the Nevada desert. Siegel and a guy named Little Moe Sedway were partners in a small hotel in what was to become the Mob's richest jackpot. "Moe was buying up property, and they tried to get me interested. I had a place in Lake Tahoe with Lou Walters—that broad Barbara Walters's father. I was looking at Cuba and the Dominican Republic. Ben came down and visited me in Havana a couple of times," Joe says. Then he adds, almost as an afterthought, "When Ben was killed, everyone was shocked. They thought it might have been Little Moe that had it done."

"Who thought that? I ask.

"Meyer and Abe," Joe answers.

"You're saying Meyer Lansky never OK'd the hit on Siegel?"

"Please. That's all nonsense. Meyer loved Ben. I was the one who looked into it. I went out to California; I investigated it for Meyer and Abe."

"So who did—"

"Excuse me. Listen to me. I'll tell you."

Joe says he hired an ex-detective, Barney Wozinski, to investigate the Siegel killing. "There was a cigarette girl Ben was always talking to. Virginia Hill [Siegel's girlfriend] was jealous of this girl. One day Virginia Hill got that cigarette girl and beat the bejesus out of her. When Ben heard about it, he went out and got Virginia Hill and beat the hell out of her. Virginia Hill left for Switzerland.

"The night Ben was killed [June 20, 1947], there was Al Smiley and Swifty Morgan with Ben when they drove in from Vegas. They stopped for dinner at Jack's, the fish place on the pier in Santa Monica. They dropped Swifty off at the hotel, and Al and Ben drove to Virginia Hill's house. I talked to Al. He said they only just sat down, Ben on the couch, him on the side chair, when the shot came through the window. Al says, 'Believe me, Joe, I was afraid I was gonna get killed.' "

Joe insists the stories that have been written in any number of books and portrayed in movies such as *Bugsy* and *Lansky*—that the Siegel killing was a Mob hit OK'd by Meyer Lansky at a sit-down in Havana with the exiled Luciano—are fictional gangland lore gleaned almost entirely from second- and third-hand information. "We were as close to it as you could get. Whoever did it had to be a marksman that shot through the window from outside, someone that knew how to handle a rifle. The police found casings from a military-type rifle. What we found was that the one that killed Ben Siegel was Virginia Hill's brother. He hated Ben, and Ben hated him."

Joe learned Hill's brother was a sharpshooter in the marines. He had a rifle he kept in the gas station down the street. "The day after the killing, Barney Wozinski went to the gas station looking for the rifle; they called the brother. He disappeared, and the rifle disappeared."

"So the story that Ben owed all the bosses a lot of money in cost overruns for construction of the Flamingo is not true?"

"That's bullshit. Ben owed nobody money, and if he did, he was honorable, he would pay it. As far as the Flamingo, every partner in there knew they were going to make their money back many times over. Nobody was worried. We knew Vegas was going to be big."

Joe shakes his head, sighs. So many wars, so many killings, so many hits: Who can keep them all straight? But the Siegel killing, that one he remembers. "The real story came from me; I told Abe and Meyer it was the brother, and everybody accepted it. If it was a hit, that's not how it would have been done."

He imparts the methodology of a Mob hit. To kill a man like Ben Siegel, Joe says, they would send a friend, someone he would never suspect, who could get in close and shoot him in the head with a revolver. "Never walk away from a body without making sure you put one or more in the head and the party is dead." The way Sam Giancana was killed. Or in a public place, usually an Italian restaurant, send in a couple of torpedoes and blast away. Like the Carmine Galante still life, blood and pasta; or Joey Gallo staggering out of Umberto's Clam House and dying on the sidewalk on Mulberry Street. Big Paul Castellano gunned down in front of Sparks Steak House. Classic Mob hits befitting a boss. But snipers? Too risky. If you're going to kill a tough guy like Ben Siegel, you are going to make sure he's dead.

"Always empty a gun before you toss it. Someone finds an empty gun, they're likely to keep it or sell it. If they find a partially empty gun, they'll turn it in to the cops for fear of being connected with whoever got shot," Joe advises, warming to his subject, the fine art of murder. I see the other Joe Stassi, the wily killer, lurking behind the old man's kind, artistic visage.

After a moment, I ask, "How old were you when you first put a gun in your hand?"

Joe turns to look at me. "My ambition was always to be a gangster, a gunman, whatever you want to call it," he says. "What started me was school. When I went into the first grade, I stuttered. The teacher got disgusted with me. She put me in a corner and put a dunce cap on me. The kids in the class all start calling me dummy and stupid and laughing at me. With the result that I started to hate school. I hated that teacher for what she done to me. I start being a truant, playing hooky."

He licks his dry lips a few times. "I was arrested for robbing a bakery shop. After letting me off a few times, the judge had enough of me. He sentenced me to two months in the Catholic protectory." Those two months became the foundation of Joe's education as a professional criminal. "From young kids you had youth up to 16, and we were put into different yards according to age. I was in the small yard with the youngest group. I used to see the older kids, and all I wanted was to be like them."

When Joe was 14, an older boy he met in jail gave Joe his gun to carry. "He had a problem with some people that were looking to kill him. They came around the neighborhood every night around midnight. They used to come down Stanton Street and on Chrystie Street turn left, and we were waiting for them. We shot at them, and believe me, windows were cracking upstairs. Who the hell knew about a gun? You just pulled the trigger. And to make it even worse, the ones that we shot at happened to be good friends of mine."

"Did you kill them?"

"No. Thank God, we missed, both our shots. But I'm saying I wanted to be a part of it. It was all through my environment as a kid. Now," he says, sitting in the driveway and preparing for the ordeal of moving his nearly one-hundred-year-old body into the house, "I regret my life. Oh, there were some great times. It was a glamorous life. When nobody else had anything, I always had money. But looking back at it and what I been through, where I wound up—prison—it's not worth it. What have I got to show for it all?"

When he got out in 1995 after the parole violation, everyone he knew was either dead or locked up. He wound up in one room with his three dogs, trapped in the prison of his infirmities and his memories. "That's why I want to tell my story," he insists. It has become his reason for living, to unburden himself of his past. "When I went back inside, I seen these young kids, from good homes, good families, in there for murder. They wanna be wiseguys. They wanna put a gun in their hand and go out and kill somebody and impress some fuckin' boss so they can become—what? A made member." His voice rises, becomes a strained invocation. "Do they know they're gonna have to kill their best friends? They should kill the fuckin' bosses!"

"Joe," I say, "how do you feel about what you did?"

We start the trek to the front door; I remember how, inside the pen, Joe would walk for miles every day. "It was the life I chose," he says, holding my arm. "I'm not looking to be forgiven. I'm just trying to tell other young fellas what I learned."

The next day, we sit in the garden behind the house, the denture burial ground, with Joe's dogs, Grandma Rose, Lucky and Penny, at his feet and his birds, a pair of beautiful pale yellow parrots, sitting on his shoulders or his head. It's a tropical oasis in the middle of the hood. From time to time, some of the local kids drop by, all black or Latino, a few of them aspiring gangbangers. They have no idea they've got a real live original gangster in their midst. Joe gives them candy or a couple of dollars and tells them to beat it.

He wants to talk about Cuba. When he was just 22, in 1928, Joe took his first trip to Havana. He loved the place. "It was wide-open. Beautiful young whores everywhere, every street corner, every bar. In one club, there were twenty-five girls. You picked the ones you wanted to be in a live sex show." He remembers there was no crime, no robberies. Maybe an occasional knife fight. Stassi made it his business to become well-acquainted with all the top Cuban officials.

After the gold rush of Prohibition, Zwillman urged Joe to go into that other enduring vice, gambling. Stassi took over the numbers for Zwillman and began opening dog- and horse-racing tracks in New Jersey and Florida. During the Depression, when everyone else went bust, Joe continued to rake in millions in cash, socking it away in a half-dozen safe-deposit boxes in the vaults of the Manhattan Trust and other banks. "I just kept stuffing it in there," he says. "I never even had time to count it." He lived in the best hotels under assumed names, married the lovely Frances Paxton of Charlotte, North Carolina, and was out every night in the most popular restaurants and clubs—El Morocco, Copacabana, the Stork Club. In the late '30s and '40s, he took over the Hollywood Restaurant and Nightclub on Broadway between 48th and 49th, which became one of the hottest spots in town. He went to every major heavyweight fight. He hobnobbed with movie stars and celebrities: Jack Dempsey, who was a close friend; Jean Harlow, who had a long, torrid affair with Longy Zwillman; Joe DiMaggio, who took to hanging out in Newark with Richie the Boot; Frank Sinatra, whom Joe first met at Willie Moretti's club in New Jersey; Toots Shor and any number of other savvy denizens of New York nightlife. Joe remembers being unimpressed by the young crooner when he first heard Sinatra sing. "To me, he was nothing compared to Bing Crosby."

But it was Havana that kept drawing him back.

"I used to go there practically every New Year's Eve," he says. "People would come from all over the world to celebrate at El Floridita in Havana." Joe remembers drinking with Ernest Hemingway, whoring with Ben Siegel and other gangsters who came to the island to visit him. By the '50s, Stassi was in partnership with Tampa boss Santo Trafficante Jr. in the Sans Souci casino and with Philadelphia godfather Angelo Bruno in the Plaza Hotel and Casino. "Meyer told me Santo was looking to open up the Sans Souci. Meyer was waiting on the license to open the Nacional, and he asked if I'd be interested in going in on the Sans Souci with Trafficante. I said, 'Yes, lemme meet him.' " It was around this time that the FBI began keeping close track of Stassi's movements. Some of the earliest FBI reports on Stassi, sent to FBI director J. Edgar Hoover from the FBI's legal attaché in Havana, note that Stassi's son, Joseph junior, married the daughter of a Cuban senator, Miguel Suarez Fernandez, who was a close friend of Fulgencio Batista's.

Stassi, Lansky and the boys underestimated Fidel Castro; they lost millions when Castro's men came down from the mountains and drove the gangsters off the island. "The Plaza was one of the first places they wrecked," Joe says, and shakes his head wistfully. The FBI reports I received say Stassi's casino was singled out because of his close ties to Senator Fernandez, who was one of the first people Castro executed. Joe put his wife and young daughter on a boat to Florida. He and Joe junior, Trafficante and a few others lingered on the island to see if Castro might want to play ball. "One night I went to the movies," says Joe. "The people that were with me went back to the Capri Hotel [the scene of Hyman Roth's rooftop birthday party in *The Godfather II*.] That was when they raided."

Castro's men arrested Jake Lansky (Meyer's brother), Santo Trafficante and a few others. And they were looking for Stassi. "I called the Capri, and they told me, 'Joe, don't come here. They just pinched everybody.' " Before that, Joe says, he got arrested every week, but they never held him. The fact that they had arrested Jake Lansky and Trafficante—Joe knew this time it was serious. He lay low for a while, then fled the island in April. "There had been revolutions before. I thought Castro would last only a year or two," says Joe. "My son stayed on another year. But in the end, I lost everything I had invested there. I had bought a lot of real estate for little money. I had bought a copper mine. I heard the mine became very productive—for the Russians."

In 1961 Jack and Bobby Kennedy came into power. Prior to the Kennedy administration, J. Edgar Hoover adamantly refused to acknowledge the existence of an organized-crime cartel. Ignoring Tom Dewey's racketeering prosecution of Luciano in 1936; the Murder, Inc., trials in the '40s, when Abe "Kid Twist" Reles first revealed the existence of the national crime syndicate; and the revelations of the Kefauver Committee Hearings in the 1950s, Hoover dismissed the notion of the Mafia. Only after the Apalachin debacle, when dozens of gangsters from all over the country were caught meeting in upstate New York, would Hoover reluctantly admit the possibility that there were criminal groups operating in concert to control nationwide illegal enterprises. The G-men went from pursuing Reds and bank robbers to stalking racketeers. From then on, *FBI* would stand for Forever Bothering Italians.

When I ask Joe about Hoover, he tells another Swifty Morgan story. Swifty used to run into Hoover while out walking his dog. Joe remembers Swifty as a comedian who would pull stunts like pretending to wipe his dog's ass with a $100 bill, switching it to a one at the last moment. He used to carry one or two items in his pockets that he would offer to sell Hoover. When Hoover said he'd pay $50 for a pair of cuff links, Swifty replied, "Fifty dollars! The fucking reward is more than that."

Joe says he knew, they all knew, that Hoover was gay, that his lover was his right-hand man, Clyde Tolson, and that he was a gambler. "I used to see them at the track together," he says. And he heard there might have been photos, but he never saw them, so he won't confirm whether the Mob was blackmailing Hoover. Joe says it was a matter of priorities. In the '40s and '50s, the priority was Nazis or Communists; in the '60s it was organized crime. What he will confirm is that it was Zwillman who met with Hoover to negotiate a deal for the surrender of notorious Murder, Inc., boss Louis "Lepke" Buchalter. Walter

Winchell became the Mob's middleman and went along for the scoop on the night Lepke got into Hoover's car on a New York street after two years in hiding. Hoover promised he would keep Buchalter in federal custody and give him ten years on a tax charge. Joe says Hoover told Zwillman he would see Buchalter was not turned over to Dewey and New York prosecutors, who wanted to give him the electric chair. Hoover didn't keep his end of the deal. Buchalter became the first and only Mob boss to be executed for his crimes.

Nothing had prepared Stassi and the other mobsters for the zeal and power of young Bobby Kennedy. Bobby's drive on organized crime had the tenor of a vendetta with Irish Catholic overtones. Many believe the beef went all the way back to the days of the patriarch, Joseph P. Kennedy Sr., who made his stake as a rumrunner and held on to the distribution rights for Haig & Haig whiskey from England after repeal. He would later be named ambassador to Great Britain. Joe says Kennedy senior was known as a double-crossing, vindictive son of a bitch. He remembers his early brush with the man whose son would be murdered in Dallas.

Stassi was living at the Warwick Hotel at 54th and Sixth, where Joe Kennedy also happened to reside. Stassi tells of a cocktail lounge at the Warwick where he would sometimes meet a woman whose last name was Rogers, coincidentally the same name as Stassi's alias. Joe Kennedy also knew Miss Rogers; indeed, she was his mistress at the time. One time, Kennedy came into the cocktail lounge and found Joe Rogers sitting tête-à-tête with Miss Rogers. "Are you two related?" Kennedy asked with a wry smile.

Joe smiles faintly at the memory. "A fella I knew well tells me, 'I was speaking to the law and was told to advise you to move out. The management doesn't want you. You're gonna get put out, maybe arrested to get you out.'" Joe heard later that Kennedy might have had something to do with Stassi's wearing out his welcome at the hotel. "Joe Kennedy was law in the Warwick Hotel. If he made a suggestion . . . " Joe gestures, cocks his head. "I moved out. Later I'm told Kennedy said I was one of five people in his life he hated."

"Because of Miss Rogers? Seems kind of extreme."

Joe says he doesn't know if it's true any more than he knows why Bobby's office saw fit to frame him on narcotics charges. The nexus between the boys and the Kennedys was long-standing and byzantine, and then it morphed into an unholy covenant. At Kennedy senior's behest, the Mob helped get Jack elected in 1960 by swinging the vote in the West Virginia primary. The CIA and at least two high-ranking mafiosi, Johnny Roselli and Joe's partner Santo Trafficante, with the connivance of the White House, were plotting to hit Fidel Castro. And to make it personal, Jack Kennedy and Chicago boss Sam Giancana were sleeping with the same woman, Judith Campbell Exner. Joe Kennedy's dictatorial influence, his habit of turning on former partners who had helped him along the way and his self-professed bigotry were channeled through the loyal scions.

Stassi was one of the first to fall. After he decamped Havana, Joe was approached by the FBI. He agreed to speak to them with the proviso that he would not discuss anything to do with his personal business or that of his friends; he would talk only about what he knew of the political situation in postrevolutionary Cuba. "They asked me, 'Are you a good American?' I said, 'Yes, I'm a good American.' " According to the FBI report, Stassi gave them very little information. He said he was returning to Cuba to visit his son and would talk to them on his return. He never did. In 1962 Stassi was named by Joe Valachi during testimony before a Senate committee as a member of La Cosa Nostra. By then the FBI had already classified him as a Top Hoodlum and opened an extensive investigation. Soon after, he was indicted on a heroin-importation case out of Corpus Christi, Texas. He went on the lam and lived for three years as a fugitive sought around the world in one of the most extensive FBI manhunts of the time. Finally, brought to ground at the Canada Club in Pompano Beach, Florida, Joe would spend the next thirty years insisting he was framed on the narcotics charges and fighting to regain his freedom.

In November 1962, almost a year to the day before the Kennedy assassination, Joe met in New York with Santo Trafficante and Carlos

Marcello, the New Orleans Mafia boss who was hounded out of the country by Bobby Kennedy. Among conspiracy theorists, Marcello and Trafficante are the prime suspects in alleged Mob plots to return fire on the Kennedys. "What did you talk about?" I ask him, scanning the FBI report of the meeting.

"Nothing. We had breakfast."

"C'mon, Joe. You never met with anyone without discussing something."

He holds up his hand. "I don't remember."

"The Kennedys?"

"We might have talked about all the heat."

"Do you believe Trafficante was involved in the assassination?"

"Please. Santo wouldn't have the balls," Joe says. He is obfuscating.

"I'm not saying him personally."

He shrugs. "Santo was a piece of shit."

Joe has nothing good to say about Santo. Cheapest man he ever met. Whenever there was money owed, Trafficante was nowhere to be found. His own people told Joe that Santo screwed them out of money all the time. FBI reports bear out there was rancor among the partners.

"What about Marcello?"

"Knowing Carlos and Santo, no. Unless they had some fool to do it for them."

"Or some patsy."

"Anything is possible," Joe allows. He believes money would have been all the motive they needed, and he admits the Kennedy Justice Department's offensive against organized crime was putting a serious crimp in the bosses' lifestyle. The Mob had never known such heat.

Arnold Stone, a trial attorney with the Organized Crime Section of the Criminal Division, whose bailiwick included Texas and New Jersey and who oversaw the Stassi investigation and prosecution, remembers he was in a meeting with Robert Kennedy at the Justice Department to discuss their Mob offensive on November 22, 1963, the day President Kennedy was assassinated. When I ask Stone about Joe's case, he says the Trafficante connection is off-limits. He'll talk about Joe on the record but not Trafficante, because talking about him could compromise ongoing investigations. I press the issue: "Investigations of whom? Santos is dead." Stone says he simply does not know enough about Trafficante to talk about him intelligently.

According to Stone, the atmosphere in the Kennedy Justice Department was one of professionalism and dedication to honest and just law enforcement. He doubts anything like a vendetta motivated Robert Kennedy, whom Stone remembers as a brilliant and hardworking man with a strong sense of fair play. Stone, who is now in private practice in North Carolina, denies Stassi was the target of a malicious prosecution solely intended to get at Trafficante. Stassi was a target in his own right. "Of course we wanted Stassi, but for the crimes he was committing. Would we have liked to talk to him about Santo Trafficante? Of course we would." Then he adds, "And Vito Genovese. And Lucien Rivard and Paul Mondolini"—two of the original architects of the French Connection. Stone believes it is Stassi's guilt that prevents him from admitting his involvement in heroin trafficking. "Better he should be remembered as a killer of five or six gangsters than a contributor to the miseries and slow deaths of thousands of heroin users, otherwise innocent children and adults."

After the Kennedy assassination, Stone went to Florida while Joe was in the wind and made overtures, through Joe's son, for him to come in and talk to them. No matter how much he may have despised Santo, Joe held true to his vows and refused to cooperate. The Feds responded by turning up the heat. The files are rife with reports on the manhunt. Stassi is described as "armed and dangerous" and a "vicious killer." There is almost no mention of Stassi in connection with narcotics.

I'm in New York when the call comes. Joe is in the hospital complaining of severe chest pains. "You better get down here," he orders.

I find him in the Cedars-Sinai Medical Center, sitting on the edge of the bed trying to put on his pants. "Get me out of here," he tells me when I walk in. It turns out the pains were caused by bruised ribs sustained when he took a fall; his heart is still going strong. I talk to the nurse, commandeer a guy with a wheelchair, and we're out. Something in my Karma has me liberating this man from large institutions.

Joe isn't ready to die yet. He's not prepared for the final liberation; he wants to go to the International House of Pancakes first. Afterward, I take him home.

"Dutch Schultz," Joe says when I have him settled on his bed.

The murder of Dutch Schultz on October 23, 1935, like the Siegel killing, is one that has long captured the popular imagination. Just 33 when he died, the Dutchman was one of the most celebrated and feared gangsters of all time. *Kill the Dutchman! The Story of Dutch Schultz*, by Paul Sann; E. L. Doctorow's *Billy Bathgate*, made into a movie starring Dustin Hoffman as Schultz; and any number of other portrayals of the infamous bootlegger and racketeer whose real name was Arthur Flegenheimer—the son of a German Jewish saloonkeeper—carry us inevitably to that October night in the Palace Chophouse and Tavern in Newark when Schultz was gunned down. Mortally wounded, Schultz lingered for twenty hours in a Newark hospital surrounded by cops, a stenographer recording his dying words. No less a literary outlaw than William Burroughs, the godfather of the Beats, wrote a film script based on Schultz's rhapsodic deathbed dithyramb.

"Who shot you?" a cop asked Dutch.

"Please crack down on the Chinaman's friends and Hitler's commander," Schultz raved. "I am sore, and I am going up, and I am going to give you honey if I can. Mother is the best bet, and don't let Satan draw you too fast." He died without naming his killers.

One of my favorite Schultz stories has him in a meeting with leaders of the Syndicate, Luciano presiding, when a vote was taken on some important piece of business. Dutch, who was suffering from a bad case of the flu, had been sitting off in the corner so as not to infect the others. Everyone voiced his opinion except Joe Adonis, who stood at the mirror combing his hair. Adonis, whose real name was Giuseppe Antonio Doto, had assumed the alias in deference to his conceit that he was the handsomest of criminals. With the other mobsters waiting for him to weigh in, Adonis finally turned away from the mirror and announced, "The star says yes." At which point Schultz leaped up, rushed over to Adonis and grabbed him in a headlock. He slobbered mucus all over Adonis's face and said, "Now, you fuckin' star, you have my *joims!*" Adonis was laid up for a week with Schultz's flu.

Joe hated Adonis, and for good reason. Adonis once called a sit-down that, had it not gone Stassi's way, would have ended in his death sentence. Adonis resented Stassi ever after. There was also an issue over a girlfriend. To Joe, Adonis epitomized the power-crazed boss who orders his soldiers to kill on a whim.

"You killed Dutch Schultz?"

"I got the contract," he says.

At the time, Joe used to meet secretly with Abe Zwillman and Meyer Lansky in out-of-the-way spots so no one would put them together. Prohibition had ended; the underworld was in transition. Luciano, Lansky and Zwillman were intent on establishing a new order and putting an end to the unbridled murder and mayhem of the '20s. The Dutchman was a throwback to the violent era of the celebrity criminal.

Schultz was trying to sell his New York brewery to raise cash to pay his lawyers and keep his corrupt police and political allies from jumping ship. Hoover's FBI had named Schultz Public Enemy No. 1 after he beat an IRS case. Schultz's legal woes were far from over, however; he was awaiting trial in Jersey on new charges, and Dewey had vowed to put him and Tammany Hall power broker Jimmy Hines behind bars. Schultz fled New York and took up residence in the same hotel where Zwillman and Richie the Boot kept apartments, the Robert Treat in Newark, around the corner from the Palace Chophouse.

Once Joe had been given the contract, he told Schultz he might have a buyer for the brewery. Joe said he would speak to the party and get back to the Dutchman in a day or two. Schultz was pleased with Joe's help, never suspecting it was all part of an elaborate setup. Joe arranged to meet Schultz at the Chophouse.

Stassi says he was too well-known at the tavern to carry out the hit himself, so he brought in two of Murder, Inc.'s most accomplished triggermen: Charley "the Bug" Workman and Emmanuel "Mendy" Weiss. "Abe was tight with Richie the Boot," Joe says. "They had made peace, and it was decided Richie would provide the other men. We used Gyp DeCarlo and a guy, I can't remember his name, we called him Stretch. I gave them a rifle. 'What's this for?' Gyp asks. I says, 'If you're being chased, use it.' "

Here Joe becomes even more sotto voce. "We wait till after rush hour, around eight o'clock. DeCarlo's partner is behind the wheel. Workman and Mendy walk in, and right away the shooting starts. Dutch has three or four of his men in there, and they all have guns. They're shooting at each other. Workman doesn't see Dutch, so he ducks into the men's room. Dutch had just finished taking a piss, he was washing his hands when the shooting started. Workman shoots him as he turns from the sink, then he robs him, which he wasn't supposed to do. Workman never followed orders. That's when Gyp comes with the rifle, and they shoot all Dutch's men. Mendy and Gyp run out and get in the car. 'Where's Workman?' Mendy doesn't know, lost him in the confusion."

The next day, Workman showed up. He told Joe he had run out the back door and hopped a bus a few blocks away. Workman was eventually arrested for the Schultz hit on the testimony of Abe Reles, the notorious Murder, Inc., killer who turned informant. Reles testified that Workman had bragged to him about killing Schultz; Joe believes Reles made up his testimony.

Stassi says he fixed Workman's trial in Newark. "There was no chance in the world he could get convicted. It came as a shock to everyone when he pled guilty." Workman served twenty-three years in prison for the killing and died without revealing who had orchestrated the Dutchman's demise. A lifetime later, Stassi's confession clears the books on one of the Mob's most spectacular hits.

"Go on, Joe, who else did you murder?"

After a long pause, he says, "Max Hassel."

"I thought you were close to Max."

"You don't listen. That's what I'm trying to tell you."

But I have been listening. I want him to say it again.

Max Hassel was one of the first men who befriended Joe when he took up with the New Jersey bootleggers. Hassel trusted Joe implicitly; Joe was considered part of the inner circle and took a suite on the floor below Hassel's headquarters at the Elizabeth Carteret Hotel in Elizabeth. Joe had gone over to meet Max at the hotel one day and ended up staying fourteen years. What Hassel didn't know was that Joe was even closer to Meyer Lansky and Longy Zwillman.

Joe was summoned to a meeting in New York. Adonis was there, Zwillman, Lansky—the bosses. They told Joe that Hassel and his partner, Max Greenberg, must go. They were trying to take over; Max Greenberg was cheating people. Joe was shaken. " 'Kill Max Hassel?' I said. 'Why, Max is no more of a threat to you than a cockroach.' Adonis says, 'Yeah, well, that's all he is, a cockroach. So kill him.' " Joe closes his eyes, fighting back tears.

"Max Hassel had been talking to me," he continues after a few moments. "If there's a war, who do I think would win? he says. I used to tell him, 'Max, as far as you're concerned, nobody's gonna bother you.' And I meant it, because everyone knew Max Hassel never cheated anyone, never hit or beat no one. Greenberg was the one; I could understand Greenberg. I heard him bragging, 'I fucked them with a pencil!' That was one of his famous sayings. Greenberg was taking everything, bullying everybody. They all had reason to kill him. But not Max Hassel."

Hassel had paid all Joe's bills when Joe was just getting established in Jersey. He was one of several Jewish gangsters Joe would work closely with over the years. And now he was going to kill him.

"I loved the guy . . . " Joe says.

But he knew that to refuse the order or even to show weakness in carrying it out would give Adonis the ammunition he needed to have Stassi killed. It took all Joe's will to keep his long-simmering hatred of Adonis from boiling over.

"Abe was telling me the trouble they had. They was scheming for months to kill Max Greenberg. They couldn't get a handle on it; it would have to be done so openly. They knew I was the only one who could arrange it. They were all looking at me. What did I have to say? I started laughing. They said, 'Why are you laughing?' I told them, 'It's the easiest thing in the world.' "

Joe once had a woman in his rooms at the Carteret Hotel who became hysterical. She was convinced her husband had followed her and was outside waiting for her to come out. A room-service waiter showed Joe a rear service entrance, and the lady slipped out unseen. It was the crucial piece of information needed when it came time to plan the hit of the two Maxes. Getting in was not the problem; they had the element of surprise. The escape route is the key to a successful hit.

Waxey Gordon, a well-known bootlegger and Lansky rival, was at the hotel visiting the two Maxes. One popular retelling of the killing has Waxey spared because he was in another room with a woman named Nancy Presser, who would go on to prominence as one of the star witnesses against Luciano in his prostitution-rackets trial. Joe says that's not true, the woman is a lying stool pigeon. Waxey was there, but they didn't kill him because the contract didn't call for him to die.

"No one was ever prosecuted."

"Who did it?"

"It's not important. What I'm trying to say, anyone who wants to be a gangster, a wiseguy, a made Mafia soldier or whatever you want to call it is going to have to face what I went through."

He licks his thin lips several times. "I killed my best friend on orders from Abe and Meyer," he says.

"Max Hassel?"

"No. Another party."

"Who?"

"I'll tell you . . . "

But he can't quite bring himself to say the man's name. It was his best friend; that's all we need to know. It was the ultimate test of his loyalty, and his treachery.

His friend loved diamonds. Joe used the pretext that he had some stones to sell to lure him to a rendezvous at a train station. This killing, too, was part of the larger power struggle. Joe, being the independent operator he was, had friends on both sides of the conflict.

"I don't believe in killing for money," he says. "There was always another reason, cheating or talking to the law, disobeying orders. They had a reason, even if the reason wasn't always right."

He knew why this killing had been ordered, but he didn't agree with it. Joe protested to Zwillman, who said he agreed, but it didn't matter; they were outvoted by the others, who believed Joe's friend was in the wrong. Joe believes it was all part of a power play by Nick Delmore to take over running the Jersey operations for the syndicate. The hit had come from Vincent Alo, who took over for Adonis when the latter was deported to Italy. Alo also inherited Joe's hatred for Adonis and went on to provoke plenty of his own. Joe is ready to fight when his name is mentioned. And Delmore? "I'll say it to the whole world: Nick Delmore was no fucking good."

Delmore was supposed to provide a getaway car but didn't. Fortunately for Joe, his friend drove to the station instead of coming by train. Joe killed him in his car, shot him in the head, then used the car to dispose of the body.

"That's how they came to have such trust in me."

"Abe and Meyer. Because you killed your best friend . . . "

He nods. "If you ask me, 90 percent of killings take place between close friends. Nick Delmore," Joe hisses, full of venom. "Later, they made this no-good rat bastard a boss. One regret I got in life: I should have killed Nick Delmore."

In 1959, at 60, Longy Zwillman went into his basement one night with a bottle of whiskey and some antidepressants. When the drugs and alcohol wouldn't exorcise his demons, Longy hanged himself from the rafters with an electric cord. There have been persistent rumors that the suicide was actually a hit. Joe, who was in Cuba at the time, doubts it. He says Longy had no real enemies, except the U.S. government, which had indicted him for bribing a juror in his trial for tax evasion. He was on the inevitable ride to prison. Besides, Joe says, if it had been a hit, they would have shot him in the head, to his face, a death befitting the high regard in which he was held. And not faked a suicide in his home, with his wife and children upstairs asleep.

"The FBI reports call you a 'vicious killer,' " I tell him. "Is that true?"

"No." He shakes his head. "I killed on orders."

"How many people have you killed, Joe?"

He waves his hands, closes his eyes. "So many . . . I can't remember."

It's as though a weight has been lifted. Joe has unburdened himself of his most cumbersome memories. He has rolled aside the boulder at the mouth to the cave of his past. The effort has left him spent and at peace.

"Tired, Joe?" I ask, and help him lift his swollen legs onto the bed.

"No. I'm fine," he says. But in a moment, he has dozed off and I am left to contemplate his ancient face. I see the shamed stuttering little boy in his dunce cap, the lonely kid who wanted desperately to be like the big boys, the bold young soldier who served his commanders, the honorable old don who kept his vows, went to prison, did his time and lived to tell about it. I wonder what other dark secrets lie within this living relic of the century that gave us organized crime.

In this era of *Sopranos* mania, here is the New Jersey mobster incarnate at the end of his days, and I am at once drawn to him and repelled, fascinated and horrified, like the rest of America watching Tony Soprano blast his friend Big Pussy into oblivion.

Loud hip-hop music from outside invades the stillness of the afternoon. Joe stirs. I think of the young rappers appropriating mobster monikers like Capone, Gallo, Gotti. The gangster persona is omnipresent in our culture. Joe shunned the limelight. He says John Gotti was his own worst enemy, he embodied the ambivalence: Am I a movie star or a mobster?

Joe insists there was no glamour, no glory in that moment when he put the gun to his best friend's head.

Sparks
from Gotti: Rise and Fall
by Jerry Capeci and Gene Mustain

Jerry Capeci and Gene Mustain spent nine years reporting on John Gotti—perhaps the best-known gangster of his generation. When Gotti wanted Paul Castellano's job as head of the Gambino crime family, Gotti set up a public execution in midtown Manhattan.

The assassins gathered in a park by the East River as the purple gloom of a wintry twilight fell across the city. It was December 16, 1985. Christmas displays were twinkling on in the windows of a giant public housing project overlooking the park. Twenty blocks north along the curving East River Drive, many tens of thousands of office workers were exiting the great mountain range of skyscrapers in midtown Manhattan.

Four of the ten men, the designated shooters, wore identical tan trench coats and Cossack-like fur hats. The outfits were meant to confuse potential witnesses and cause recollection of coats and hats but not faces. The other six men, backup shooters and getaway drivers, were dressed for anonymity.

John Gotti had given everyone their assignments the night before, in a meeting at a storefront in Bensonhurst that Sammy used for his construction businesses. But now as they huddled in the park, with its barren trees and the East River's treacherous currents rushing past, Gotti—with Sammy at his side—went over the details one final time.

In a few minutes the team would be leaving for the ambush site—a street outside an elegant midtown restaurant. Although they had made the correct assumption, some of the assassins did not officially know who it was that they had been summoned to kill; it was for their benefit that Gotti said: "It's Paul who's gettin' popped. So this gotta go right. We ain't allowed no misses."

The assassins were all soldiers or associates loyal to the Gotti wing, including Angelo Ruggiero and two others stamping their feet against the cold, John Carneglia and Anthony Rampino.

"Whoever else's there has to go, probably be Tommy," Gotti added, meaning Paul's loyalist and driver, Thomas Bilotti. But Bilotti—Paul's newly named underboss—was almost as important a target as Paul. To increase the odds of his agenda, a family takeover without a fight, Gotti had to eliminate Bilotti too.

Gotti turned to the designated shooters. In unintentional but revealing fashion, he had selected four drug dealers as the triggermen; they included two men under indictment with Angelo in the heroin case—Carneglia and Edward Lino, a Bonanno associate who wasn't facing as many serious charges as Carneglia and the rest, since he had not been caught uttering too many incriminating words at Angelo's house.

"Once you make a move, don't leave until they're dead. If you don't get 'em there, we lose. We're all gonna be dead."

As Gotti spoke, Angelo dragged on a Marlboro and fidgeted with one of the team's walkie-talkies. "These fuckers gotta be the same channel," he said to no one.

Sammy stood beside Gotti, calm, resolute, dead-serious. He hardly said a word, beyond reminding the shooters of the lethal certainty of "head shots."

A few days before, right after revealing his plans to break up the Gotti crew, Paul had handed the Fist this opportunity by scheduling a dinner meeting with five captains, including Tommy Gambino, Carlo's son, and James Failla, an elder loyalist from Carlo's era. Fatefully, he also invited a capo he believed was loyal—Frank DeCicco, who quickly alerted Gotti and Sammy.

Now DeCicco was already en route to the restaurant; after the ambush, he was to discourage reprisal and encourage unity by telling the other capos they need not fear for their own lives.

The restaurant, Sparks Steak House, was on East Forty-sixth Street between Second and Third Avenues, in midtown, one of the most pedestrian-congested areas in the world. The anonymity and bustle of midtown, however, made East Forty-sixth an ideal stage for surprise, particularly at a going-home hour.

"Sparks, 5 p.m.," read an entry in Paul's diary, which also contained reminders about meetings with his defense lawyers in the DeMeo trial, which was in recess for the holidays.

That week, Sparks had been rated the city's top steakhouse by *New York* magazine, and it was popular with businessmen and diplomats and spies from the United Nations complex two blocks east. The year before, it also had been the topic of a tirade by Paul, in which the doomed millionaire moaned in the presence of the FBI bug then in his mansion that Sparks's management had not given him anything on the house during previous visits—despite his influence in the union that represented Sparks's employees.

"Ya know who's busy makin' a fortune?" Paul said to two union fixers. "Fuckin' Sparks. What those guys do is good for a hundred grand a week. Me, I don't get five cents when I go in there. They don't even buy you a drink."

The plan was to shoot Paul and Bilotti as they pulled up beside Sparks and the two stone lions on the sidewalk—strong lions, but not wise like foxes to traps—and turned over their car, as they inevitably would, to a parking attendant.

Carneglia, Eddie Lino, and the other two designated shooters would pair off and approach from either side of the car. Rampino, backup shooter, would loiter across the street, in the unlikely event that the victims escaped the fusillade. Angelo and two other backups would position themselves toward the Second Avenue side of East Forty-sixth, where two getaway cars would be waiting.

Gotti and Sammy Gravano would be watching the hit from a car on the Third Avenue side of East Forty-sixth Street, with Sammy ready to jump out and begin firing a .357 Magnum if the victims somehow managed to evade the shooters and Rampino, and flee toward Third Avenue.

It was an excellent plan—the targets boxed in, a kill zone worthy of a military-style ambush. Later, people were surprised that Gene Gotti was not on the team. But as in the Army, the borgatas had a rule against sending brothers into combat together.

"Let's go," John Gotti said as the run-through in the park ended. "Don't fuckin' forget, whoever's with Paul has to go too. If fuckin' somethin' goes wrong, and we miss 'em goin' in, we go into the restaurant and take the motherfuckers there."

Until now, Sammy had given assassins last-minute reminders. But Gotti had taken command and Sammy was comfortable taking a backseat. He had what his ego required—he had been chosen to be alongside as the Fist arrived at the point of no return.

After DeCicco expressed reservations early in the plot, Sammy also had dwelled on the question of whether Gotti was the right person to lead the Gambino family. Gotti was overbearing, flashy, temperamental; and because he had spent so much time in jail, he lacked the hands-on know-how of men his age, men like DeCicco—and even Sammy, who was five years younger.

Still, underneath Gotti's bluster, Sammy thought he saw a man of Cosa Nostra, a man of daring if not know-how—especially after DeCicco said, as the plot thickened, that they had no choice but to support Gotti.

"I could be John's underboss, but he could never be mine," DeCicco had said. "His ego couldn't handle it; if I was boss, we'd just have the same problems again."

Sammy accommodated himself to Gotti's ego too, for his own good and the good of the family—the equation he felt he always tried to make, despite how difficult it sometimes was.

Anticipating vengeance from Paul loyalists, Sammy had moved with two other men, pistols, and ammo into the basement apartment of an associate on Staten Island. Gotti had mulled over similar plans but was gambling they wouldn't be necessary.

"Sammy," Gotti said on the way to Sparks, "nobody'll give a fuck about this *cazzu*—not enough to fuck with us, you watch."

"I don't know, John. Killin' a boss."

"Paul ain't a real boss. Never was."

With Gotti at the wheel, they departed the park in a black Lincoln with tinted windows. The shooters and backups; left in the getaway cars. With Frank DeCicco already at Sparks, only two members of the Fist were absent—Joseph Armone, the aging capo recruited for post-assassination politics, and soldier-at-large Robert DiBernardo, the Teamsters fixer. Armone was too infirm to be on the street in an ambush; Deebee was young but not a shooter, and so he had been told to take a trip to Florida.

The drive uptown took ten minutes. Recalling it a few years later, Gotti told Sammy that Paul was to blame for what was to happen because he resented strength and talked behind people's backs and was so jealous of Neil that he was afraid to let Neil be a good underboss.

"He wasn't half the man Neil was. He never understood Neil was happy bein' underboss. He should've blown the guy, but he was geloso. He wasn't a man. If you're a tough guy, he hated you. And any time he could knock you, he knocked you."

Sammy recalled the story of being at a Christmas party at Paul's and how Paul upbraided him when he said he was leaving to attend a Christmas party at Neil's, and then Gotti said how much he hated going to Paul's mansion.

"Every time I went there on a Saturday, I hated it. I hated the fuckin' world, because whoever was there before me, as soon as they left, he cursed them out. You know when you leave, he's gonna say it about you."

In the end, Gotti said, Paul just did not know "the life." He was "a fuckin' fish on the desert, a fish outta water."

In midtown, after circling the block once, Gotti and Sammy pulled into a parking space that opened on the northwest corner of Third Avenue and East Forty-sixth, a one-way eastbound street. The vantage point was ideal; they could look across Third at the entrance to Sparks, which was only a few doors east of the southeast corner of East Forty-sixth and Third.

From inside the Lincoln, Sammy saw backup shooter Rampino lurking by an office-supply store directly across from Sparks and, amid the hubbub of pedestrians, a mailman emptying a box at the corner. Furtively, he clicked on one of the team's walkie-talkies and notified the others where he and Gott were parked.

In the next instant, a nearly identical black Lincoln pulled alongside the parked Lincoln with Gotti and Sammy, and stopped for a red light; when Sammy glanced to his right, he was startled to see Paul, and Tommy Bilotti, who was at the wheel of the second Lincoln and reaching for something in the glove compartment.

"Holy fuck," Sammy whispered, like he had just witnessed a supernatural event. He briefly felt like he had at his induction, like he was floating in a dream, but the adrenaline pouring into his stomach jolted him alert.

He turned toward Gotti and flicked his head back, to point Gotti to what he had seen, but the light changed and Victims No. 9 and 10 on Sammy's murder ledger moved off.

Sammy whispered again into his walkie-talkie: "Paul and Tommy are coming through the intersection now."

It was an advantageous heads-up for the designated shooters. They could stop strolling back and forth in their long tan coats and fur hats, trying to become part of the swelling crowds of Christmas rush-hour shoppers, and get ready to kill.

The killing began as soon as Bilotti drove across Third Avenue and stopped in front of Sparks. He and Paul never had a chance. The two shooters assigned to Paul fired six bullets into his head as he stepped out of the car on the curb side.

The gun of one shooter assigned to Bilotti jammed, but the others did not, so Bilotti was shot as he, frozen in surprise, saw Paul shot. Carneglia assigned to Paul, saw the gunman on the other team unable to fire; calmly, he walked around the front of the car and fired be-sure shots into Bilotti's head.

Pedestrians began scrambling every which way. When the light on East Forty-sixth changed, impatient drivers carried Gotti and Sammy inconspicuously through the intersection, across Third, right alongside the bodies, then past the shooters high-tailing it east to Second Avenue and the getaway cars.

Some later wondered whether it was foolish for them to have risked being seen on the street or hemmed in by stalled traffic. But at the time their faces were not well known. And if somehow they had gotten trapped on the block and cops sought to question them, they had a simple explanation; They were on their way to a dinner meeting with Paul.

Unimpeded, Gotti cruised down the block, then turned south on Second Avenue and melted into the anonymity and bustle of mid-town before anyone thought to dial 911.

Sammy tuned the Lincoln's radio to 1010 WINS, an all-news station. "Maybe there'll be a bulletin," he said.

"They better make it an obituary!" Gotti said, slapping the wheel of the car. "Those fucks are gone! What a piece of work!"

"Everybody did okay. How it's supposed to go."

Gotti guided his Lincoln down to Thirty-fourth Street, over to East River Drive and down to the entrance to the Brooklyn-Battery Tunnel at the tip of Manhattan, then through the tunnel to Sammy's con-struction company office in Brooklyn.

Meanwhile, hearing gunshots inside Sparks, DeCicco and two capos hastened to leave. Outside, they saw Paul's car and the bodies and hur-ried away. One of the capos, James Failla, the elder loyalist who prac-tically ran the city's private sanitation industry, began to shake.

"I could've been in that car with Paul," he said to DeCicco. "They were gonna give me a lift."

"But you weren't, and you don't have another thing to worry about. Let's just keep on walkin' out of here."

Down the block they ran into Tommy Gambino, Paul's nephew; a few minutes late for his dinner meeting with Paul, he was walking toward Sparks, vaguely aware of some commotion ahead.

DeCicco motioned him to turn around, then fell in beside him. Gambino was a man of boarding schools and country clubs who was worth a hundred million dollars; he was likely one of the few men in the family who had not been required to "make his bones"—commit a murder—before his induction.

"Your uncle's been shot," DeCicco said.

"Is he dead?"

"He is, so's Tommy."

"Jesus, what's going on?"

"Don't worry, everyone else is okay. Got to your car and leave. We'll be in touch."

DeCicco went to his car and drove to Bensonhurst to meet Gotti and Sammy at Sammy's construction office. There, before DeCicco reported on his conversations with Failla and Gambino, everyone embraced and kissed each other on the cheeks.

"I told them no one else is gonna get hurt," DeCicco said.

"Good; they got the fuckin' message right there," Gotti replied, still pumped with excitement.

"But we could get hurt, we could all be dead in six months."

"You worry more than Sammy! I'm tellin' you, no one fuckin' liked Paul except maybe his nephew, but that's blood and Tommy ain't gonna give us problems. We did everybody a favor!"

"We could have a massive war with Jimmy Brown and them," DeCicco said, referring to James Failla by his nickname.

"Forget about it, Jimmy Brown's an old *cazzu* too! We ain't runnin' scared of him!"

"We just took out the boss," Sammy said. "But I'm ready. We're ready. We gotta be."

"We'll all nose around tomorrow and see what's what," Gotti

said, calming down. "But we didn't come this far to be lay-down Sallys now."

Back on East Forty-sixth Street, the shooters had slipped away east toward Second Avenue and hopped into the getaway cars.

A public relations executive leaving his office had taken a long look at the most deliberate shooter, Carneglia, the one who calmly strode around the front of the car and fired into Bilotti after finishing with Paul. A delivery man for a photo finisher got a good glance at one of the backups, Rampino, whose sunken eyes and acne scars made for a hard-to-forget face.

A retired cop walking on Third Avenue toward East Forty-seventh Street when the gunfire began had followed the shooters toward Second. But they were in the getaway cars and gone when he reached the corner and dialed 911.

One of the witnesses did not recall any fur hats. One said the tan trench coats were dark. The two who were not former cops were not eager to talk about the faces they had seen, and the ex-cop had not seen any faces.

In the heart of midtown during a Christmas rush hour, the Fist had boldly executed what looked to be a perfect crime.

The double murder was the biggest gangland story since 1957, when Carlo's predecessor, Albert Anastasia, had been assassinated; the city's noisy media went after it with almost the same gusto as a mayoral murder. The court files of several pending Cosa Nostra cases contained a few references to intrigues in the Gambino family. The information was vague and confusing, but enough to feed an inky avalanche that lasted several days.

Even the most casual readers and viewers were introduced to the name John Gotti, who was identified in most of the stories as the probable culprit. Overnight, he became more of a public figure than Paul or Neil had ever been.

In one widely distributed remark, Remo Franceschini, boss of an NYPD detective squad in Queens, cast the murders as a grab for power and flatly predicted, "Gotti will emerge as the head of the other capos."

High-minded outrage kept the avalanche going. "The decent citizens of this country are demeaned in the eyes of the world if brazen cold-blooded murders can be perpetrated on a street in New York," said federal court of appeals judge Irving J. Kaufman, chairman of the president's Commission on Organized Crime.

"The waste of a human life is shocking, no matter who it is," added United States district court judge Kevin Duffy, who was presiding over the DeMeo case, as he adjourned it for three weeks to weigh motions from Paul's codefendants for a mistrial (they were eventually denied).

Reporters who tried to contact Gotti at his home in Howard Beach were told he was not available. A lawyer who had recently begun representing Gotti, however, said his client had declined a request from the FBI to submit to a voluntary interview because he knew "nothing about the murders." Such unequivocal denials would eventually become almost a full-time occupation for the lawyer, Bruce Cutler, a loquacious former prosecutor with a likable and shamelessly outrageous style.

Without much detail to go on, many reporters wrote stories that emphasized how young Gotti was compared with the other Cosa Nostra bosses and went on about his style, looks, and penchant for showy double-breasted suits. Thus, words such as "youthful," "dashing," and "dapper" became part of his early public image.

Paul was buried a few days later in Brooklyn, where he had been born to Sicilian immigrants seventy years before. Citing the life Paul had lived, the local Catholic bishop denied him a funeral mass. Only personal family members attended his wake, because by that time the transfer of power in his Cosa Nostra family had begun, and even ardent loyalists were afraid that an act of respect might be seen as portending an act of vengeance.

The transfer of power had begun two days after the murders when— even as detectives continued to canvass offices along East Forty-sixth Street and Third Avenue for witnesses—almost all of the borgata's capos gathered for a tense meeting at a restaurant owned by Sammy and others twelve blocks north on Third.

Technically, the meeting was convened by the only surviving member of the Gambino administration, the seventy-five-year-old in-house adviser, consigliere Joe N. Gallo. But Gotti was telling him what to do. One captain about as old as Gallo failed to show; he had checked into a hospital for treatment of a sudden nerve disorder. Another, Tommy Gambino, was given an excused absence.

"I sent a message to Tommy that it was okay for him not to come," Gotti told Sammy. "I told him what happened with Paul was business, but with him being Paul's nephew, it would be a little awkward for him here. Tommy's a sweetheart. We want him to know we got nothing against him."

Gotti intended to take over no matter what happened at the meeting, but he preferred an "election" by the caporegimes—and so before the meeting he had sent old-time capo Joseph Armone, recruited into the plot for just such a purpose, to Gallo and others with a simple message: Gotti was taking over, and the family risked a hor-rible war if anyone resisted.

Gallo, a Carlo holdover who had never regarded Paul too highly, got the message. He had not managed to achieve the distinction of never having been charged with a crime by taking chances, and so now he did not risk offending Gotti by asking any questions about the mur-ders. In the winter of his life, he was happy just to be well enough to be alive during a critical time.

In that vein, before the meeting Gallo explained to Gotti and the other conspirators the Cosa Nostra rules that apply when the rule that a boss cannot be killed without approval from the four other Commis-sion bosses is broken. The Fist had contacted only acting bosses in only three of the four families—and then only, on an "off-the-record" basis, meaning, in Cosa Nostraspeak, that the contacts were never made.

"You cannot ever tell the truth about this," Gallo advised. "The Commission has a rule, you must have its permission to take a boss down. You broke that rule. You can't ever admit that to anyone. Sooner or later, you'll have to come up with a story about what happened, but you can't ever admit it."

Against that wonderland backdrop, the meeting—held around a conference table in the restaurant's basement—began. Most of the captains had brought bodyguards, but the bodyguards had been told to remain upstairs—by Sammy and Angelo, the only soldiers in the room; they made it clear that they were armed and as Gallo spoke they stood behind the table like a stony palace guard.

It was all the takeover evidence the capos needed, but the seating—Gotti on one side of Gallo, DeCicco on the other—provided more.

"It's terrible, what's happened," Gallo began. "But we don't know who killed Paul, we're investigatin'. Nobody feels worse for Paul's and Tommy's families than me. But we're a family too and we have to stay strong. So that's why we called you here."

None of the captains believed him, of course. But the armed sentries and seating arrangements made reassurance more important than truth. Nobody had any questions about the murders; Gallo, speaking for Gotti, gave them the only answers they wanted.

"Everyone in this room is gonna be all right. Nobody is in trouble. Nobody is gonna get hurt. We don't want nobody carrying guns or overreactin' to anything."

The election could have been accomplished right there, but Gotti had already decided to give anyone who wanted to challenge him an interval of opportunity, so Gallo announced that after a few more days of investigation, he would call another meeting, at which Paul's successor would be chosen.

In the meantime, this was to be a private Gambino matter. "We don't want no discussion about this outside the family. We don't want nobody getting involved in our business. We will elect our own boss."

Still, Gotti felt compelled to say something to the other Cosa Nostra families, to pay some deference to the tradition of cooperation and communication—and so over the next couple of days, Angelo and Sammy were dispatched to give the other families the same messages Gallo had given the Gambino capos, plus one more. With so many cops and FBI agents investigating the murders, now was not the time for loose talk.

Three families—Luchese, Bonanno, and Colombo—responded positively. Paul's crazy-like-a-fox-friend, Genovese boss Chin Gigante, was more quarrelsome—and not just because the murder of his construction partner meant that he was likely to lose money. He sent a return message saying that while he accepted the situation "for now," a Commission rule had been broken; someday, someone would have to pay.

"Chin's just blowin' smoke," Gotti told Sammy. "He's too smart to mess with us."

"He'd get others to do it."

"We gonna be all right. As long as we keep denyin', nobody's got proof of nothing."

Still denyin', John Joseph Gotti Jr. was elected boss of the nation's biggest Cosa Nostra family when the caporegimes convened a second time, just before New Year's Day, 1986.

Gotti was scheduled to stand trial in two cases in the next couple of months; one, the case in Queens state court arising from a street fracas with a refrigeration mechanic over a double-parked car in 1984, was more embarrassing than worrisome; in the other, Diana Giacalane's RICO case in Brooklyn, he faced forty years in prison with little chance of parole until he had served twenty-five years—a de facto life sentence, if he was convicted, since he was now forty-five years old. But no one with a vote dared cite that albatross as a liability.

Frank DeCicco—who had said that while he could be Gotti's underboss, Gotti could never be his—nominated Gotti. With the deck so stacked, the other capos followed suit and gave their own seconding speeches. Without having to fire another shot, or duck one, the King of Queens became king of the volcano.

Men of Honor

by R i c h a r d   B e n   C r a m e r

Fighting organized crime in the United States isn't easy, but in Italy the task is even more difficult—and dangerous. Richard Ben Kramer in a 1993 piece for Esquire *described the life and career of anti-Mafia prosecutor Giovanni Falcone.*

First you'll have to be rational. Giovanni Falcone, with his computer brain, divined that the Mafia was an organization of thoroughgoing logic. Second, if you want to understand, you'll have to know about Sicily. Judge Falcone (every bit a Sicilian) said the values of Cosa Nostra were no more, no less, than the values of Sicily—taken, perhaps, to the extreme.

Third, and most important: You'll have to look upon the men of the Mafia with respect and empathy. Judge Falcone (the only one they'd talk to) said they played by the rules and they didn't lie. He said they were the only men who meant what they said absolutely, and who lived by their beliefs.

Ha said they were what they called themselves—Men of Honor.

How do we know the judge was right?

Because he and his wife and their bodyguard were blown to bits of char by a bomb planted under a highway by the boss of bosses, Totò Riina.

Anyway, they supposed it was Riina—the cops and judges who were supposed to know. Of course, no one could know for sure, because no one talks. That's the heart of the problem, *l'omertà*. The word is commonly rendered in English as "silence," or "code of silence." A literal translation is "manly stoicism," which offers a clearer idea of how Men of Honor see themselves. It's no accident that the Mafia code word for the law is feminine: *la sonnambula*—"the sleepwalker." That gives a clear idea of how far out front was this one wakeful lawman.

Before Falcone it was perfectly acceptable for Sicilians (or big Italian pols, from the safety of Rome) to declare that there was no Mafia: It had died in the dim rural past or had withered in the fluorescence of modern Italian development. It was acceptable (even respectable) for judges to maintain the convenient and slumberous fiction that the Mafia might exist, but just as handful of disparate bands—no better than hooligans . . . who mostly killed one another, anyway. One such somnambulist was Judge Antonino Meli; the govenrment made him Falcone's boss.

It was Falcone's spectacular achievement to prove the existence and structure of the Sicilian mob, the mother of all mafias, as a unity. In fact, he created the entire code and hierarchy of the Mafia, first in his head and then on paper, with such thoroughness and clarity that he could lead a panel of his peers past doubt. He did this through a feral decade's work, living always in mortal danger, unstoppably sifting and linking thousands of previously unconnected facts. That's why his colleagues recall his mind as a computer: Nothing got lost. But Falcone's work had less in common with technology than with art: Like a great novelist, he was God of the universe of his own imagining; he was so much master of the world under his pen that he could reconstruct whatever detail he required to make it come alive for all to see.

That it was a narrow and brutish universe he never had a doubt. Though he descried honor in it, risked his reputation and safety to defend its soldiers when they honored him, he never "went over." He remained always, in the halting English of one colleague, "a very, very judge." Falcone's words for himself were plain: "I am just a man of the State." The shrug that went along was not meant to diminish the job—to which, he was aware, he'd given up his life. It only showed he had found no choice, as the Men of Honor had found none in their lives. It was the measure of his comprehension that he saw even his own role in the drama, a role that could end only with his death.

In his 1991 book, based on his interviews with the French journalist Marcelle Padovani, he recalled the judges and police officials whom the Mafia had killed. Most, he said, died from ignorance or inattention; some gap in their knowledge proved fatal. Some simply failed to share their knowledge, which meant the Mafia could kill a whole investigation for a tiny price, the death of one man. Falcone always tried to surround himself with a team of judges; in the end, he tried and failed. "One usually dies because one is alone . . . because one is not given support. In Sicily, the Mafia kills the servants of the State whom the State has not been able to protect."

Some of these "illustrious corpses" underestimated the danger or tried to live a "normal" life. Falcone made no apologies for the armored door to his bunker office, his bulletproof Alfa Romeo, his siren-screaming escort of carabinieri soldiers in Kevlar vests. "I do not believe I should give a gift to the Mafia by offering myself as an easy target." (When he went for coffee, he'd order ten, then pick one to drink. No one could know which to poison.)

Yet, he knew, some few of the State's dead servants had perished not from lack of knowledge, or want of caution, or even isolation within a justice system that seemed not to care. One was a Judge Chinnici, who brought Falcone into the anti-Mafia war and who was blown up by a car bomb outside his home in 1983. Falcone spoke of the case with characteristic dispassion. "Yes, Rocco Chinnici's was only to be expected. . . . Even though he couldn't improve on his tactics, he fell into a trap and lost his battle. The Mafia proved itself to be stronger and more able than he was."

You could say Falcone wrote his own last chapter there. He was the best. And he lost.

But it was also true that he'd been isolated; the State couldn't or wouldn't support him. It might be that even Falcone let his guard slip one fatal notch—once the pols and his fellow judges drove him from his Palermo bunker, gave him a fancy title and a "normal" life in Rome. Falcone might even have concluded, in the end, that he lost by failure of knowledge—or that he ran out of time: He could not learn enough, fast enough, about the Beast, Totò Riina. For instance, where was he?

Corleone doesn't look like the town we saw in *The Godfather*: those leafy villas, each with its soft-spoken don dozing in a chair on his sun-dappled patio (unaware of the knife blade flashing toward his neck). No, Corleone is a hard huddle of menace on a slope of gray rock. The houses are concrete, small, gray like the rock beneath, and ingrown, with their dirty blank backs turned to the narrow streets.

Ingrown is the structure of the place, the jumbled filigree of streets and houses crowding ever tighter into a fold of the mountain until (it seems perforce, by their pressure) there erupts, from the heart of town, an eerie o'ertowering outcrop of rock. Atop this forbidding, slag-colored butte stood for centuries the local jail, now converted into a monastery for barefoot Franciscans who beg alms on the stone streets below and feed in return the sullen conviction of the *Corleonesi* that their town is unfairly famed just for the Mafia: *Why will no one write about our monks?*

Unfairness is a birthright here, enforced not just by strangers—the trickle of tourists who gawk and leave (film fans frustrated by this cheerless mob theme park)—but reinforced daily by the old twisting risky roads that never got improved by the Italian State; by the promised jobs that never arrived; by the land reform that gave the peasants plots too small for survival; by the absolute inequality of the world in town to the world on TV: In the town of Corleone (population twelve thousand), there is not a restaurant, there is not a theater or a cinema (there is one porno house); there is no library, gallery, museum; there is not a nightclub, dance hall, pool hall, swimming pool, public gym, tennis court, basketball court; no place to court love, licit or illicit; there is no place to go, and no place to forgather in joy, save perhaps the church, with its bleeding saint in a glass case on the front wall.

Of course, it was worse in the '30s and '40s, when young Salvatore Riina came of age. That was before power and plumbing, so the matrons in their mourning black spent their hours with washtubs at the spigot that was called a fountain. That was before land reform, so at dawn the men had to hitch up their donkeys to carts full of tools and troop for miles to the great estates of the barons before they could start work—if there was work. One study estimated the average field hand found only ninety to one hundred days of paid work in a year. And that counted weeks for the harvests—grain in August, grapes in September, November for the olives—when men wouldn't get home at all: They'd take turns sleeping with a rifle at hand atop the day's work, to keep it from thieves. The shepherds got home less: They'd stay with their beasts weeks at a time on the baking rock hills, in endless hegira for grass that somehow survived the killing ten months of sun—nursing, meanwhile, the patent unfairness of all those acres gone to waste in grain and grapes. In Corelone, the Mafia could always count on shepherds to help settle scores with the all-encroaching farmer. Such a young shepherd was Salvatore Riina.

He had the normal upbringing—that is, a childhood without advantage. He left school in the fifth grade. He could read; that was plenty for a shepherd's son. He was just a few years out of school, hanging out with friends, playing bocce, when an argument turned into a fight. Riina pulled out a pistol and shot another boy in the leg. The boy died from loss of blood. Riina was fifteen when the court sent him to prison in Palermo, for six years . . . finishing school, in the view of the mob, or mobs, in his hometown.

Even in those days, just after Mussolini's war, Corleone was unfairly blessed with two Men of Respect, who represented two distinct styles, or as some would have it, the Mafia past and Mafia future. There was, already in place and pride, the traditional agrarian Mafia capo, who, like so many of his peers and predecessors, was a man of professional attainment, which set him apart from his peasant soldiers. This was Dr. Michele Navarra, the town's leading physician. At the same time, there returned to Corleone a younger, flashier exemplar of honor, one Lucciano Liggio, back from his youth in America, where his attainments ran more toward modernist improvements like striped suits, .38 Specials, and machine guns. Of course, they were great friends in those days, when there was so much business and power to divide: The mob had struck a deal with the U. S. Army to ease its wartime invasion of Sicily and in gratitude, in occupation, Uncle Sam turned over every town hall (along with precious gasoline and hundreds of firearms permits) to handpicked mafiosi who would, it was said, keep the peace.

For example, Dr. Navarra obtained from the Yanks enough transport for his civic-minded project to "organize a meat commerce" with Palermo. In other words, he got a stranglehold on meat for the capital . . . and, of course, Liggio helped out: He organized the shepherds (who flocked to *him*) to control the vast State-owned hills of the Ficuzza forest, where they grazed and guarded the stolen herds. Just for another example, Dr. Navarra wanted to become the director of Corleone's hospital. Liggio helped out as best he could . . . when he and a couple of shepherd-boy lieutenants killed the former director . . . and Dr. Navarra got the job. That was the way they stayed friends, though the doctor seemed hopelessly old-fashioned to the dashing Liggio, who also had great plans for the capital, Palermo . . . without all those stinking animals in trucks.

When it came, the trouble started with a woman. It happens often: Cosa Nostra is particular about the honor of women. In fact, one great cause of estrangement between the Sicilian mother-mob and its rich young American issue cropped up when the U.S. branch went into prostitution. That was unthinkable in Sicily, where tradition must be kept in mind. For example, Sicily's murder method of choice is the *lupara bianca*, the "white shotgun," which is not really any type of gun but disposal of the cadaver so it can never be found. The disappearance is significant and loathsome not because it protects the killers from discovery (the cops don't enter into this calculation) but because the absence of a corpse prevents the family females from kissing the wounds and vowing upon the beloved body: *Thus will we drink the blood of his killers.*

In the spring of 1958, the female in question was the lovely Leoluchina Sorisi, who had captured the heart of Lucciano Liggio. Alas, Leoluchina was already affianced to a local boy, also of note, named Placido Rizzotto. Rizzotto was one of those brave and lonely union types trying to organize the peasants to demand the breakup of great feudal estates. It was a tribute to his talent and grit that he was actually making progress. That's all the eager Liggio talked about when he proposed to old Dr. Navarra that they should rid the town of this union creep, who was putting strange ideas into peasant heads. Dr. Navarra consented. Liggio did the job—that was the easy part. Maybe Luccianuzzu took it a little too easy, because a boy from a neighboring village saw the whole thing, to the moment when Liggio dumped the corpse down a well The boy was brought, prostrate from terror, to the local hospital, where Dr. Navarra administered a "sedative," and, strangely, the boy died. Still, it was trouble, because the boy's babbling sent the peasants to the well, whence they hauled to town the body of Rizzotto, upon which the lovely Leoluchina vowed: *I will eat the heart of the one who did this to you!* (It should be noted, however, that when Liggio was arrested, some years later, he was found at her house.)

Real trouble came when Dr. Navarra discovered that Liggio cared not a fig for unions . . . and that he, Michele Navarra, Man of Honor, had been gulled to countenance a murder for sinful purpose, i.e., the defloran of a local female. He ordered Liggio killed. The doctor's men were sloppy, too. They got Luccianuzz' out of town, into the countryside, but when they tried to take care of him, he got to his gun and they shot it out in a bloody mess. Liggio, wounded, crawled to the next village, where he obtained the protection of some local Men of Honor and sent them as emissaries to beg reprieve from Dr. Navarra.

Of course, it wasn't finished. But it ended that same year, when Liggio and two shepherd lieutenants—the best shot in town, Bernardo Provenzano, and his friend, back from jail, *u Curtu* ("the Short One"), Totò Riina—pumped 110 bullets into Dr. Navarra. Liggio became the boss of the *Corleonesi*. Totò Riina became a made man.

That was the year, '58, when Giovanni Falcone had to make a choice. He made it wrong. He was unlucky sometimes, when his heart got mixed up in things. Falcone made all his big decisions with his heart. He was coming out of high school and had to pick his path. He chose Livorno, the Italian naval academy. He'd decided to go to sea.

You had to know how the kid grew up—the air in his house . . . Years later, when he was a Mafia-busting hero, people often said that Falcone understood because he was raised in an old quarter of Palermo, among the very people who would become his passion and prey. The Italian papers wove splendid fantasies about the young Giovanni, honing his young computer brain on the penny-ante black marketeering that was everywhere in the old *quartiere* in the years of scrambling and shortage after the war . . . all nonsense. There was never scrambling or shortage in the old *palazzo* of his mother's kin. There was plenty. There was duty. There was history.

That it loomed on a dark street in an old part of town—La Kalsa, near the sea, still bore an Arab name from a millennium past—only enhanced its distinction. It was the house of his mother's grandmother's brother, who was mayor of Palermo when the Italian State was young. It was a house built by and for the power of the State, as the nearby Church of the Magione had been raised to glorify another power. In nearer history, in tinted photographs on the walls of the tall dark rooms loomed two uncles: Both his mother and father had hero brothers who'd died in the Alps in World War I. No Falcone child could ever forget that the mother's brother had falsified his age, at seventeen, to give his life for Italy. But Giovanni and two sisters were not raised just in duty of death: Their father, doctor of chemistry, served the State every day as chief of the Office of Hygiene. In the neighborhood, therefore, he represented the State, and was accorded the admixture of respect and antipathy that Sicilians always reserve for authority (coming, as it always does, from outside their ken).

A little stranger, then, was Giovanni, the doctor's son—a bit apart and admirable in the *quartiere*; dutiful, as became the only boy; romantic, like any child who finds friends in books. Giovanni was devoted to the serial stories. His particular friends were the Beati Pauli, who were members of a monkish and sacred sect of adventurers who would meet in caves (always wearing hoods, so they never knew who the others were), who strove, by guile and swordsmanship, to protect the poor against the greedy rich and a neglectful State. . . . Them and Zorro. In the family's grand reception room, beneath the frescoed ceiling, the walls were cloaked in ornate cloth, which Giovanni, seven years old, further decorated with his wooden sword in a pattern of z's. (After his punishment, he complained to his sisters: "How did they know it was me?")

He was bright in school, reserved and correct. He was a pest protecting his older sisters. His sports were passionate solos: gymnastics, canoeing, swimming. He adored the sea. He would never quit. He used to say a man with his will could arrive at anything. And by his teenage years, he was rippled all over with the long muscles of the marathon waterman. That's when he decided that his duty his destiny, called from the bridge of a ship of the line in the Italian fleet. So he took the naval-academy test. His score ranked fifth in the nation. He went to Livorno . . . and hated every minute.

The discipline was stupid. The officers were stupid.

He arrived in the fall; by Christmas he'd written to his father, asking, if it were not disgrace, if he would not lose a term, whether he might not, after all, enroll at university. His father wrote back that he was already enrolled—the doctor had seen to that, back in the fall. This naval business was crazy from the first. So Giovanni brought his destiny of duty to the faculty of law at the University of Palermo. And he did not lose time. He graduated at twenty-two. At twenty-three he took the test for magistrates—judges and prosecutors in the Italian courts.

At twenty-four, he was a magistrate, the youngest, most avid servant of the State's law.

And there was love. Two loves, actually, for he also married at twenty-four. She was eighteen, another decision of his heart, a woman of understanding, he thought (she would become, by profession, a psychologist). . . . But after years, she would not be able to understand what he felt he had to do. In time, she would lose out to the longer, more passionate love of his life, the State. He was, even at the start, the most thorough young magistrate, meticulous in his preparation, exacting in his briefs and memorandums of sentence . . . informed, precise, relentless. He routinely put in twelve-hour days. He worked without breaks, with absolute focus . . . "like a panzer," they say in Sicily—where memory may fetch up an image of the swift and unstoppable German tank.

You could say he lived for the work, and in it, though the few hours outside might be pleasant enough: He still went to the sea, when he could; he loved to eat, though he cut back ruthlessly when his figure changed from *robusto* to stocky; he shaped himself to the role in every way. Or maybe he had no choice, it shaped him. His accustomed reserve sat well in a judge's robe (which counts in Italy, where magistrature is not just a job but a style). When youth was his hindrance, he grew a beard for "authority." (Years later, he'd shave to luxuriant moustaches, for the same goal.) Now he was ever *Il Dottore* Falcone, or *Professore*, or *Vostro Onore*—which seemed to him fitting. (Even in Palermo, he discouraged *Dottore* Giovanni, which smacked of false intimacy. He became that "very judge" in the courthouse, and in life. His family always figured it cost him his wife, but that was later: Divorce came in '79; by then it was just a ratification.

By that time, Judge Chinnici had called. Falcone switched from the civil section to the criminal, the anti-Mafia war. What else could a romantic young judge from Palermo give his life to? What compared in importance? . . . And better still: He would become the founding member of an anti-Mafia pool of judges, who were all young legal adventurers, whose work was top secret, known only to themselves.

They lived (so the papers dubbed it) *la vita blindata*, the hooded life; they'd meet, every day, in their bunker . . .

Falcone was not unlucky with his true love.

They called it incredible good fortune for Riina—no one could explain it—to win such a girl as Antonietta. It wasn't just her connections, though her family, the Bagarellas, was a potent local Mafia clan. The mystery was, Ninetta was so bright, educated as a teacher. She could have had a career, respect. What could she see in . . . him? The way they always tell the story, a friend told Riina that Ninetta's family would never accept him. "Well, then," he's supposed to have said, "I'll kill them all."

No one gave Riina credit for his brains. The hyper-eloquent and title-loving Italians are always confusing intelligence with education. (The judges and police officials of Palermo would only credit Riina with *furbezza*, a sort of animal cunning, after he'd made monkeys out of *them* for twenty years.) But as usual, Riina had the long view. He and Antonietta were considered engaged when she was thirteen.

Riina had something better than diplomas, in Corleone—another sort of respect. He had power, after he helped to kill the boss, Dr. Navarra. In the world of Cosa Nostra, prestige attends such a killing; honor accrues to ruthlessness. As Falcone said in his book: "For the Men of Honor what counts is the courage displayed by the assassin, his professionalism. The more cruel, vicious, and crude a murder appears to our eyes as ordinary citizens, the prouder is the Man of Honor, and the more he will be praised for his valor from within the organization." In fact, though its business is profit, the organization is all about power. To see this difference—crime for power versus crime for profit—is to see the difference between Cosa Nostra and any other organized crime. If money were the goal, Sicily's most wanted could just take their millions and escape. They do not. They'd rather go underground on their own turf, with their power . . . as did Ninetta and Totò.

They were married in '66 (by a Mafia priest, a member of the

Coppola clan); they honeymooned in Venice. A photo of Totò on the grand piazza there—a happy tourist, a pigeon on his arm—was the last picture anyone saw. They came back to Sicily, and soon . . . they disappeared.

It wasn't hard or even inconvenient. Many men disappeared, and never left town. So ingrained was the Sicilian habit of not seeing anything that was unhealthy to see, it didn't matter how often these fellows were seen. There were always stories in Palermo about this capo or that one, with a trapdoor in his office or a tunnel that led for miles to the sea (especially after one mafioso was caught in his skivvies as he tried to escape through a secret door in his shower). But it really was simpler. When Antonietta's brother, Leoluca Bagarella—feared and famous for his murders of a carabiniere colonel and the head of Palermo's police Flying Squad—was finally picked up in a random road check, the sum of his precautions was a false driver's license and a pair of shades. As for Totò, his children were born in Palermo's best clinic. (Two births were registered there under the surname Riina.) Later, those children were driven every day to private school . . . no matter: the Riinas were not seen.

But, in time, his hand would be everywhere apparent in the capital. When the *Corleonesi* moved in on Palermo, the whole city changed—much for the worse.

It was Liggio who won the first beachhead, the pool halls . . . and that was all for a while. Palermo already had ten Mafia families with the power to claim seats on the ruling Commission. They didn't want any help on their own territory. Liggio decided to help, anyway. And he had the power, with his two chief weapons—Bernardo Provenzano and Totò Riina. In fact, Liggio relied more on Provenzano—for good reason. "Provenzano shoots like a god," Liggio told one fellow mafioso. "It's a shame he has the brain of a hen. Riina, on the other hand, would like to bite off morsels bigger than his mouth."

Of course, back then, in the '70s, no one knew what Liggio said. Before Falcone and the pool got going, no one outside Cosa Nostra could be sure of the existence of the Commission . . . much less the upheaval in it when the boys from Corleone started making moves. There were murders and disappearances; sometimes in bunches. (These were chalked up to unspecified "factional conflict.") It was known, mostly from the protests of U. S. lawmen, that Sicilians were moving into the drug trade: They'd come to dominate the heroin traffic into North America. In Sicily, it was obvious the Mafia was pouring new, uncounted billions into "legitimate" business—construction, real estate. The profile of Palermo was physically changing. Where the capital had always hugged the plain between the sea and the mountains in quarters of ancient Arab geometry, the sky was now carved into dirty canyons by wall-to-wall apartment houses—ugly, cheap concrete boxes, oversized—all illegal, of course. Anyway, it should have been obvious: There was no more building control under the administration of Mayor Vito Ciancimino—previously a barber in the town of Corleone.

But on the largest scale, this cancerous "boom" was also not seen. If it was discussed, it was as a side effect of the long-awaited "development"— that is, as Sicily's cure. Italian law enforcement was focused on the Red Brigades, the threat to the State from terror. The few anti-Mafia triumphs ("Lucky" Liggio, for example, was sent to jail a couple of times) were often reversed by higher courts, without public or political protest. The fact was, the Mafia had purchased protection: There was a placid and profitable marriage between the ruling Christian Democrats and the mob—especially the Palermo families, who believed in taking care of business quietly. The State delivered fat public contracts and, when required, court rulings. The Mafia delivered untraceable cash and votes by the millions to keep the DC in power.

That was destined to change with the ascendance of Totò Riina. Jail time had begun to erode Liggio's influence. Riina was left on the outside to follow his own ambitions. That's when he started to show his penchant for the longer view. Slowly, and with a delicacy that even his fellow mafiosi never imagined in him (when his plan came clear they still protested: It must be Ninetta!) . . . he began to insinuate men faithful to him into the *Palermitano* families. By '81 he was ready, and Palermo awoke to a Mafia war that could not be ignored.

A thousand people would die in a year, and those were just the bodies that were left around to be counted. From Rome came vows: Such violence *must be stopped!* . . . It didn't stop. Riina was moving on the old Palermo families one by one; he'd promise peace whenever he needed time. He'd assassinate the boss and clean up the faithful who could be found. For the promise of peace, his own men in that family would move up to command of that territory. In April and May of '81, Riina killed the top two bosses of central Palermo, Stefano Bontade and Salvatore Inzerillo. His third nemesis, Gaetano Badalamenti, escaped Sicily with his life, but Riina's fatal influence extended overseas. According to information later developed by Falcone, John Gambino soon arrived in Sicily (as ambassador for the U. S. boss, Paul Castellano) and received the request—which was respected—to eliminate the escapees who had sought haven in America. Nothing was safe from Riina, not even tradition. Two bosses, Tommaso Buscetta and Salvatore Contorno, the only strongmen who might have contested Riina militarily, had their relatives killed, boys and women, too. There were fifty funerals within those two families.

Of course, there was the tradition of the Christmas amnesty. Even Riina could not ignore it. He declared a peace and hosted a spectacular party at a private villa. There must have been forty or fifty guests. He even invited the old Palermo boss, Saro Riccobono (with whom relations had been sour, owing to the disappearance of a couple of Riccobono's friends) . . . and nothing was spared: There was music, food, wine—*feasting* . . . after which Riccobono, for one, stretched out on a couch in the living room to rest. Four of Riina's men set upon Riccobono. "Saruzz'," one was heard to mutter, "your story finishes here." They strangled him to death on that couch. At that moment, other Riina men ran through the house and garden, finishing with guns all the friends of Riccobono. In Palermo, that same evening, fifteen Riccobono men were gunned down at their homes, in bars, in garages, on the street and brought to the villa, where they disappeared in a tank of acid.

There was another new wrinkle in Riina's rule: Gone were the days of private business quietly arranged through connections in government and politics. The provincial secretary of the DC was killed; he'd threatened the power of the friendly former barber, Ciancimino. Six months later, it was a former parliamentary deputy who'd come back to Palermo to "stamp out the Mafia." Five months later, the president of the region of Sicily who had vowed to clean up public contracts . . . then a particularly inflexible judge . . . then the Communist deputy who proposed a law permitting confiscation of Mafia profits. That was '82, at which point the government in Rome had to act, if only to silence the hostile press. The State sent to Palermo its hero, General Carlo Alberto Dalla Chiesa, the conqueror of the Red Brigades, *Uomo di Ferro*, Man of Iron . . . who was celebrating his one-hundredth day on the job, along with his pretty, pregnant wife and a bodyguard who was driving, when they all were shot to pulp by a hail of bullets from Totò Riina.

What a strange life it was for the four young judges of the pool, squirreled away with their secrets in their corner of the Ministry of justice building in Palermo, behind the steel doors with TV cameras to offer a view of the hallway outside, where the escorts sat splay-legged, cradling their submachine guns, waiting for the moment when their judge would emerge to trot through the echoing Fascist acre of marble to the front entrance, where ramps had been built so the armored Alfa sedans could roar up the steps, and their doors with the darkened windows would fly open, nearly touching the bulletproof Lexan of the building's doors so the judge would never stand exposed for one instant before the sirens wailed, again and the engines screamed, as the soldiers at the wheel dumped their clutches and skidded down the ramp, leaving in the sunshine only ache in the ears and an acrid double track of burnt rubber . . . time for lunch.

Or maybe it was dinner, or breakfast, for there was no clock, and a schedule for more than a day or two was dangerous. Judge Chinnici had been blown up just at that moment of fatal regularity, when they knew (whoever they were) he would leave his apartment for the office. There were soldiers on the streets in front of the judges' houses thereafter, to make sure no one could leave more cars packed with TNT. Of course, that increased the judges' isolation: Now they were pitted against their neighbors on the desperate matter of parking. (The grateful citizens of Falcone's building signed a letter proposing that the State make alternative arrangements for the judge—a secure building somewhere, they suggested, perhaps a jail.) But it wasn't just neighbors. Politicians complained in print that the ministry's focus on *supposed organized* crime was feeding the ancient slanders against Sicily—this was another *attack from the North*. And it wasn't just politicians. Within the ministry, a high-ranking magistrate suggested to Falcone's boss: "Bury him under mountains of minor trials—that way, he'll leave us in peace."

It was clear Falcone was in the lead, though all four judges of the pool were within a year in age, all shared knowledge of investigations, all shared the same hobbled and hooded life. Something about Falcone drew attention—a self-possession, a self-sufficiency, a conviction about his worth and work caused envy, or admiration, curiosity at the very least, and . . . curious, too: That untouchable conviction of self-worth was the sign Sicilians had recognized for years—something they had to notice to stay out of the path and the business of their local Men of Honor.

It wasn't that he took on the values of the mob—quite the reverse. He was, if anything, less tolerant of the small complicities that were woven into the life of Palermo—things everyone did to get along: the "recommendations" for jobs, for contracts, for positions of advantage . . . the little *pizzo* paid to do business (the word is Sicilian for "beak," as in the phrase "just enough to wet my beak") . . . the all-pervasive habit of not seeing—*after all, everybody has to live.* It was as if the terminal unsureness of his hold on life required from him more conviction and correctness, a tense and inflexible certainty—of course he bothered people. At a party in Palermo one night, an old friend counseled him: "Giovanni, why don't you ease up—live and let live, enjoy!" Falcone turned on him with a chill that stopped the man in his tracks. "If I didn't know you," said the judge, "I'd say you were working for the other side."

The strange part was, he was enjoying; he was alive as some men never get to be. At last, he'd found a way to share his excitement—his wartime romance, his second wife, Francesca Morvillo. She was the daughter of the head of Palermo's Trimunale, another child of the State and now a judge herself—divorced, as was Falcone, committed and meticulous in work, as he was. She was beautiful, graceful, admired everywhere in the ministry (even where he was not) . . . but she understood exactly what he had to do. She was not confused about the life she was choosing to share: They would never be able to travel, never go out, never even take a stroll together. She, too, would live in constant danger—at least in a constant state of impending widowhood. The letters that arrived for him with bullets in the envelope . . . or a picture of his coffin with his date of birth and a date of death (always coming right up!) . . . or coded threats he'd hear from mafiosi ("You do a dangerous job. If I were you, I'd even take my bodyguards to the bathroom with me"). . . . These were confirmation for Falcone—he was getting warm, they were starting to sweat. These workdays of twelve, fourteen, sixteen hours, were what he was put on earth for. He gave a nickname to his pool colleague, Giuseppe Ayala, who'd get to work sometimes at 9:00 a.m.—Sleepyhead. Sometimes, at 10:00 or 11:00 p.m., Falcone would look up with a start from the stacks of paper on his desk and call down the hallway of the bunker: "Hey! It's night! Don't you think it's time we removed this thorn from the side of the State?" Then, with sirens wailing, he'd go home and talk about the Mafia with Francesca till 2:00 in the morning. What was the point of sleep?

Falcone was coming to know his opponents: This life-on-alert was their habit of existence; sureness of knowledge was their stock-in-trade. The difference between the Man of Honor and the population of sheep (whom he fleeced) was that he knew what happened, and why. Falcone had to match that sureness to survive.

For four years, he'd pieced together the few available facts. He figured that if the Mafia was making billions from the drug trade, there had to be traces in Sicilian banks. That reasoning won him his first convictions. And he'd reasoned from the other traces the Mafia left behind: When ballistics tests on the bosses Bontade (killed with a shotgun and a Russian AK-47) and Inzerillo (also an AK-47), were compared with bullets from the body of Dalla Chiesa, it was clear the same Kalashnikov had been used in all three killings. To Falcone, then, it was also clear: There were two factions in the Mafia war and the winners had also killed the General.

Falcone's instinct was toward unity. His mind rebelled against the mess of rumor that washed up in the wake of every killing. It was not sufficient for him to list the profusion of Mafia names as so many mysterious flora, to speculate on their authority or their family connections, like some pre-Mendelian botanist monk. He knew better science was bound to reveal a structure in which the creatures dwelt. At the same time, he rejected the romance of grand conspiracy: the whispers that the Mafia was really led from Rome, from the government—these bosses were but puppets. (This theory gained steam from Dalla Chiesa's assassination: That hero was *allowed* to beat the Red Brigades, so the saying went, because they threatened the State from the outside; the Mafia, on the contrary, was the hand of the State itself . . . and so the Man of Iron had to die.)

At bottom, Falcone respected his foes: Why would Cosa Nostra— born as a struggle for control against the government—suddenly bow to orders from Rome, from men it could not control? That made no sense. . . . Nor did fantastic tales of "ritual killing," supposedly meant to terrorize the population. (Chinnici, according to this sort of theory, was car-bombed to show that the Mafia could "turn Palermo into Beirut.") No, Falcone assumed the Mafia killed as it was able. (Chinnici was car-bombed because that was the efficient way.) And killed only when it had to. The bosses were not puppets or monsters; their actions had to make sense in their world.

He came to think of them as "people like us," or maybe a bit better: They told the truth. As he explained in his book, the organization has an absolute respect for facts; truth telling is life and death. "If a mafioso does not respect the obligation to tell the truth in the presence of another Man of Honor, it is a sure sign that one or the other is soon to die." The Man of Honor speaks only when he is sure of the facts, when he has the right to speak, when the information concerns him. "Otherwise he places himself beyond the rules and at that point no one—nothing—will protect him." It occurred to Falcone, the Mafia state was much more efficient, more capable of requiring respect, than was his State, than the nest of half-truth and compromise that was his ministry. If other judges thought Falcone crazy when he claimed, 'The Man of Honor is obliged always to tell the truth" . . . that did not matter: He knew what he knew.

It was respect he showed to mafiosi he interviewed. He wouldn't burst into their cells (as the cops liked to do) to demand that they talk, or else. Unlike so many elegant judges, he'd never use the contemptuous second-person pronoun, *tu*, but always the formal *lei*—as he expected them to call him judge or Your Honor. He'd take care to acquaint himself with their "human situations," their families, their histories, relatives killed, their own situations within Cosa Nostra. He'd ask specific questions about specific crimes of which they had knowledge, and would never indulge in "fishing ("Tell me what you know about this Mafia!"). He was Sicilian enough not to ask about things that weren't his business. . . . Sicilian enough, too, to understand their answers: the shrugs, silences, and cryptic sayings in dialect. Above all, he told the truth. "You can say whatever you like," he'd begin. "But remember, this interview will be a calvary for you, because I will try by any means to make you contradict yourself. If you manage to convince me of the truth of what you say, then and only then will I be able to consider the possibility of safeguarding your right to life—protecting you from the bureaucracy of the State and from Cosa Nostra."

It was respect that won Falcone his big break, in '84—the cooperation of Tommaso Buscetta. Buscetta was famous within the mob for his courage and ferocity, though he was not a *capofamiglia* (female trouble again: Buscetta had shown himself incapable of emotional control . . . he'd married three times). In the war with the *Corleonesi*, Buscetta was driven out of Sicily to Brazil—in fact, he was driven out of Cosa Nostra by the serial murders of his kin. Still, he never would have talked if he hadn't met Falcone.

He told the judge at the start: " . . . I don't trust anyone else. I don't believe the Italian State really intends to fight the Mafia. Then he added: "I warn you, Judge. After these interviews with me you will become a celebrity. But they will seek to destroy you, physically and professionally. And they'll do the same to me. Don't forget, an account opened with Cosa Nostra can never be closed. Do you still wish to interview me?"

They talked for months at a time. Buscetta was the first of the great *pentiti*, the "repentants" who were to teach Falcone the language, method, and manners. . . . Buscetta was the confirmation of all that Falcone had imagined in the Mafia—unity, rationality, control; the shortened distance between saying and doing (if they said, it was done). . . . And Buscetta was the turning point in another sense. Unlike the handful of mafiosi who had talked before, he didn't come to the State in a panic of self-preservation, but with the considered judgment that the values of Cosa Nostra were gone, trampled underfoot by the *Corleonesi* who had killed his two sons. In that he was a prophet: Falcone soon had other *pentiti* who found they could trust him more than their fellow Men of Honor. And he did not lose time. With his fellow members of the pool, he piled up interviews and evidence, thousands of pages. He filled his head with Cosa Nostra until he could see it whole . . . and then he indicted it whole.

In November '85, the judges of Palermo's pool issued an "instruction" accusing 476 defendants at once. They would mount the biggest trial in the history of Italy. They would construct an enormous concrete bunker-courtroom within the walls of Palermo's Ucciardone prison, with underground tunnels from the cell-blocks to steel-barred courtroom cages, in which the mafiosi would be on display.

There had never been anything like it in Palermo or anywhere else. The twenty-million-dollar *aula-bunker* was an international fascination, built in pieces, put together in a matter of months. As the trial approached—February '86—Palermo was rocked by a crime wave:

muggings, robberies, murders, bomb threats . . . as the *Corleonesi* bosses tried to stir up nostalgia for the days when the mob kept matters in hand. Unemployed workers were sent to the streets to demonstrate for the good old days of the "boom." From every part of Italy, two thousand police and special agents were shipped to Palermo for "maxi-trial" security. Journalists came from everywhere in the world. They all wanted Falcone, of course; in that, they were all disappointed. Falcone and his closest colleague, Judge Paolo Borsellino, had been spirited from their apartments one night, taken for a pretrial "vacation" at the Asinara prison on the island of Sardinia. There they could work their sixteen-hour days in peace—that is, without further exertion by Italy's security forces.

As the trial began, schools were empty; parents feared the Mafia would have to mount a massacre to strike back. Italy all but stopped while citizens watched TV to catch a glimpse of the faces that belonged to such well-known names of terror. There, in his cage, was the putative head of the Commission, Michele Greco, whom Liggio had nicknamed the Pope because he only stood there, to bless the business, while the *Corleonesi* ran things. There was old Liggio himself, pacing like a lion, an effect heightened by the ruff of fur collar on his leather coat. There were hundreds of Mafia "soldiers," button men, enforcers, drug couriers, drug, chemists, drivers. . . . Just reading the roster of defendants and charges would occupy the first hour of every day in court.

And the trial would last for eighteen months. Every witness, every defendant, would be questioned in the dock on the minute particulars of Mafia life. ("So how was it decided that Mr. Michele Greco would be godfather to your second son? . . . ") Then the question and the answer would be summarized by the presiding judge and taken down in longhand by clerks arrayed in front of the bench. Documents would run to a million pages. Every boss, every soldier, was considered by name, accused of specific crimes that Falcone proposed to prove. And not just the hundreds of defendants in court: By Italian law a criminal did not have to be in custody. Falcone would convict Totò Riina—still in hiding after twenty years—of three counts of murder, and would win from the jury three life jail terms.

In all, by late '87, the maxi-trial would sentence 338 defendants to total jail terms of almost three thousand years. But the individual convictions, even the massive totals, did not measure the triumph. For the first time in history, the Italian State had taken the measure of the Mafia. For the first time, Falcone had proved the methods and shape of the organization, its purposes, profits, logic, rigor, and chain of command. He robbed it of the mystery that made up so much of its power. Any schoolchild in Italy could now see in newspapers a chart detailing the members of the Commission, with x's next to eight of the eleven names to show the bosses then in jail.

And something else: There were no massacres, no bomb blasts, no litter of bodies in the streets. It was as if the octopus was stunned. From Rome, no less than Prime Minister Craxi proclaimed the demise of the Mafia. Falcone thought otherwise: He knew about the men still on the outside—Riina, the Beast, for one. Falcone knew the Mafia was clever enough, disciplined enough, to let the State beat its chest in triumph until the focus was lost . . . while the mob regrouped, while it cleaned itself of traitors and weak links, while it worked invisibly on judges of appeal who would reconsider the jail terms. Falcone insisted the work had just begun. Now was the time for the State to move fast, to take advantage of new *pentiti*—they were coming to him steadily now. (One of the best, Antonino Calderone, told the press: "I collaborated with Falcone because he is a Man of Honor.") Falcone insisted new pools must be formed, not just in Palermo, all over the nation . . . but for reasons that never quite came clear, it didn't matter what Falcone said anymore.

When the top job of his Office of Instruction came open in 1988, Falcone was the heir presumptive. Suddenly an older judge, Antonino Meli, was convinced (by unseen powers) to withdraw his application for the presidency of the Tribunale and apply instead for the Office of Instruction. Meli got the office and promptly voiced his opinion that the Mafia was not a unified command—just a collection of hooligans.

At the same time, judges from other courts in Italy initiated learned and finicky reviews of procedure in the maxi-trial. Perhaps the convictions were not valid (so one theory went) because of the extraordinary length of proceedings; defendants were not judged with the promptness they deserved. In the Ministry of Justice building, in Palermo, there was a growing school of thought that Falcone—good man, good worker—was nevertheless afflicted with delusions about the Mafia: He thought Cosa Nostra was involved in everything; he'd take over every investigation in Italy! By '89 the local papers were retailing, on the front page, anonymous letters (signed by "the Crow") that accused Falcone of using *pentiti* as "killers for the State." Courts of appeal were reversing the maxi-trial sentences. Greco was let free. Totò Riina was absolved. Of course, the government vowed to reappeal, in an effort to reinstate convictions . . . but no, perhaps not with the prosecutors from Palermo. That year, the pool was dissolved. Judge Meli said it was better to let individual magistrates work on individual cases—in their local jurisdictions, of course. That was the summer of 1989, when fifty sticks of dynamite were found in front of Falcone's beach house, minutes before he emerged for his morning swim.

Clearly he got the message. He was under attack. His credibility was steadily eroding. He was alone. . . . From Rome, the Minister of Justice was calling: Perhaps Falcone would consider another job—a splendid title, a coordinating position—Director of Penal Affairs. With a bitterness of which he never spoke in public, Falcone accepted transfer to Rome. Before he left, he got a bill from the Stateroom and board for his "vacation" in Asinara prison. Falcone paid . . . and demanded a receipt, which he framed and mounted, ever after, on his office wall.

On May 23, a sunny Saturday in the spring of '92, Falcone decided on the spur of the moment that he and Francesca would fly down to Palermo. He called ahead for escorts. He got a secret-service plane. He arrived in high spirits . . . Even he had to admit, a year or two outside the cauldron of Palermo hadn't been bad: He'd decompressed. He still lived with escorts, drove in armored cars. But he'd recaptured a few of life's pleasures—a meal in a restaurant, a stroll home from dinner. . . . Still, he could not give up his life's love.

From the ministry in Rome, he was pushing for a new anti-Mafia directorate (modeled on America's FBI), a new national superprosecutor, and a law (like the U. S. witness-protection act) to give his *pentiti* financial support, security, and new identities. Falcone was five days past his fifty-third birthday—still, a long way to go. He said the law would prevail, he had to keep faith. Just three months before, Italy's supreme tribunal, the Corte di Cassazione, had stunningly affirmed the verdicts of the maxi-trial, reinstating the convictions and jail terms for the bosses.

At the Palermo airport, Falcone greeted his escorts, then held out his hand for keys—he'd drive. He took off for the city on the eight-lane superhighway—gunned the Alfa up past eighty miles an hour . . . and that was the last he did.

As Falcone's car and two escort vehicles passed over a culvert in the road, a ton of dynamite exploded beneath them.The bomb was detonated by remote control from a hillside overlooking the highway. (Investigators would come to believe Totò Riina himself was on that hill.) The trap had been laid with such care that Mafia experts had padded the sides of the culvert with mattresses so all the force of the blast would shoot up through the road.

The road was gone, replaced in a split second by a twenty-foot crater. Falcone's car was twisted and mashed to a fatal steel brioche, hurled to earth in an olive grove, two hundred yards away. His two escort cars and two civilian vehicles were also blown away. Falcone died on his way to the hospital. Francesca died five hours later.

In the quick profusion of professions-of-grief, plans-of-action, promises-of-eternal-remembrance, there was a depressing familiarity. The ministry issued brave assurance that Falcone's work would go forward. Priests called for understanding that, of course, would not diminish our resolve. Political leaders weighed in with demands for an end to the system that would tolerate such tragedy. Italian officials had practiced this drill too many times—for police chiefs, carabiniere colonels, Judge Chinnici, General Dalla Chiesa the awesome moral suasion of each death had faded, down to a phrase between commas in the paragraph about "illustrious corpses."

But three days after Falcone died, in a driving rain in Palermo, ten thousand people tried to push their way into the funeral mass for Falcone, Francesca, and their bodyguards. Politicians who came were hissed and spat upon. They had to sneak out a back door. In an electrifying display of grief, rage, and *Sicilianità*, the young widow of one bodyguard took the pulpit to demand that the Men of Honor get down on their knees before her, to beg forgiveness, to show they could change. She screamed to the crowd *"But they never change!"* The citizens of Palermo, in the San Domenico Basilica, drowned out Mozart's *Requiem* with their cry: *Justice! Justice! Justice!*

The Carabiniere research team spent months getting settled into Palermo, learning the *quartieri* that were home to the Men of Honor . . . and picking out a few men to follow. That wasn't hard. You can always see the air of confidence on a mafioso.

So they studied each one—Whom did he meet? . . . Who was more important—he or the guy he met? . . . Who came over to whom to shake hands? . . . Who got up when that guy came to the table? . . .

The Special Operations Group, just two years old, was the sort of national strike force Falcone had been trying to create. They were pros, patient and careful. They studied the places the mafiosi went—that bar, that garage, that butcher shop (which never sold any meat). After months, they knew the places by heart—who lived there, who owned that . . . then they followed people from those places: Whom did they have to visit?

By the end of last year, they were bearing down. Carabiniere technicians mounted video cameras to survey that bar, this corner, that shop. . . . They had to work carefully. They'd install at night, with lookouts on nearby streets, in contact with radios. (*Stop. Here comes somebody—okay, go ahead.*) When they followed people, they'd break off early so they'd never be "burned." If it happened, they were dead.

Next day, they'd follow two minutes longer, one block farther, then they'd break off again . . . They videotaped their hot spots twenty-four hours a day, then watched the tapes for patterns: It was behavior of submission they wanted to see.

Still, it could have gone on forever. No one knew what Riina looked like. The FBI computers in Washington had "aged" his last picture—that twenty-five-year-old snapshot from the grand piazza in Venice—but what if he'd had an operation? What if he'd left Palermo? What if he knew every move they'd made and was patiently watching them advance, block by block, into his trap? . . .

Then fortune descended, in the person of a Mafia "soldier" named DiMaggio—he got arrested and started to sing. Actually, it was more complicated: women trouble again . . . Baldessarre DiMaggio was a mafioso in the town of San Giusepe Jato, part of the Giovanni Brusca clan, which owed allegiance to Riina and the *Corleonesi*. Doing well, DiMaggio was—a mechanic by trade, with a villa and a swimming pool—but then he fell in love with a girl from his town and left his wife and children. The wife went straight to the boss, Brusca, who called in DiMaggio and ordered him back to his family. DiMaggio refused. And so—for want of respect, as well as morals—Brusca banished him from Cosa Nostra. DiMaggio went to Riina to appeal his termination . . . and Riina refused him. That's when DiMaggio knew he was a dead man. Termination, to Riina, meant termination. So DiMaggio headed north and turned himself in to an officer he knew. After that, he was pointing out places and people for the cops.

And that's when Riina's luck changed: He ran into his own sort of female trouble. The carabinieri saw her, and they knew: It had to be Ninetta. Nobody knew what Totò looked like, but Ninetta Bagarella—she looked exactly the same. A little thicker, maybe, lines around the mouth, but she kept her hair black . . . same eyes . . . same expression.

From headquarters in Rome, Colonel Mario Mori gave the order to lock onto her. Watch her house, never let it go. They didn't have to wait long. The next morning, 8:30, the first car that drove in was a silver Citroën. A man came out of the house, got into the shotgun seat—a gray-haired short man.

The carabinieri were stunned. Is that him?

Got to be him.

Jesus! It's him!

They followed. Up the street, a second chase-car swung in behind. At the first light, the lead carabiniere car pulled up next to the Citroën; the Special Ops glanced over . . . he didn't look like their picture.

Who else could it be? . . .

Orders came straight from Mori: Take him—*now.*

The third light was the circle at the Motel Agip—always miserable traffic. The Citroën got stuck between a truck and a bus. The carabinieri jumped out and surrounded the car, covered every window with sub-machine guns.

They didn't ask, they told him: *You are Totò Riina. . . .*

They were yelling. *Riina! Out of the car!*

He protested, there must be some mistake. He presented an identity card in the name of Vincenzo Bellomo.

Out of the car!

They cuffed him, frisked him, told him he was under arrest. After twenty-five years, it was over in five minutes. He never even raised his voice. In their car, when they hit the siren and got out, he murmured, yes, he was Riina. Later, as he left their station house for jail, he turned to his captors and told them quietly: "Congratulations."

In front of Falcone's apartment building in Palermo, there is a tree, a tall, curving ficus that rises alone, unlikely, from a patch of dirt between slabs of broken concrete. Without declaration, unbidden by any committee or official, Sicilians made this his shrine. Cut flowers and bouquets carpet the concrete, fresh batches every day. To the tree trunk are pinned pictures of Falcone, with what Sicilian women call his eyes of velvet, and a smile that fills his cheeks around his moustaches. And there are pictures of people he never knew. They put their like-nesses on the tree with messages to him: "Falcone, we want to hope again." There are multipage ballads from Sicily's poets, and two-line letters from school kids: "You didn't want children! I would have wanted you for a father." Every tree-inch is covered with greeting cards, rosaries, crosses, and pictures of saints, banners made on computer printers, paintings, drawings . . . and there is one placard, bold writing on poster board, nailed to the tree. It's dated January 16, 1993, the day after Riina's capture.

"Giovanni: Your tree has borne its first fruit."

Riina's new picture has become an Italian icon, too. There he is, in the carabiniere station, with a framed portrait of the martyred General Dalla Chiesa looking down upon him. Riina stands, head bowed, hands folded, like a peasant who's been called to the padrone's house to talk about next year's crop. The newspapers ran the photo day after day, with stories that trumpeted the triumph of the State:

MAFIA: THE END OF THE LINE?

Riina is on trial now, facing a series of murder charges that will occupy him and the judges for the rest of this century. He comes from his cell to the *aula-bunker* every day, and sits in his cage. He's a sawed-off, stocky figure; maybe five foot three. A new law prohibits court-room TV cameras from showing a defendant's face, so when Riina breaks in on the proceedings, Italian viewers see only a digitized fuzz where his head should be, and two hands leaping and stabbing the air in indignation.

Riina says he knows nothing about Cosa Nostra. It's all an invention of newspapers and TV.

No one seems too upset about that. Italy is in a crisis of investigation already. One sixth of the Parliament is under suspicion of corruption—along with businessmen, bankers, party officials, bureaucrats . . . while the archetype of Christian Democrat power, the seven-time prime minister, Giulio Andreotti, is being investigated for links to the mob. In the ministry building in Palermo, they say if Riina talks now, the Mafia would crumble . . . but so would Italy.

For the moment, the State is safe.

Ninetta took the children back to Corleone, to the house of her sister, behind one of those blank walls. She'll be safe there; people will take care of her. But it's not just her safety. As Falcone said: "Everything is a message, everything is charged with meaning in the world of Cosa Nostra." Ninetta's presence in Corleone is Riina's guarantee: He will not tell the law anything.

Anyway, to whom would he talk?

Tongs
from Chinatown
by Gwen Kinkead

Authorities have worked hard to bring down the Mafia, but have done little to control Chinese gangs known as tongs. Gwen Kinkead's (born 1951) discussion of tongs in her 1992 book about New York City's Chinatown suggests that the tongs exercise great power there.

The tongs are even stronger now than they were fifty years ago, and are doing their best to keep Chinatown isolated. They overwhelm the community, influencing every aspect of its life—business, politics, journalism, tourism. The reason is simple: some of their members sponsor crimes that terrorize and cow the community. Some crimes are the traditional ones—smuggling of aliens, prostitution, extortion, loan-sharking—but now, instead of smuggling opium, which faded around the Second World War, members of tongs import gargantuan quantities of heroin, generally through Bangkok or Hong Kong. Along with independent traffickers, they have in the last six years taken over from the Cosa Nostra the business of smuggling the drug.

The tongs' influence is pervasive partly because of their open structure: anyone who pays $30 can join a tong and will be inducted in an elaborate ritual that includes the burning of paper vows; chanting oaths before Gung Gong, the god of war; offering incense to the gods of hell; and swearing blood brotherhood to avenge all wrongs done to other members and to die before cooperating with police. Not all tong members are criminals, of course. Thousands of waiters, merchants, laundrymen, businessmen, seamen, garment factory workers, even journalists belong to tongs for the muscle to enforce their business deals, for protection, and for revenge: any member of a tong can call on a gang's services in a dispute. A tong member in trouble doesn't have to ask. He receives a telephone call. The message is simple. "Do you need help?" the voice says. A Chinatown elder explained why people join tongs: "You have so-called peace of mind. You think the tong is behind you. That's the psychological reason. You think also maybe it will help your business. You know more people, you will meet all the other members. As a member paying thirty-dollar dues a year, it's okay. But if the tongs tap you to become part of their hierarchy, then you have to deliver." One tong member told me, "When people look at me, they have more respect. The respect is fear." While it is true that tongs also do some good—for instance, they translate for new immigrants, sponsor the dragon dancers at New Year's, and sports leagues, and housing for some elderly—their crimes far exceed their beneficence. Their power is such that no one in Chinatown wants to discuss tongs—especially with outsiders.

Nearly all of the Chinatown tongs are national groups with chapters in cities throughout the United States, and each has tens of thousands of members. Their New York chapters are often the largest because New York has the largest Chinese community in the country. For the same reason, several tongs have their national headquarters in Chinatown. The top men in a tong (women are not permitted to join) are its board members and its elders—the wealthy and influential in a community. Board members are elected because they are prominent: they may own a large business, or give to charity, or simply have charisma. But power resides in a tong's elders and its presidents, whether or not they are important outside the tong.

The so-called godfather of Chinatown is Benny Ong. (His real name is Kai Sui Ong, which means Good Prophecy Ong.) He is the adviser-for-life of Hip Sing, Chinatown's most powerful tong. Ong is eighty-four years old, a thickset man with a sagging moonface and hands like square blocks. He is often called Uncle Seven, because he was his parents' seventh child. Born into a poor family in Harbin, he emigrated at age twelve, worked in a Chinatown laundry, and became a Hip Sing in the 1920s. He spent the years from 1935 to 1952 in jail for second-degree murder, and thereafter resumed active membership in Hip Sing, which was then under the presidency of his brother Sam. After Sam's death in 1974, Benny took over. He was jailed again briefly in 1977 and 1978, for bribing police and government officials; in conversations recorded by investigators, he boasted that he was *the* payoff man in Chinatown and had numerous friends among district attorneys, police inspectors, and chiefs of detectives.

Hip Sing's big rival is On Leong, which has its headquarters in New York and is run by the national president, Wing Wah Chan, and the local president, Albert Moy. Tung On, headed by Clifford Wong, is a new group, with headquarters in Chinatown. In addition, there are the Chinese Freemasons, Chih Kung, and the Fukien American Association, run by Alex Lau; the last was formed in the early eighties by people from the Chinese province of Fujian, and is said by law enforcement officials to be heavily involved in heroin trafficking and the smuggling of aliens. It is pro-People's Republic, unlike the other tongs, which support Taiwan. Except for Chih Kung, each tong is affiliated with a gang, and it is the gangs—the equivalent of standing armies—that carry on the tongs' power struggles.

The tongs' turf is rigidly divided. Law enforcement officers assigned to cover Chinatown and others working on Asian crime have maps of Chinatown with streets colored to indicate tong control. Hip Sing controls Pell Street; On Leong controls Mott. A tong member on the wrong street is a provocation, just as it was in the 1890s, and a gang member ripping off another tong's gambling parlor still starts a war.

"Chinese invented the Mafia, and then Marco Polo took it to Italy and the Italians reinvented it," a Chinatown insider explained to me. "The tongs are the families—everyone knows who's a member. You don't want to cross them. Each has about fifty prominent members. Real bosses, about ten each. They post elected officers. If you're a Chan or an Eng, it's quite possible you belong to one of them. Chans or Chens are On Leong Engs or Ongs are Hip Sing. The tongs run the gangs and the gambling houses, and they settle disputes in the old-fashioned way: you give me face, I'll give you face; if you don't listen to me, I'll break your face. Uncle Seven is the elder statesman of the underworld, but his power has been eroding for some time. He's from the previous generation, and many mavericks have been challenging the structure. Also, there are the Vietnamese gangs—the tongs have no control over them."

The Vietnamese gangs, new to Chinatown crime in the last few years, are greatly feared in the area; they are considered more violent and vicious than Chinese gangs, who hire them as muscle. They are mostly young refugees who have dropped out in frustration at being unable to learn English or have run away from foster homes. As refugees, they can't be deported. Members of the most notorious gang, Born to Kill, are often tattooed with the initials BTK above a coiled snake. Born to Kill has upset the longtime order of Chinatown organized crime because it is not backed by any tong and because its members speak dialects none of their victims understand, and prey on merchants who have already paid tongs anything from $50 to $1,000 a month in "lucky money," or protection money.

"It's chaotic now," Mrs. Kong, who owns a large family-run retail soybean business in the center of Chinatown, told me. "Different gangs come to store and ask for protection money. Usually, a store has to pay the tong, and then its gang doesn't bother them. But now the Vietnamese gang shakes the store down, and other gangs do, too."

Mrs. Kong's daughter Tina added, "We know a policeman who is more powerful than the gangs, so we don't pay. It depends on your business and who your friends are. We pay lucky money at New Year's, but it's nothing—fifty or a hundred dollars. Of course it's a bad problem. People is very afraid about it. To set up some business if they know no friends! I just try to protect our interest—not stop it. A lot of people complain, but they never do anything to stop it."

Another merchant told me, "It's cost of doing business here. Maybe one percent of places getting extorted are unhappy. It's status quo. I'm upset now because we're in first phase of disorganized crime. It's so serious it's terrifying. Those kids come in. We have no one to negotiate with. You can't b.s. your way out, or make a deal. This is new. In eighty years, this is new. We don't know who they are—it's not the same guys each time. We think it's free-lance kids. Vietnamese don't respect anybody. Things are changing."

This same merchant explained why he preferred the organized crime of the past, when gangs extorted weekly or monthly payments for themselves and the tongs with clockwork regularity: "If it's organized crime, and one wild kid says, 'I want to sell you an orange tree'—you know extorting me, demanding a lot of money for the lucky New Year's plant—I say, 'Don't break my face, are you kidding?' I know the management of the tong that controls my street, its general, and its lieutenants. To save face, I'll complain to its second rung, not the top. The kid gets taken care of. If I have a really big problem, I go to see the top people: on Division Street, I go to see Clifford Wong. On Pell Street, I go to see Benny Ong. On Mott, I see Wing Wah Chan. I'm for tranquillity. I'm not looking for reform. I'm typical, I think. Chinese are the richest people on earth, you know. All these guys out there are getting rich. They don't view themselves as enslaved by gangs and associations. The IRS enslaves me, not the gangs."

Further complicating turf in Chinatown are several gangs from Queens—the Green Dragons and the White Tigers—which are allowed by Chinese gangs to operate on some streets and run some gambling parlors. Neither Queens gang is affiliated with a tong. But probably most feared in Chinatown are members of the Hong Kong triads, here in advance of China's takeover of the colony.

Crime is worsening in Chinatown. According to a study published in 1991 by Ko-lin Chin, a sociologist at Rutgers University, and two colleagues, eighty-one percent of the restaurants and two-thirds of all the businesses in Chinatown are victimized by gangs.

Everyone knows who the gang kids and the tong bosses are, but no one revolts and turns them in. Those who do make complaints won't testify in court. Few crimes are reported; fewer still go to trial. Police make cases only with great difficulty. A sergeant in the Fifth Precinct, which includes Chinatown, said, "Chinese don't cooperate—although the little they're doing now is better than the nothing they did before.

"Let me give you some examples," the sergeant, who spoke to me on the condition that he remain anonymous, went on. Here's a double homicide that went down at four fifty-five p.m. on a warm afternoon at 277 Canal. All our witnesses are American. Canal Street is wall-to-wall people at five p.m.! And there were no Oriental witnesses? It took us a year and a half to find the guy—Lam Trang, a Vietnamese, Born to Kill. He shot two Chinese-Americans, sixteen-year-olds, Flying Dragons. It was a turf war. Trang jumped across the country. The Vietnamese have no roots—they jump from community to community.

"The situation with the Chinese is unique. I've had them come into the precinct house to do lineups, and look at the floor. They never cooperate in identifications when we go out canvassing. Off the top of my head, I can think of only one complainant who has gone to court for us. She's the only one.

"Here's another example. We had a witness in a homicide four years ago but she was so fearful of reprisals that it took us three weeks to get from her an identification of the suspect and then she moved away." The witness was a poor Burmese-Chinese woman, a cook in a restaurant, the sergeant said. "A Burmese guy strangles a twelve-year-old Chinese girl from down the hall in her building and stuffs the body in a sleeping bag in this woman's closet. She sees the body. The killer calls and says, 'I have something of mine in your closet, don't open it.' The woman is here illegally. He threatens to report her to Immigration. She's terrified and leaves the apartment to stay with a friend. Her building on Eldridge has no heat, so no one found the body for a while, and the Burmese guy eventually threw it out the window. The witness is an acquiescent type. She's used to being browbeaten. There is no women's lib in Burma, you know. She didn't report the crime.

"How many Americans do you feel if they found a body in their closet would not call the police?" the sergeant asked.

"They're funny people to deal with—they're used to having the government shoot criminals. That's how the Communists deal with them in China. The perpetrator isn't going to come back and haunt anyone. All the time, they ask when I say so-and-so is in jail for a few years, 'In jail for only two years?'

"Finally, we got an ID by appealing to this woman's religion. We got a former police commissioner from Burma to sit with her, we put Burmese music on, and he sat patting her hand. He told her, 'You're a Buddhist, you have to assist the police if you know something.' She actually jumped up and fell at our feet and started kissing our feet, saying, 'I understand.' The burden was off her—it was like repentance."

Nancy Ryan, the chief of the Trial Division in the Manhattan District Attorney's office—she is known in Chinatown as the Dragon Lady—adds, "In fifteen years, I have had less than two dozen merchants testify in open court. Not until 1983 did we have any civilian testify in a murder case. We had to arrest him to get him to court. And I've had just one civilian identify the murderer in a homicide. It's a very complicated problem—the Chinese are deeply frightened. They know there are armed thugs on the street and they can't have twenty-four-hour police protection. They don't understand our system, and they can't conceive of a system where cops know who the gang members are and let them roam the street, or a system where if someone is charged with a crime he's out on bail in a week. They don't trust public officials. Chinese have many proverbs that exhort people not to trust public officials. They come here with their shirts on their backs and their dreams, and they struggle in a way we can't conceive of, because we are too spoiled by affluence. I find it hard to imagine that anyone else in these very adverse circumstances would be more noble about testifying."

William Calhoun, who until the beginning of 1991 was the captain of the Fifth Precinct, added, "It's not 'Will there be retribution?' but 'When?' Ten years is not too long for Chinese to wait, I'm told. This community is faced with people bent on havoc. It's organized retribution."

In one of the latest instances, in the spring of 1990, a beauty shop worker and her boyfriend were murdered and their bodies dumped on an estate on Long Island. The woman, a former girlfriend of a gang leader, had testified five years earlier in a gang-related trial in Brooklyn.

"We go crazy with this stuff. We make the Sicilian vendetta look like nothing. We'll wait twenty years to get you back," says a young Chinese.

Chinatown has four Chinese-language daily newspapers, but most of them don't report such crimes. Journalism in Chinatown is a warped, submissive creature, as emasculated as it is in China. Journalists risk firings and death threats for reporting the news. Ying Chan, who has been one of Chinatown's most respected reporters and is now on the staff of the *Daily News,* told me, "There's no tradition of independent journalism in Chinatown—everyone is so scared. The papers represent political interests, which are tied to economic interests. You can't cover the tongs—we did the best we could. Every time we tested the limits, people got beat up. The gangs called me in the early 1980s and told me they were waiting for me on the street. In 1988, my publisher told me that Benny Ong had asked him to fire me and said he would give him thirty thousand dollars' worth of advertising." This sort of intimidation, Chan added, was standard practice in Chinatown. "The publisher didn't fire me—he asked me not to cover Chinatown. The unwritten rule is: No names of tong members or gang members. We print their English names, or use phonetic Chinese to confuse everyone, or give just their Chinese surnames. Or we blank the name out—it's standard to put 'XXX' for a witness's name."

In 1978, Hsin Yuan Cheng, then a Chinatown columnist, was badly beaten on the street one night by five young men. He is sure he was attacked because he wrote so many stories about the community. "At that time, I am young, and I try to correct everything," Cheng told me. In 1984, a member of Hip Sing's gang, the Flying Dragons, walked into the Chinatown office of the editor of *Sing Tao Jih Pao*, a large Hong Kong–funded daily, and demanded at gunpoint that a reporter who had written about a dispute over an extortion be taken off the story. She was. In 1987, the now-defunct *Center Daily News* dropped its coverage of a landlord-tenant dispute involving the gangs when its reporter was harassed. In 1989, a reporter from *Sing Tao* did not observe the unwritten rule and wrote up the testimony of an On Leong boss in a murder trial. The reporter was fired but was rehired after he apologized personally to the On Leong boss and the paper, in abject apology, sent the tong a roast pig, a traditional offering of respect. A Chinese TV reporter who shot footage of an On Leong gambling joint in the late eighties was told he would be killed if the story was shown.

Another incident that occurred outside Chinatown still has a chilling effect on news gathering in Chinatown. In 1984, San Francisco journalist Henry Liu was murdered after finishing a critical biography of Chiang Ching-kuo, the son of Chiang Kai-shek, who was then Taiwan's president. A United States federal appeals court, upholding the sentences of ten members of United Bamboo, a Chinese gang from Taiwan, called the murder a political assassination. The court ruled that the international boss of United Bamboo had flown to San Francisco "so as to be able to provide Taiwanese government officials with support here in the event that those officials needed to flee their country and be safeguarded in the United States. Additionally, at the suggestion of Taiwanese officials," the boss "planned to murder Henry Liu, a Chinese journalist who had become an American citizen, because he was considered to be a traitor to Taiwan. In addition to eliminating Henry Liu and silencing his critical writing, the murder was designed to serve as a warning to others in the United States whose acts were considered subversive to the interests of officials in Taiwan. . . . In return for his efforts to develop the United Bamboo gang as a base for putative fleeing Taiwanese officials, and for the murder of Henry Lin, [the boss] and the United Bamboo gang were to receive 4 billion Taiwanese dollars as well as political patronage, protection and prestige in Taiwan."

A reporter for the *Center Daily News* in San Francisco, who wrote an accurate story suggesting that the murder was ordered by Taiwan intelligence agents tied to the president of Taiwan, was transferred. So was her editor. Other reporters who might have investigated the connection between certain tongs, gangs, and Taiwan did not take up the gauntlet.

Peter Lee, a Chinatown journalist, pointed out, "If an American journalist was censored, there'd be outrage. Here, the community says we shouldn't have written that story. It's in Chinese culture to be careful of what you say, not to humiliate someone in public, to avoid confrontation. This is why tongs threaten us so freely. As the tongs see it, they have a legitimate beef when we cover them or print their names. It's a vicious cycle. The longer people tolerate this, the less freedom they have." Perhaps having second thoughts himself about talking to an outsider, Lee added, "If one day you read that Peter Lee is found dead somewhere, you can pretty much draw the conclusion that I have a big mouth. I'm only half joking. I know there is that possibility. I hope the Justice Department and the FBI will open an investigation into censorship and infringement of the First Amendment in Chinatown."

Quo Chen, a Taiwanese reporter who has worked in Chinatown, doubts whether anyone will ever do "the inner story" of the tongs and the gangs. "The damage would be too great—the dirt would be spread on everyone's head," he told me. "I mean community leaders. It's a nasty statement, but it's true. This is such a small community. We meet each other every day. No way to escape, no way. Suppose you are a publisher, you know someone who is a good friend of a tong member who's doing drug trafficking, prostitution. Because you write about it, take sides, you may lose money. Take my former paper, which comes out as a weekly in New York and as a daily in Taipei. It has enough money and manpower to investigate the tongs and the gangs—why doesn't it? Let me put it this way: these things are not a significant disease. Some of the tong members traffic in drugs, some launder money, but what is their relation to one another? We don't know. And we are not that interested in finding out. 'You have your way to survive, I have my way'—that's the dialogue among Chinese. You may belong to a tong, but I do not. I understand you, and you understand why I don't see you as a criminal—your acts don't hurt my interests."

Additionally, some Chinese see tongs as legitimate, even admirable, because they provided financial backing for Sun Yat-sen's 1911 Revolution and then for the Guomindang. Chiang Kai-shek used triads, secret criminal societies on which the tongs were modeled, to assist the Nationalists in the civil war against the Communists. After 1949, many triad members fled with him to Taiwan. Others formed the underworld in Hong Kong, maintaining ties to their American cousins, the tongs. "It would take a dissertation to explain the admiration for these people," Quo Chen says. "They're not looked down on: they're always against the government, which in Chinese history is always corrupt. The connection between the Guomindang and the gangs has its source in Sun Yat-sen. In a feudal society to make a revolution you have to have organizational power and the triads—also called the Green Gangs—were it. So you see it in the government. In China and Taiwan, they say, 'You are in the black way, the dark root.' That means gangs. Now, Uncle Seven, tongs, overseas Chinese—all are attached to the Guomindang. It's nasty but it's understandable if you know our history."

"Tongs have shut down journalism in Chinatown," another journalist told me. "You can say that. I can't, it's too dangerous."

One story the Chinatown press stayed away from was a bitter dispute several years ago between City Hall and the CCBA. In the early eighties, Mayor Edward Koch had proposed an addition to the Manhattan Detention Complex, known as the Tombs, a prison on the western edge of Chinatown. The community rose against it. As a compromise, housing for the elderly and several shops were added to the proposed addition. Representatives from the community, including the CCBA and the Chinese-American Planning Council, were elected to the board of a corporation overseeing the construction and management of the addition.

When the CCBA arranged the election of several tong members to the board, howls of protest from the Chinese-American Planning Council and other board members reached Richard Mei, Jr., an adviser on Asian affairs to Mayor Koch. Mei led a fight to remove the tong members.

Mei told the Koch administration in a memo that the city could no longer support the project if the tongs remained members. Mei recalls, "We were afraid that they'd control the community space in the project or charge rent or protection money. Also, we had some fear that they'd monopolize the selection of tenants. One of the problems is that it has always been very difficult to gather evidence against the tongs." The city tried to shame the tongs off the board, saying that the CCBA had elected "unacceptable" members, including some associated with organized crime. Manhattan District Attorney Robert Morgenthau read the riot act, charging that the police believed that the tongs were connected to youth gangs that served as enforcers for criminals controlling gambling, drug dealing, and extortion in Chinatown. "Ridiculous, the CCBA responded, in the *New York Times*. There had been fighting among the tongs' youth "groups," it admitted, but now all that has changed." Benny Ong shot back, also in the *Times*, that the CCBA "will not lower its head to this evil" or "tolerate this type of defamation."

The city won on a technicality—it took the CCBA to court for stacking the board. Richard Mei, who is now with the State Department, said, "I was vilified in the Chinese press. They said I was a yellow dog and a traitor to the community. The CCBA put a notice on its door banning me from its premises." The project is finally going forward after years of delay.

Another subject that Chinatown journalists have avoided is the tightening of the tongs' control over the CCBA itself. The tongs have long been able to dominate the CCBA through its executive council; but until recently a gentlemen's agreement barred them from electing one of their members president. In February 1990, however, Benny Ong, the Hip Sing elder, and Wing Yeung Chan, the former national president of the rival On Leong, shocked Chinatown by voting as a bloc at the CCBAs annual election. "It's time for a change," Uncle Seven said. "All the past presidents have been corrupt. None of them have spoken English." He proposed raising the president's salary and extending his term from a year to two years. A former president of the New York City chapter of On Leong nominated a former president of the New York City chapter of Hip Sing. This nomination was seconded by the national president of another tong, the Chinese Freemasons. Wing Yeung Chan nominated Paul Yee, a businessman close to On Leong, and Yee's nomination was seconded by the national president of Hip Sing. Several hours later, the other candidate withdrew, citing "health reasons," and the CCBA, over the objections of its outgoing president, who reminded members that they weren't permitted to vote on only one candidate, elected Yee.

A Chinatown reporter observed, "It was the first time these rival tongs cooperated and endorsed the same candidate and forced him down our throats. Usually, they don't cooperate and no one votes for their candidates. The *World Journal* "—one of Chinatown's newspapers—" and *Sing Tao* sanitized and glamorized the election and said it was great for Chinatown. That is ridiculous. You have a puppet handpicked by the Chinese Mafia running the CCBA, Chinatown's governing body. Imagine if the mayor of New York was handpicked by John Gotti!"

After the election, journalist Ying Chan noted, "Everyone knows there is a story here—but it's hands off. People don't want to get into trouble."

Within a few months of the election, Benny Ong flexed his muscle over CCBA. He proposed expelling twenty-four members of the organization, thereby eliminating many of the staunchest supporters of Taiwan. Paul Yee called a general meeting without the twenty-four members that Ong wanted expelled, and the motion passed. Once again, breaking precedent, On Leong and Hip Sing voted for the explosive change. Much later, after threats of litigation by the ousted members, Uncle Seven withdrew his proposal. "In the CCBA, who has the right to expel any members?" one representative fumed. "It is almost the twenty-first century in the United States and we have this dictator! You look at the Mafia in the 1890s, and they ran over their own people. It's the same here. But what can you do?"

Crimetown USA

by David Grann

David Grann's 2002 piece for The New Republic *illustrates how organized crime can set the tone for a city's politics and culture.*

There was a certain tidiness to the killings in Youngstown. Usually they happened late at night when there were no witnesses or police and only the lights from the steel furnaces still burned. Sometimes neighbors would hear the short, sharp sound of gunfire and then nothing, a silence you can't describe unless you've heard it, which if you're lucky you haven't.

Everyone suspected who the killers were—they lived in the neighborhood, sometimes just down the street—but no one could ever prove anything. Sometimes their methods were simple: a bullet to the back of the head or a bomb strapped under the hood of a car. Or sometimes, like when they got Mr. Magda, they allowed for the more dramatic, tranquilizing their victim with a stun gun and wrapping his head in tape until he could no longer breathe.

Yet the most frightening method, the one that captured the city's imagination, was the most immaculate: the disappearance of people in broad daylight. They were the city's ghosts. Police found their cars empty on the side of the street, the engines still warm, or their dinner tables still piled with food. They had, in the most classic sense, been "rubbed out." The only sign of the killers was an artistic flourish: the dozen long-stemmed white roses victims often received just before they vanished.

So, when Lenny Strollo ordered the hit that summer night in 1996, there was no reason to believe it would go down any differently. As the top Mafia don in Ohio's Mahoning Valley, he presided over the killings and disappearances in and around Youngstown from his farm in nearby Canfield, where he tended his gardens and ate vitamins to quiet his heart. His reach extended over nearly an entire corner of the state, a stretch of land that was home to more than 200,000 people and that had become, by all accounts, the most crooked county in America—a place, in the modern era, where the Mafia still held sway over every element of society, from the police to the judges to the politicians. Only months earlier, Strollo had ordered his main mob rival mowed down as he drove to work. But this time his choice of target was more brazen: the newly elected county prosecutor, Paul Gains.

The Mafia didn't ordinarily "take out" public officials, but the 45-year-old prosecutor had so far resisted all the customary overtures, bribes, and campaign contributions, and it was now widely rumored that he planned to hire as his chief investigator the man the Mafia hated most: Bob Kroner, the local FBI agent who had spent 20 years pursuing the mob. In Mafia fashion, Strollo employed endless layers of authority so that nothing could be traced back to him. First he gave the order to Bernie the Jew, the man he relied on for all his muscle. Bernie, in turn, hired Jeffrey Riddle, a black drug dealer turned assassin who was obsessed with the Mafia and, according to friends, boasted that he'd one day be the first nigger ever inducted into the family. Riddle then brought in his own two-man team: Mark Batcho, a fastidious criminal who ran one of the most sophisticated burglary crews in the country, and Antwan "Mo Man" Harris, a crack dealer who, though he still lived with his mother, had already committed at least two other murders.

That Christmas Eve, as Batcho and Harris later recounted, the three men loaded up on everything they needed: walkie-talkies, ski masks, gloves, a bag of cocaine, a police scanner, and a .38 revolver. Around eight o'clock in the evening, they drove out to the prosecutor's home, in a Youngstown suburb dotted with strip malls. The houses glowed with Christmas lights. But, when they arrived, no one was home. Batcho got out of the car and waited behind a lamppost near the garage. He attached a speed loader to the revolver to enable him to shoot faster and tested the voice-activated walkie-talkie. No one responded. He tried again. Nothing. He couldn't believe it. Here they were asking him to carry out the premier Mafia hit in years and the equipment was busted. He ran back to the car and said he couldn't kill anyone without "communication."

Batcho, Harris, and Riddle regrouped at the Giant Eagle Supermarket on Route 224 and programmed two of their cell phones so they could dial each other at the touch of a button. As they eased up in front of the house again, they noticed that a car was in the driveway and the kitchen lights were on. "OK," Riddle said, shoving the gun back in Batcho's hand, "get out and go do this."

Batcho jumped out of the car, carrying the bag of cocaine Riddle had instructed him to plant on the body to make it look like a drug-related killing. He crept up to the house, his heart pounding. The garage door was open, and he said, "Hey, mister, hey, mister," but no one answered, and he kept walking. The side door to the house was open, too, and he could hear someone speaking. He decided to go in. Creeping down the corridor, he heard Gains talking on the phone in the kitchen. Batcho rushed in, pointed the gun at the prosecutor's midsection, and fired. As Gains fell to the ground, Batcho fired again. Blood spilled from two wounds—one in his forearm, the other in his side. Batcho took another step closer as Gains put up his hands to ward him off.

Batcho aimed near Gains's heart and pulled the trigger. But the gun kicked back in his hand, jamming. *Jesus fuckin' Christ!* Batcho turned and ran out of the house, stumbling into the woods in back. He tripped and fell and, getting back up, hit the button on the cell phone, screaming, *It's done! It's done! Come pick me up!* As he came out of the woods, he saw the car approaching down the street and lurched toward it, jumping into the backseat. He crouched down, shivering. "Did you kill him?" Harris and Riddle asked.

"I think so," Batcho said uncertainly.

"You don't know?" Riddle said.

"The gun jammed," Batcho said, "the gun jammed."

Harris looked at him coolly. "Why didn't you go in the drawer and get a steak knife and stab him to death?" he asked.

Riddle said they had to go back and finish the job, but just then the police scanner crackled with news of the shooting. Riddle hit the gas and started swerving along the back roads. Fearing they'd get pulled over, Harris took the gun and threw it out the window. But the speed loader was missing. *Where the fuck is the speed loader?* they started screaming at each other. Then from the scanner came even worse news: Gains was still alive.

It was one of the least skillful murder attempts in the valley's history: the speed loader was found outside the house, along with a clean footprint; a sketch of the shooter appeared in the paper within days. But, ironically, the crime scene was so messy that investigators couldn't believe Strollo's people were behind it—not even Gains, who told friends, *If the mob had done it, I'd be dead.* Batcho, who had begun to wear disguises around town, slowly emerged from hiding. Amazingly, it looked as if these murderers would get away as well, until one spring night the prosecutor got a phone call at home. "Are you Paul Gains?" a woman asked.

"Yes," he said, "who's this?"

"I know who shot you," she said.

When the woman rattled off details about the crime that few could have known, Gains called the police, who brought in the FBI. "I know everything," she told the agents who rushed to her apartment the next day. "I know other people they shot. I know everything."

And so it happened. The call, from the ex-girlfriend of an associate of the hit men, helped solve a mob hit for the first time in the valley's history. But, coupled with a three-year covert operation by the FBI, it would ultimately help uncover something far broader. It would slowly untangle what authorities describe as one of the last truly mob-run counties in the country: a place where the Mafia still controlled a chief of police, the outgoing prosecutor, the sheriff, the county engineer, members of the local police force, a city law director, several defense attorneys, politicians, judges, and a former assistant U.S. attorney; a place whose residents had grown so used to a culture of corruption that they viewed it casually, even proudly; a place, in a sliver of America, where a malignant way of life was left largely untouched for almost 100 years. Now, after more than 70 convictions, the investigation has wound its way to the most powerful politician in the region, a man whom the FBI caught on tape with the mob nearly 20 years ago but who has eluded them ever since: United States Congressman James Traficant.

Today, the Mahoning valley is one of the most depressed corners of America. But it wasn't economic bust that first brought the mob to the valley; it was economic boom. In the early years of the twentieth century, the valley—a thin corridor of land that twists and turns its way through northern Ohio—was the heart of an industrial empire. Steel mills stretched as far as the eye could see, their furnaces streaking the sky with 15-foot flames. For more than 50 years, their lights drew immigrants—Poles and Greeks and Italians and Slovaks who thought they had found the Ruhr Valley of America—as well as a burgeoning class of racketeers who thought they had found their own "Little Chicago." Youngstown's streets were lined with after-hours joints, where the steelworkers drank and played Barbut, a Turkish dice game, and where capos, dressed in white-brimmed hats and armed with stilettos, ran the numbers, or "bug," as the locals called it. Youngstown in the 1940s wasn't particularly unusual. Like Chicago, Buffalo, or

Detroit, it had a teeming immigrant population accustomed to arbitrary and violent authority, a booming economy, and pliable local politicians and police—all the ingredients the mob needed to flourish.

But, unlike those larger cities, Youngstown was too small to have a mob family of its own. And, as a result, it turned into a battlefield. By 1950, as the rackets mushroomed into a multimillion-dollar industry, the Pittsburgh and Cleveland Mafia families began fighting for control of the region. Bombings began to ricochet through the valley—warnings to those who allied themselves with the wrong side. It got so bad over the next two decades that the local radio station ran public-service ads featuring an earsplitting bang and the slogan "Stop the bomb!" In 1963, *The Saturday Evening Post* dubbed the area "Crimetown U.S.A.," noting: "Officials hobnob openly with criminals. Arrests of racketeers are rare, convictions rarer still and tough sentences almost unheard of."

Shortly after Bob Kroner arrived in the valley in 1976 as a 29-year-old FBI agent, a full-scale war broke out. On one side was Joey Naples's and Lenny Strollo's faction, which was controlled by the Pittsburgh Mafia; on the other were the Carabbia brothers—known in town as simply "Charlie the Crab" and "Orlie the Crab"—who were aligned with Cleveland. "It seemed like you'd get up every morning and get in your car and hear someone else had been murdered," says Kroner.

First there were "Spider" and "Peeps"—two petty cons hit within a few weeks of each other. Then came one of Naples's drivers, shot as he changed a tire in his driveway, and a crony of Peeps's, who was gunned down outside his apartment. Then, poor John Magda, who was discovered, his head wrapped in tape, at the dump in Struthers, and, next, a small-time bookie who refused to go easily—he was first bombed and later shot through his living-room window while he watched television with his wife. Then, Joey DeRose Sr., killed by accident when he was mistaken for his son, a Carabbia assassin; and finally, a few months later, the son, too. "Oh my God, they got Joey," his girlfriend screamed when police told her they had found her car burning on a country road between Cleveland and Akron.

• • •

A former high school math teacher who turned in his books for a badge in 1971, Kroner quickly plunged into this underworld. He could be seen in town, in his neatly pressed suit and tie, trailing reputed hit men and banging on the doors of the All-American Club. Though he came from a family of cops, Kroner didn't look like one: he was too tall and slender, almost delicate, and he lacked the easy manner of the police who played craps in the shadow of the courthouse. He wore penny loafers in a city where most people wore boots, and he had a certain stiffness, as if he were a substitute teacher who feared he might lose control of his class.

Unlike his FBI predecessor, who, according to the agency's own affidavit and informants, had allegedly consorted with gangsters and was later appointed Youngstown's chief of police at the Mafia's behest, Kroner was hostile to the local dons. Prickly and shy, he spent hours alone in his small office, smoking cigarettes and listening to intercepted conversations between the different gangs. He made little diagrams of each family, to which he added further details whenever he received a tip from an informant. He did everything he could to bring down their enterprise: tapping their phones, tailing their cars, subpoenaing their friends. In other words, he was, as Strollo and his cronies put it, a "motherfucker."

One day in the spring of 1981, not long after Charlie the Crab, the head of the Cleveland faction, disappeared without a trace, Kroner searched the apartment of one of the city's most notorious assassins. The apartment was cluttered with knickknacks, and Kroner and his partner went through each room carefully. In a cabinet, Kroner noticed a bread box and opened it. Inside, tucked amid the stale bread, was an audiotape. When he played it, he heard vaguely familiar voices: "He's a scared motherfucker." And: "You either play our fucking game or you['re] going to be put in a fucking box." Two of the voices, he was sure, belonged to Charlie and his brother, Orlie the Crab. But there was also another voice, one Kroner thought he recognized from television and radio. Then it dawned on him: It was Youngstown's newly elected sheriff, a former college football star named James Traficant.

• • •

Later, acting on a tip, Kroner and his partner drilled open the Carab-bias' sister's safe-deposit box, where they found a similar tape with a handwritten note that said: "If I die these tapes go to the FBI in Wash-ington. I feel I have more people after me because of these tapes and . . . I pray and ask God to guide and protect my family." At headquar-ters, Kroner and his colleagues listened to a jumble of voices arguing about which public officials were allegedly being paid off by the rival Pittsburgh mob.

"You believe they got all them fuckin' people?" Orlie said.

"I know they got [Mayor] Vukovich," Traficant said.

"Oh, they definitely got Vukovich," said Charlie.

"I know they got Leskovansky," Traficant continued. "I know they got Haynes. I know they got Morley. I know they got Gilmartin."

"They don't have Gilmartin," said Charlie.

Traficant paused, as if running through the names in his mind. "I don't know all of them," he finally said. "But I know it's a fuckin' fistful."

With its Pittsburgh rival controlling many of the valley's politicians, the Cleveland faction knew it needed some pols of its own. And the tapes, apparently made by Charlie the Crab at two meetings during the 1980 sheriff's campaign, appeared to show them buying Traficant, a rising star. "I am a loyal fucker," Traficant informs the Carabbia brothers at one point, "and my loyalty is here, and now we've gotta set up the business that they've run for all these fuckin' years and swing that business over to you, and that's what your concern is. That's why you financed me, and I understand that."

The arrangement, according to the tapes, was an old-fashioned one: Traficant acknowledged receiving more than $100,000 from the Cleveland faction for his campaign. In exchange, he'd use the sheriff's office to protect the Carabbias' rackets while shutting down their rivals. "Your uncle Tony was my goombah. . .," said Charlie, "and we feel that you're like a brother to us. . . . We don't want you to make any fuckin' mistakes." Traficant assured his benefactors that he was solid and that, if any of his deputies betrayed them, "they'll fuckin' come up swimming in [the] Mahoning River."

But, according to the tapes, Traficant wasn't primarily worried about his deputies; he was worried about the Pittsburgh mob. As Charlie knew, Traficant had accepted money from Pittsburgh, too—some $60,000, the first installment of which came with the message, "I want you to be my friend." The young candidate for sheriff was double-crossing the Pittsburgh family (he had just given over at least some of their money to Charlie the Crab to prove his loyalty), and he knew that, when they found out, they would retaliate. "Look, I don't wanna fuckin' die in six months, Charlie," Traficant said.

On the tapes, Kroner and his colleagues could hear Traficant hatching a plan to protect himself from the Pittsburgh Mafia—and the officials they controlled. "Let's look at it this way, OK?" he said. "They do have the judges. . . . They can get to the judges and get what they need done. . . . What they don't have is the sheriff, and . . . I'm one step ahead." On the day he was sworn into office, Traficant said, he'd take some of the money the Pittsburgh family had given him and use it as evidence to arrest them for bribery. What's more, he described what he and the Crabs would say if their secret dealings were ever exposed: "I was so fucking pissed off at this crooked government, I came to you and asked you guys if you would assist me to break it up, and you said, `Fuck it . . . we'll do it!' OK? That's gonna be what you're gonna say in court."

"Orlie too?" asked Charlie. "He's got a bad heart—"

"*Look. . . ,*" said Traficant. "I'm not talking fucking daydreams. . . . If they're gonna fuck with me, I'm gonna nail them." Traficant was taken with the audacity of his plan. "If you think about it," he mused at a later point, "if I fuckin' did *that—*"

"You can run for governor," said Charlie.

They all broke into laughter.

After Kroner and his superiors reviewed the tapes, they called Traficant down to headquarters. Kroner had never met the sheriff before, and he watched as he settled into the chair across from him. Traficant was an imposing figure, with wide shoulders and thick brown hair that stuck up on top so that, at first glance, it looked like a wig. You could tell from his muscles that he had once worked in the mills, and he walked as if his joints had been worn down to the bone. As they exchanged pleasantries, Kroner told Traficant he had grown up in Pittsburgh and watched him play football at the university there—where Traficant had starred as a daring quarterback who, as one NFL scout put it, "at the most critical point in a game . . . will keep the ball himself and run with it," bowling over anyone in his path.

What happened next is in dispute. According to sworn court testimony from Kroner and other agents present, Kroner asked the sheriff if he was conducting an investigation into organized crime in the valley. Traficant said he wasn't. Kroner then asked him if he knew Charlie the Crab or Orlie the Crab. Traficant said he'd only heard of them.

You never met them? Kroner asked.

No, Traficant said.

You never received money from them?

No, he said again.

Then Kroner popped in the tape:

> Traficant: "They have given sixty thousand dollars."
> Orlie the Crab: "They gave sixty. What'd we give?"
> Traficant: "OK, a hundred and three."

After only a few seconds, Traficant slumped in his seat. "I don't want to hear anymore," he said, according to Kroner. "I've heard enough."

In the FBI's version of events, Traficant acknowledged he'd taken the money, and he agreed to cooperate in exchange for immunity. In front of two witnesses, he then signed a confession that read, in tiny, cursive letters: "During the period of time that I campaigned for sheriff of Mahoning County, Ohio, I accepted money . . . with the understanding that certain illegal activities would be allowed to take place in

Mahoning County after my election and that as sheriff I would not interfere with those activities."

According to the FBI, it wasn't until several weeks later that Traficant recanted his confession, after learning that he would likely have to resign as sheriff and that the reason for his resignation would become public. "Do what you have to do," he told Kroner, "and I'll do what I have to do." Or, as Traficant later told the local TV station, "All those people trying to put me in jail should go fuck themselves."

The FBI did what it had to first, arresting the 41-year-old sheriff for allegedly taking $163,000 in bribes from the mob and for willfully and knowingly "combin[ing], conspir[ing], confederat[ing], and agree[ing]" with racketeers to commit crimes against the United States. Incredibly, facing up to 23 years in jail, Traficant decided to represent himself in court, even though he wasn't a lawyer and even after the judge warned him that "almost no one in his right mind" would attempt such a thing.

On the day of the trial, pacing the courtroom in a short-sleeved shirt, Traficant told the jury just what he had vowed he would say on the Carabbia tapes: that he was conducting "the most unorthodox sting in the history of Ohio politics." In a role that he said deserved "an Academy Award," Traficant told the rapt gallery that he had been acting all along as an undercover agent, trying to convince the Carabbia brothers he was on their side so he could use them to shut down the more powerful Pittsburgh faction. "What I did, and what I set out to do very carefully," he said, "was to design a plan whereby I would destroy and disrupt the political influence and the mob control over in Mahoning County."

Though he admitted taking money from the mob, Traficant said he did so only so that his opponent in the campaign wouldn't get it. And, though he acknowledged that his voice was on the tapes, he claimed they were doctored to incriminate him. And, though he agreed he had signed "a statement," he said it was different from the fraudulent "confession" the FBI introduced into evidence. And, though he confessed he had initially lied to the FBI about the sting, he said it was only because he couldn't trust its agents—one of whom, back in the '60s, was allegedly tied to the mob. Indeed, he insisted that, if the FBI hadn't intervened, he would have cleansed the most corrupt county in the country. "The point of the matter I want to make is this," he said. "I got inside of the mob." Then: "I *fucked* the mob."

It was a stunning performance. When Kroner finally took the stand and testified that he had seen Traficant sign the confession, the sheriff jumped out of his chair and yelled, "That's a goddamn lie!" During cross-examination he taunted his FBI adversary, saying, "Oh, I see" and "No, Bob." Half crazy, half charming, he referred to himself as "my client" and asked reporters, "How am I doin'?" In a region instinctively wary of outsiders, he became, by the end of his defense, an emblem of the valley. In Youngstown, people held parties on his behalf. His supporters sold t-shirts touting his heroic struggle. It didn't matter that the IRS would later find Traficant liable for taking bribes and evading taxes, in a civil trial in which he took the Fifth. Or that the money he had allegedly taken as evidence for the sting was never turned over. Or that one of his deputies claimed on the stand that Traficant had repeatedly asked the deputy to shoot him to make it look like an attempted mob hit. Traficant understood his community better than anyone else. It took a jury four days to decide to acquit. Charlie the Crab was wrong about only one thing: Traficant wouldn't become governor. He would become a United States congressman.

By the time Traficant went to Washington, D.C., in 1985, the valley was already disintegrating. The worldwide demand for steel had plummeted, plunging the area into near-permanent recession. Mills barricaded their doors. Department stores closed. At least one airline discontinued its service to the region. By the end of the decade, the population in Youngstown alone had fallen by more than 28,000, while the sky, leaden for half a century, turned almost blue.

Traficant, reelected to term after term in Congress, railed against the closings, sometimes even sounding a little like Charlie the Crab. When one of the last steel mills in the region filed for bankruptcy in the late '80s, Traficant warned: "I think this is beyond all this talking phase. If [the owner] rips off the last industrial facility . . . then someone should grab him by the throat and stretch him a couple of inches." But there was nothing he or anyone else could do.

And if prosperity had brought the mob to the valley a half-century earlier, depression cemented its rule. The professional classes that did so much to break the culture of the Mafia in Chicago and Buffalo and New York in the 1970s and '80s practically ceased to exist in Youngstown. Much of the valley's middle class either left or stopped being middle class. And so Youngstown experienced a version of what sociologists have described in the inner city. The city lost its civic backbone—its doctors and lawyers and accountants. The few upstanding civic leaders who remained were marginalized or cowed. Hierarchies of status and success and moral value became inverted. The result was a generation of Batchos, kids who worshiped the dons the way other children worshiped Mickey Mantle or Joe DiMaggio. (Batcho even tattooed a picture of a legendary mob boss on his left upper arm, telling people proudly, "[I'd] take a bullet for him.") Meanwhile, Lenny Strollo and his partners, in need of players for their cash-strapped casinos, began catering to the local drug dealers and criminals, who were the only people left with money to spend.

The mob, which had once competed with the valley's civil society, largely became its civil society. As late as 1997, in the small city of Campbell, Strollo controlled at least 90 percent of the appointments to the police department. He fixed the civil-service exam so he could pick the chief of police and nearly all the patrolmen. The city law director literally brought the list of candidates for promotion to Strollo's house so the don could select the ones he wanted. "Strollo," says an attorney familiar with the city, could "determine which murderers went to jail and which ones went free."

In 1996, while three mob hit men, including Mo Man Harris, were on their way to kill their latest target, they were pulled over by the Campbell police for speeding, according to people in the car. In the vehicle the cops found an AK-47 rifle, a .357 Magnum revolver, and a 9 mm pistol. One of the killers used his cell phone to call Jeff Riddle, who rushed to the scene and told the police the men were running an errand for Bernie the Jew. The cops let them go.

In the rare instances when the police arrested a reputed mobster, Strollo and his associates simply paid off the judges. There was such a sense of impunity that once in the spring of 1996, when an incorruptible judge prevented Strollo from fixing a particular assault case, he dispatched Batcho with a walkie-talkie and a silencer to wound the defense attorney so they could get a mistrial. "I said, 'Are you attorney Gary Van Brocklin?'" Batcho later recalled. "And he said, `Yes, I am.' . . . And I shot him right in the knee." "I don't know how an honest defense attorney could make a living in this town," says Kroner's boss, Andy Arena.

And, of course, Strollo's tentacles reached the valley's representative in Congress as well. Until he was exposed in 1998, Traficant's top aide in the district, Charles O'Nesti, served as the "bagman" between Strollo and the city's corrupt public officials. (Traficant had hired O'Nesti in 1984, despite his claims on the infamous tapes that O'Nesti was a mob crony whom he would arrest as part of his so-called sting to clean up the valley.) While working for Traficant, O'Nesti would meet Strollo at the don's farm or talk with him on the phone. The two even conspired to steal a stretch of city pavement as it was being laid down. "The hold that the mob has had here to this day," says Arena, "I don't think you'll see anywhere else in the United States."

The FBI sting that would start unraveling this web of corruption began in 1994. Kroner, now middle-aged, had given up smoking through hypnotism and put several pounds on his slender frame. One morning, as he met with other agents in their cramped office in nearby Boardman Township, he could barely contain his frustration. He had just witnessed the disintegration of one of his few triumphs: 14 months after he'd nailed Strollo for gambling, his nemesis had reemerged from prison and reasserted his power. Even when we bust them, Kroner thought, they just come back.

So, after years of disappointment, Kroner and his colleagues opted for a new approach: rather than attack the mob from the top, as they had in the past, they'd start at the bottom, with the number runners and the stick handlers at the Barbut games. The investigation was based on the theory of carpenter ants—if you didn't eliminate all of them, even the smallest ones, they would simply multiply again. "We set forth right in the beginning that we were not going to stop until we got to the nest," says Kroner, "and if it meant having to work deals with people we had lots of evidence against, that's what we were going to do if it would lead us up the chain."

One of the first people they persuaded to cooperate was a local bookie named Michael Sabella, who worked in the markets and always smelled of fish. After being questioned by the feds on another matter, he agreed to wear a wire around the county's gambling dens. Eventually, he gave them enough evidence to get wiretaps on several low-level members of Strollo's sprawling enterprise, who, in turn, gave them enough evidence to tap more phones, and so on. As the number of intercepted conversations mushroomed into the thousands, Kroner and his partners, John Stoll and Gordon Klau, spent days sifting through transcripts.

But, after more than a year of sleepless nights, they still hadn't penetrated the Mafia's innermost circle. Hoping to "shake the tree," as Kroner put it, they started raiding gambling joints, which finally gave them enough evidence to install bugs in Strollo's kitchen and telephones. They began picking up snippets of incriminating conversations. They heard what sounded like a plot to shake down a priest and what some "asshole did before . . . he got whacked."

At one point early in their investigation, Kroner got a tip from an informant that Strollo was going to kill one of his rivals, Ernie Biondillo. Feeling a moral obligation to warn Biondillo, he picked up the phone and called him. "This is Bob Kroner," he said. "You know who I am?"

"Yeah, I know who you are."

"Well, I need to sit down and talk to you alone."

They met that night in a parking lot. Kroner hoped the warning would encourage Biondillo to cooperate with the investigation. But Biondillo just kept saying, *Who the fuck wants to kill me?*

Kroner studied him hard. "I can't tell you that. I'm not out here to start a war."

Unable to get an answer, Biondillo drove off in his Cadillac. Several months later, as Biondillo turned down a deserted street, two cars boxed him in, and two men wearing rubber masks opened fire. By the time Kroner got to the hospital, Biondillo was already dead.

Though Kroner was sure the hit was ordered by Strollo, the FBI still didn't have enough evidence to arrest him. But, by the summer of 1996, the authorities were finally starting to close in, and Strollo, sensing it, became more and more paranoid. On the phone, he began speaking almost exclusively in code and, suspecting Kroner was listening in, would say, "Bob, can you hear me? Can you hear me?" Once, upon meeting one of his oldest and most trusted confidants, Strollo had a sudden premonition that the friend was wearing a wire. Another time he decided a plane was following one of his bookies. When someone tried to calm him down, he snapped: "This is my life you're talking about . . . I got to fight for survival."

Strollo grew obsessed with Kroner. He sent one of his men to find out if the FBI agent's father, an old-fashioned city cop, could be paid off to control his renegade son. But word came back that the father was honest, like his kid. Knowing the FBI was tapping him, Strollo began to plant evidence against his nemesis to suggest Kroner was on the take. He told associates, almost nonchalantly, that Kroner had received bribes from "Little Joey" and was running drugs through the valley.

Then one day Kroner's partner heard Strollo grow more and more menacing. "I don't know what I'm going to have to do about these guys," he said, referring to the FBI agents. Not long afterward, unbeknownst to the FBI, Strollo ordered the hit on Gains, the county prosecutor who, the Mafia believed, was about to hire Kroner as his chief investigator.

But the bungled hit, of course, only created a bigger problem: In spring 1997, Gains received the phone call fingering the hapless assassins. On the basis of information from the caller—"the scorned woman," as Kroner gratefully called her—Bernie the Jew, Riddle, and Harris were all charged with attempted murder. One day, as Batcho was leaving his house with a friend to go to Jay's Hot Dogs, an unmarked car pulled up behind him. "Are you Mark Batcho?" two men said, jumping out of their car. "No, I'm not Mark Batcho. I don't know him," Batcho replied. But, in spite of his protestations, they took him into custody, where he eventually became, as he put it, "the lowest form of life there [is]—a mob rat."

On a cold morning just before Christmas 1997, dozens of FBI agents fanned out through the valley, arresting more than 28 other mob associates. When Kroner showed up at Strollo's door with an arrest warrant, Strollo said, "Are you happy now, Bob?"

In the end, nearly all of Strollo's underlings pleaded guilty and turned evidence against one another, except for Bernie the Jew and Riddle, the two men who had adopted the old Sicilian code even though they could never be officially inducted. "The only ones who had any balls were a *shvartsa* and a shine," said one of the lawyers familiar with the case.

Bernie insisted there was nothing to worry about: Strollo would never turn on them and break his oath of silence. But just before the trial, even as Bernie was speaking, Strollo's lawyer was leading his client upstairs, where he cut his final deal with the prosecution and told Kroner, "You win."

The announcement is surely one of the strangest moments in C-SPAN's history: "I will probably be under indictment" in the next few months, Traficant says, staring into the camera. It is March 2000, almost 20 years since his last arrest. The congressman has put on a somber black coat and tie for the occasion, but his hair is slightly tousled and his trademark long sideburns make him look like an aging biker. In his 16 years in Congress, Traficant has earned a reputation as a fiery, eccentric populist who often appears on the House floor, in polyester suits, to champion the working class and rail against the IRS. In a city without memory he has become known simply as "the honorable gentleman from Ohio," an almost cultish figure who sleeps in his office to save money and closes his speeches with the line "Beam me up, Mr. Speaker."

But today he looks as if he hasn't slept in weeks, and he says he's scared to death. "Hawks are circling, buzzards [are] circling, sharks [are] circling . . . trying to kill the Traficant election," he stammers. He pauses, his cheeks flushed. "Let me tell you what: Twenty years ago—not quite—I was the only American in the history of the United States to defeat the Justice Department. . . . They have targeted me ever since." Suddenly he points his finger into the camera: "I'm targeting *them*. They better not make a damn mistake . . . I am mad and . . . I'm going to fight like a junkyard dog in the face of a hurricane, and . . . if I beat them you're now watching one of the richest men in America, because I'm going to sue their assets all apart."

Even stranger than his warnings to the Justice Department and the FBI—and his admonition that he'll shoot any unexpected late-night visitors to his house—are Traficant's threats to his own party. He warns that if Democratic leaders don't stand by him, he'll switch parties—a critical defection that could undermine the Democrats' chances of regaining a House majority this fall. And, as further compensation for his loyalty, Traficant demands a list of favors for his district: "I want an empowerment zone from the president of the United States—and I expect it this year—and I want additional appropriations. . . ." On national television, he seems to be extorting his own party.

Traficant doesn't say what the indictment will be for; nor will the FBI. But his C-SPAN announcement comes on the heels of a six-year investigation into organized crime in the Mahoning Valley that has already led to convictions against Traficant's former aide O'Nesti, a disbarred attorney who had advised him for several years, and a former deputy in his sheriff's office. According to news accounts first detailed in the Youngstown *Vindicator* and the Cleveland *Plain Dealer*, investigators are looking into, among other things, whether the congressman received illegal contributions—including the use of a Corvette—from associates in the valley. They have recently homed in on two brothers, Robert T. and Anthony R. Bucci, who own a paving company in Traficant's district and allegedly delivered materials and did construction work on the congressman's 76-acre farm. Both brothers appear deeply enmeshed in the city's network of corruption. On one of the FBI's wiretaps, O'Nesti conspires with Strollo to steer a million-dollar contract to the Buccis' company. Robert Bucci has since apparently fled the country after allegedly transferring millions of dollars to an offshore account on the Cayman Islands.

Through it all, Traficant has steadfastly maintained his innocence, and the valley is bracing for a second showdown. "Here's what I'm saying now," he insists grimly on C-SPAN, "and I'm saying this to the Justice Department in Cleveland, Ohio. . . . If you are to indict me, indict me in June so I can be tried over the August recess, [because] I don't want to miss any votes."

When I arrive in Youngstown on a recent, cold spring morning, there is an odd sense of déjà vu, as if the old tapes have been rewound and played again. As Traficant campaigns for a ninth term in Congress, he once again faces the old accusations: bagmen, illicit favors, payoffs. I head downtown, trying to find someone to ask about the allegations, but the city is bizarrely empty, as if people had been called away on a last-minute errand and never came back. Finally, after rows and rows of boarded-up stores and deserted sidewalks, I see a light in one of the shops. In the window, Italian suits hang with handkerchiefs in the pockets. An old man is folding clothes by the cash register. When I ask him about Traficant, he stiffens. "Ain't no one gonna get rid of Traficant," he says. "Traficant's too sharp." Far from being angry about the city's history of corruption, he seems almost proud of it. He recalls fondly the "henchmen," including Strollo, who bought their suits from him. "They didn't wear red or pink [ones] like they're coming out with now," he says. When I press him about the local corruption, he shrugs. "Who cares? If you're working and making a living and nobody is bothering you, why are you going to butt in?"

Later, at my hotel, several elderly men are sitting around a table arguing about Traficant. "Traficant produces," says one. "That's what counts." "Damn right!" says another. They are all in their seventies and eighties and have lived in the valley for decades.

"When I was eight years old," one of them says suddenly to me, as if to make a special point, "I delivered newspapers downtown, and I would always go by this speakeasy on Sunday afternoon. Well, one day the owner says, `I want you to meet someone.' So I went over and it was Al Capone." He pauses, shaking his head in awe. "Al Capone."

"You see this," another man says, referring to the last speaker. "This is typical Youngstown. Here's an educated man, an attorney, and Traficant is a god of his, and he's still raving about meeting Al Capone."

When I stop at Youngstown State University to talk to Mark Shutes, an anthropologist and one of the only academics who studies the region, the first thing he says is, "You're not gonna write some crap about how we're all victims of gangsters, are you?" Shutes contends that, after so many years of eroded civic institutions, the community has come to rely increasingly on mobsters, who play the same role in civic life that the police and the political establishment do in other cities. "We have socialized ourselves and our offspring that this is the way the world is," he says. "This is our little safe part, with our community and church, but in order for it to be safe, you need these people to be brokers." Indeed, in a world where corruption is normal, he says, values prized in other cities are, in the valley, deemed counterproductive. "We don't see high ideals as being a benefit," he explains. "We see [them] as being a weakness. There is no sense in this community in which gangsters are people who have imposed their will on our community. Their values are our values."

So much so that, despite two opponents railing against his alleged mob ties and an FBI investigation reportedly closing in on him, Traficant won the March 7 Democratic primary with more votes than his two main competitors combined. Traficant seems so unbeatable in November that some congressional Republicans have decided to defend him, apparently hoping he'll follow through on his threat to switch parties and cement their fragile majority. "Jimmy Traficant is not being done right by," Republican Representative Steve LaTourette of Ohio told the Cleveland *Plain Dealer*. "There isn't a finer man, there isn't a finer member of Congress, there isn't a finer human being . . . than Jim Traficant. God bless you, Jimmy Traficant, and I hope to serve with you for many years."

Emboldened by his popular support, Traficant is doing what he's long done so well: rallying the valley against the outsiders trying to besmirch its name. Over the last year, he has defiantly called his convicted former top aide, O'Nesti, a "good friend" and championed a local sheriff convicted of racketeering, arguing that he should be moved to a prison closer to Youngstown to be near his ill mother. "[T]hese sons of bachelors will not intimidate me," he likes to say of the FBI, "and they won't jack me around."

Though he has retreated from reporters—"I'll only make an official statement when I'm actually killed," he says—the press releases have begun to pour out of his Washington office: "TRAFICANT BILL WOULD CREATE NEW AGENCY TO INVESTIGATE JUSTICE DEPARTMENT"; "TRAFICANT WANTS PRESIDENT TO INVESTIGATE FEDERAL AGENTS IN YOUNGSTOWN." On the House floor, where his speech is protected against suits for libel, he is bolder still: "Mr. Speaker, I have evidence that certain FBI agents in Youngstown, Ohio, have violated the rico statute and . . . stole large sums of cash. . . . What is even worse, they 'suggested' to one of their field operative informants that he should commit murder. Mr. Speaker, *murder*."

At FBI headquarters in Boardman, Kroner and his boss, Andy Arena, are trying to fend off Traficant's allegations. They are careful not to say anything about the press releases, the pending investigation of the congressman, or even the 1983 trial. But it is clear they are under siege. On talk radio, Traficant supporters denounce Kroner as a thief, a con man, a crook, a creep, a liar, and a dope dealer. "The thing that most depressed me," says Kroner, "was when I became the subject on talk radio one day and they were discussing my integrity." He folds his arms. "I just have to block out [those] things." Rather than a hero, he has become almost a pariah. "Everything is turned upside down here," says Arena.

As Kroner sits in his neatly pressed jacket and loafers, his 20-year-anniversary FBI medallion mounted prominently on a thick gold ring, he seems slightly defensive. "Every time we charge another public official, the [media] presents it as another black eye for the community," he says. "I'd prefer if they'd portray it to the community as another step in cleansing ourselves. We've got to take a look at what's being done here as a positive thing."

It is dusk by the time he shows me around the valley, and we rush past the old steel mills, past the Greek Coffee House and the Doll House and all the other gambling dens, past the place where Bernie the Jew met with his team of hit men and where Strollo had Ernie Biondillo whacked in broad daylight. "We're a part of this community like everyone else," Kroner says at one point. "We suffer the same problems if we live in a corrupt town." He pauses for a moment, perhaps because he can't think of anything to say or perhaps because he's not able to talk about the expected Traficant indictment or perhaps because he realizes that, after 25 years in the Mahoning Valley, he's done all he can do. "As long as they choose to put people in office who are corrupt," he says, "nothing will ever change."

Blood Brothers

by John Sedgwick

Boston has its share of dangerous characters and colorful personalities—and some of them help run the state of Massachusetts. John Sedgwick's 1992 profile of brothers Billy and Whitey Bulger ran in GQ magazine.

t was a raw, blustery day on the South Boston waterfront, and the retired longshoremen stood in the lee of a coffee shop with their collars up and their caps down low over their brows to ward off the cold. They eyed me warily as I approached.

Mine was a fool's errand, I suppose. I wanted to hear from them about the neighborhood's famous pair of mismatched brothers: James J. "Whitey" Bulger, the reputed leader of the Irish Mafia, whose terrifying exploits fill no fewer than fourteen volumes of reports by the FBI's organized-crime unit, and William M. "Billy" Bulger, the Massachusetts senate president, who is, after the governor, the most powerful politician in the state government. Together, the two constitute one of Boston's fundamental mysteries, a snake twisted about the heart of the city. "It's exactly as if Al Capone's brother was president of the Illinois state senate," a previous senate president named John Powers once complained, *"and nobody ever mentioned it."* Interestingly, when I called Powers to discuss the Bulgers, he refused even to come to the phone. Virtually everyone else in a position to know likewise clammed up, the ultimate tribute in a gossipy town to the Bulger brothers' overwhelming power to exact revenge, to instill fear and to silence. One South Boston hood got smacked by his father simply for mentioning the name of Whitey Bulger in the house.

Yet both Bulgers are lifetime Southie men, pure products of this harsh peninsula that reaches out like a lobster claw into the Atlantic. While both have risen to the heights of their chosen professions, neither one has ever moved out of the neighborhood of his youth. I figured if anyone could tell me the truth about the Bulgers, it was these old men down by the sea, among whom the brothers have lived all their lives. Yet obviously these men did not welcome a stranger with the wrong accent asking audacious questions about two of their own. Their weathered faces, at first incredulous, turned blank, then cold, then mean.

I moved from one to another, finally reaching a kindly looking man in tweed, who took me aside. "What's it you want to know, now?" he asked benignly. I told him, and a strange thing happened. When I asked about Whitey, he answered about Billy, speaking of the tremendous power he wielded in the senate. When I asked about Billy, he spoke of Whitey, saying how dangerous he was, how a fellow had to watch his step around a man like that. I thought the man was daft. But eventually I realized that he understood only too well. To know one Bulger brother, you have to know the other.

It's an old story, this saga of brothers who went their separate ways in life, as old as Cain and Abel. Nowadays, the tale seems almost too melodramatic for contemporary tastes, rife as it is with such old-fashioned themes as the meaning of brotherhood, the pull of blood, the twists of fate. The story of the Bulger brothers is a B-movie barreling out of the 1940s, starring Spencer Tracy and James Cagney as the good and the bad sons. And in its own way, it is a saga almost as compelling as that of another old-fashioned Boston-Irish family, the Kennedys.

So it may be inevitable that the Bulgers are rooted in South Boston, a throwback neighborhood in America's most antique city. Pass over the narrow bridge that links South Boston to the rest of the city, head down the main thoroughfare of Broadway, and you have gone back at least a generation in time. It's quiet here, almost eerily so. "Southie's safe because it's so fuckin' dangerous," one lifelong resident told me. Most South Bostonians are lifelong residents, and many of them have devoted their lives to keeping things just the way they have always been. It is this determination that propelled the long, ferocious battle against forced busing in the Seventies, a fight led by local firebrand Louise Day Hicks but ardently supported by Billy Bulger, who repeatedly condemned the "unremitting, calculated, unconscionable portrayal of each of us, in local and national press, radio and television, as unreconstructed racists." At the peak of that struggle, some protesters considered hiring thugs to blow up the bridge to the mainland and insulate themselves from change forever. As it is, the trendiness that has taken over so much of the nation has made no impression here. There are no chocolate chip–cookie stores in Southie, no croissantwich shoppes, no teddy bear boutiques, not even a movie theater. Instead, there are bars: more than thirty of them altogether, one virtually on every street corner, with good Irish names like Kelly's and P.J. Cronin's. Most of them are dreary, dimly lit places adorned with cardboard shamrocks and faded postcards of Ireland. Together with the monuments to the neighborhood's many war dead, they give Southie much of its tragic character.

Billy and Whitey Bulger are certainly not the first pair of famously disparate brothers from South Boston. The McCormacks of Andrew Square hold that honor. The gaunt, abstemious John W. McCormack rose from poverty to become speaker of the U.S. House of Representatives in 1962 and a sainted memory in the neighborhood. His 350-pound brother, Edward, a saloonkeeper better known as Knocko, offered illegal gambling upstairs at his Wave Cottage restaurant in Southie, and he ran with Paddy Coleman, the notorious bookie from Boston's South End.

Such stark contrasts should not be surprising. As with most ethnic neighborhoods, South Boston offers few routes to success, cut off as it is by geography, religion, class and temperament from the Brahmins who rule the city from Back Bay and Beacon Hill. Thomas O'Connor, a Boston College professor who grew up in Southie and has written a book about his hometown, says the career choices of an ambitious Southie resident were for a long time limited to three: politics, the priesthood and crime. In the case of the Bulger family, it was inevitable that two aspiring sons should select two different options. (As it happened, Billy Bulger briefly considered the priesthood before settling into politics.)

Looked at another way, the two Bulgers might simply be considered the heirs to both halves of the great tradition of the Irish political rogue best embodied by James Michael Curley, who, back in the Forties, served a portion of his final term as Boston's mayor in the Danbury federal penitentiary, for mail fraud. He once assailed South Bostonians as "thugs, muckers, doormat thieves and milk-bottle robbers," but the neighborhood took him as an adopted son all the same. One might say that Billy represents the upstanding, front-parlor half of Curley; Whitey, the conniving, back-alley half. At least in the public mind, the two halves make one whole. Tempting as it must be politically, Billy has never publicly disavowed his brother, never washed his hands of him. Perhaps he knows that that would never go down in Southie, whose voters are his ultimate judge. After all, as Billy himself likes to say, quoting Seneca, "Loyalty is the holiest good in the human heart." Or perhaps a brother like Whitey adds a useful dimension to Billy's reputation. Or perhaps Billy simply loves him. Whatever the reason, the two are joined for life.

But the marvel is not that the Bulger brothers have headed in opposite directions but that they have pushed to such extremes. Knocko McCormack only dabbled in crime. Whitey is by most accounts a gangster, pure and simple. He is not believed to have ever held a legitimate job in his life, with the exception of a troubled two-year stint in the air force and some custodial work that Billy lined up for him after Whitey emerged from his only prison stretch, for armed robbery, in the mid-Sixties.

And he looks the part. The few photographs of him show an aging thug with thinning hair, the long, upturned nose that is a Bulger-family characteristic, steel-gray eyes that are usually hidden behind dark glasses, and a permanently unfriendly expression. A health nut and an exercise addict, Whitey is known for a powerful physique that is startling for a 62-year-old. "He's held his years better than I," grants Billy, 57. "All I do is walk."

One has to get by on other people's impressions of Whitey, because, unlike the John Gottis of the criminal world, Whitey Bulger does not make himself available to the press. The very idea of trying to speak to him is almost unthinkable. You don't call up Whitey Bulger requesting an interview. You don't drop by his apartment hoping to have a word with him. You don't ask his friends to line something up. The reason is simple: Whitey Bulger cultivates the image of someone who might kill you, and I now choose to believe the image.

Partly because of his reclusiveness, Whitey is hard to get a fix on as a mobster. He is not perched atop an intricate hierarchy of foot sol-diers, like the usual Mafia don. But neither is he a niche player who confines himself to just one criminal market, be it marijuana impor-tation or bookmaking. Investigators believe he participates in a full run of Mob activities—gaming, loan-sharking, money-laundering, illegal liquor distribution, cocaine sales, marijuana smuggling, pil-ferage, occasional Mob hits and whatever other odd-lot opportunities for making a quick buck might come his way. But questions persist about the range and nature of his undertakings. In a city where so much is known about so many, the fact that almost nothing is known definitively about Whitey is probably his greatest asset. It has kept him out of jail and in business. The essence of his public image is his lack of one: We picture whatever scares us the most.

While every newspaper brings fresh reports of the fall of yet another rival Mob chieftain—most recently, 60-year-old Joseph Russo, whose elaborate 1989 ceremony inducting other mobsters into Boston's

Italian Mafia was taped by the FBI—Whitey has been collared only the one time, and that was at the beginning of his career. Since then, despite countless investigations by the U.S. Drug Enforcement Agency, the state police, the local police, the Internal Revenue Service, the U.S. attorney and various local district attorneys, he has neither been arrested for nor charged with a single crime, a fact that suggests that either he has been clean all these years or he has been unusually skillful. Most investigators incline toward the latter view. "The man is a career criminal," says Robert Long, a former state police detective lieutenant now with the investigative firm LCF Associates, who spent more than a decade fruitlessly chasing Whitey Bulger. "He has been the target of all these investigations, and he's still on the street. The guy has beaten the system. I don't know anybody else around here who has stayed up that high for that long. Whitey Bulger is the absolute, undisputed champion of Boston mobsters. I gotta hand it to him. He's played all his cards right—and he's pulled the right lottery ticket, too."

Long is alluding to Whitey's latest, possibly most impressive gambit, one that is designed to keep him on the street a good while longer. Whitey won the Massachusetts lottery. Or, more exactly, he was one of four men cashing in on the winning ticket of the "Mass Millions" lottery, bringing each of them $89,556 a year for the next twenty years. Although some people figure that, Whitey being Whitey, he somehow rigged the lottery (almost nobody thinks he won it honestly), the more likely explanation is that he simply muscled in on the winning ticket after the fact. After all, he used to be part owner of the building now housing the South Boston Liquor Mart, where the winning ticket was bought by a certain Michael Linskey. Whitey liked to sun himself out front of the store on summer afternoons. It wouldn't have been difficult for Whitey to introduce himself to Linskey between the Friday when Linskey learned he had won and the Monday when he showed up with the winning ticket at state-lottery headquarters. While Whitey no doubt is happy to have the money, he's happier still to finally provide a legitimate source for $89,556 worth of an annual income that had previously been completely inexplicable. As one disappointed investigator said, "[Whitey] just made himself bulletproof from the IRS."

But for a mobster, success is measured not only in dollars but also in square feet, by the territory he controls, and by that standard there is some uncertainty about just how successful Whitey is. Jerry Angiulo, the North End mobster now serving a life sentence in prison, was taped by the FBI in 1981 saying that "Whitey's got the whole of Southie" and that Whitey's longtime partner, Steve "the Rifleman" Flemmi, had "the whole of the South End." But that was probably just wishful thinking on Angiulo's part, since just the year before, Whitey had been headquartered in a garage on Lancaster Street around the corner from the Boston Garden and barely a mile from Angiulo's own North End offices. From a cockroach-infested flophouse across the way, Robert Long had watched Bulger for months, and he saw what he terms a "Who's Who of organized crime" coming by the garage— major marijuana importers, cocaine dealers, bookies, boxing pro- moters and much of the hierarchy of Angiulo's own organization. All of them paying homage, or money, to Whitey Bulger. A decade later, spooked by the many efforts that federal and state agents have made to bug his office, his car and his phone, Bulger conducts his business at night from no single headquarters, making his calls from pay phones around the city. Most law-enforcement officials believe that Whitey's turf extends through most of the eastern part of the state, from Lowell, in the north, down through Somerville, Roxbury and South Boston, south to Quincy and Brockton.

As an Irishman denied entrée to the traditional Mafia, with its arcane blood ties, Whitey has pretty much had to make it up as he's gone along. For a while, he worked his way up through the Winter Hill gang of Irish mobsters in Somerville, led by Howie Winter, but after that broke up in the late Seventies, following Winter's arrest for race-fixing, Whitey split off with Flemmi, an Italian. The two have been tight asso- ciates since, a pair of free-lancers with such fearsome reputations that they have been able to dictate terms to the more-established crime outfits, much to the irritation of the dues-paying Italians. Angiulo used to rage that Bulger and Flemmi never accorded him the tribute he expected. "When did they ever come down here and give me a quarter?" he once complained while FBI tapes were running. "I don't think they ever intend to pay it, if you want my honest opinion." There was some boozy talk one night of the Italians' going after the two with machine guns, but nothing ever came of it. If anything, Bulger and Flemmi played the Mafia's game more purely, because they didn't get bogged down in all the capo and *consigliere* crap. They forged alliances as they needed them, and broke them afterward. For Bulger, the mastermind, the situation was never fixed, but always fluid; loyalty was never permanent, but had to be reinforced—at gunpoint, if necessary—every day. Whitey never took anything for granted.

And when in doubt, he attacked with total fury. Late one night, Bulger spotted some men standing too close to his car, parked outside his place in Quincy, and figured it was some of his many enemies trying to plant a bomb. He came charging out of his house in a rage, scared the men away and then chased after them in his car, all the time screaming obscenities at them about their trying to kill him. Only when the car neared a police-operated safe house did Bulger realize the truth: The men were plainclothes police planting a bug in his car. Even then, he had a few choice words for the cops before taking off. The message was clear: Nobody fucks with Whitey Bulger.

In terms of his personal style, Whitey learned from the mistakes of the Old Guard, like Jerry Angiulo. Angiulo enjoyed playing the robber baron, with a big house in affluent Nahant and a kid in Little League. To Bulger's way of thinking, one can speculate, that life-style was what got Angiulo forty-five years for racketeering; it drew attention to him. Let the Mafia types strut and mouth off and go to prison. Whitey has laid low and stuck to basics. No house, no wife, no kids. He is an invisible man casting a long shadow. "It's almost like he doesn't exist," says one Boston police officer who should know better. "It's like there's a Whitey Bulger, but no one can find him." Few Bostonians would recognize Whitey if they passed him on the street; hardly any cops even know what he looks like. "He could walk right by me," says one thirty-year police officer, "and I wouldn't know." He has several apartments in South Boston and Quincy, all of them leased under the name of his girlfriend, making them untraceable by the IRS. The address he gave lottery officials is on Twomey Court, a modest two-story brick building in a complex filled mostly with senior citizens. Although he once splurged on a Cadillac and a Jaguar, he now drives a large blue LTD, also registered in his girlfriend's name. What money he spends, he unloads down in the Caribbean, where he won't be noticed. His invisibility has caught some people by surprise. For years, the local inflammatory radio personality Jerry Williams used to inveigh regularly against Whitey, apparently unaware that one of Whitey's crash pads was right next door to his own place in Quincy.

Although he is a notorious figure in most of the city, in South Boston Whitey is regarded as something of a patron saint. Everyone has a story of Whitey's doing something nice for somebody, whether it is helping an old lady up the steps with her bags, pressing money into the palms of grieving widows, warning young women about the dangers of walking alone at night or keeping drugs away. As one retiree puts it, "Whitey's nifty." No doubt, Whitey is capable of chivalry when it suits him, and he may even have an ennobled view of himself. In one of his few public utterances, he once told some DEA officials he came upon that "we're all good guys here. You're the good-good guys, and we're the bad-good guys."

But he has founded his professional life on something that is not so nice—his reputation as a cold, brutal killer. "Whitey handled a lot of problems that needed to be handled," says Robert Long. Problems like, guys needing to be killed? "Whatever problems there were," Long says. "I have to be careful what I say here." Whitey continues to live off of the fear that he can instill in others. Much of the cash that is toted over to him in suitcases and grocery bags, investigators say, is protection money, paying Whitey to keep other gangsters away—and, implicitly, to stay away himself. "You could see it in the way his associates approached him," says Long. "You could see that they were afraid." In one surveillance photo, Whitey stands with his legs spread, his arms gesturing forcefully. His minions cower in front of him, arms tight to their sides, seemingly scared to intrude upon Whitey's space.

They never know when his temper might blow. Investigators were watching one day as a 240-pound underling named Nicky Femia, later murdered in a gangland hit, laid out an oozy Big Mac and some greasy fries on the hood of a black Chevy for a lunch that was way too high in calories and fat for Bulger's liking. He suddenly charged at Femia, swept up the food and threw it in the startled mobster's face.

Whitey's murderous reputation has not gone unnoticed in Billy Bulger's place of business, under the golden dome of the Massachusetts State House. In the course of an interview with one legislator, I asked if the name Whitey Bulger ever comes up in conversation. The man, who refused to be quoted by name, acted as though I had pulled out a gun and aimed it at his head. "No," he hastily replied. "Never."

"Why not?" I persisted.

"Because of who he is," he answered, unnerved by the conversation.

"You mean because he's a killer?" I pressed.

He nodded.

"Do you really mean that Whitey might kill you if you spoke about him?" I couldn't believe he was serious.

"Let's just say I've heard several threats, and that's all I want to say about them," he said, eager to change the subject. I just looked at him, amazed. "It's like walking under a ladder," he concluded. "Okay, it might be that nothing would happen to you if you walked under it, but why take chances?"

There are too many stories. Recently, when a couple of small-time hoods were found dead in South Boston—one shot in the back of the head, one shot in the face—people assumed that it was Whitey's work: Supposedly, the two had broken into a liquor store in which Whitey had had an interest. In a sense, they are the lucky ones. Others who have tried to muscle in on Whitey's territory have simply vanished without a trace. "Those guys just fuckin' disappeared," says one insider. "There was no corpus delicti. Fuck that."

• • •

If Whitey is a man of the shadows, Billy is, like any public figure, a man of the light. He has the air of a schoolboy—short, bright-eyed, fresh-scrubbed, almost irrepressibly eager. But that hasn't helped his reputation. When I asked James Michael Curley's son Frank, for example, if he saw anything of his father in Billy Bulger, he curtly replied, "Good God, no." Then he added, "If his name ended in a vowel, he'd be a South American dictator or the illegitimate son of Mussolini." Bulger claims such enmity stems from his disdain for the press. "If I have any mystique," he says, "it's because I have had the nerve, or the arrogance, not always to be available for comment on all the charges that have been leveled at me. I figure I can either answer them or ignore them, and I've ignored them. But they do pile up."

He is trying to stay above it all right now. He is upstairs at Anthony's Pier 4, a waterfront restaurant known for its political connections, microphone in hand, addressing a throng of Democratic loyalists whom he has tapped for $250 each to raise money for the party's state-senate candidates. This is a matter of no small concern to Bulger, whose senate presidency depends on a Democratic majority. Tonight, he has brought out the faithful, or the obligated, in quantity. The place is as big as a basketball court, and it is jammed wall-to-wall with cheap suits. Failed gubernatorial candidate John Silber is here, former Lieutenant Governor Tommy O'Neill, most of the state house and senate leadership and—in a coup—almost the entire Democratic congressional delegation: Barney Frank, Joe Moakley, Joseph Kennedy. . . . Only Ed Markey is missing, and he called to say he was stuck at the airport. Every Massachusetts politician knows to be respectful of Billy Bulger, but the congressmen are being especially nice these days, since redistricting is coming up, and Bulger will almost single-handedly decide their political future. Bulger can hardly contain his glee. "I lord it over them," he told me on the phone a few days earlier. "It's my one opportunity. I tell them I want to see them at Pier 4. They say 'Wherever you want us.' It makes me more insufferable than before."

And sure enough, Bulger is insufferable. As with his celebrated Saint

Patrick's Day breakfasts at the Bayside Club, a tavern in South Boston, Bulger takes the opportunity to revel in his power—power to redistrict congressmen into oblivion, power to belittle them with his wit, power to hold them under his spell. Billy Bulger is a good speaker, with a voice so pleasant that when he once sang "The Isle of Innisfree" with the Boston Pops Orchestra, people snickered only at the beginning and were genuinely moved by the end. Tonight, he tosses the usual political bouquets, then he sights John Silber in his crosshairs. He helped Silber get on the ballot for the last gubernatorial election, only to see him blow his lead at the end of the campaign with some astonishingly intemperate remarks addressed to the first lady of Boston newscasting, Natalie Jacobson. Bulger assumes a cat-with-canary-in-mouth look and says he has a remedy: "Next time, I'll have a little whiff of chloroform ready." The crowd chortles. Bulger is warming to the task. He says he has nothing but admiration for Silber's aggressiveness. "If Silber had won, by now we'd have invaded Rhode Island. And by the end of his first term, all of New England would be ours." Some men watching beside me actually double over with laughter. And then Bulger spots Bob Crane, formerly the state treasurer, a job that involves overseeing the Massachusetts lottery, and one that, like so many other posts, fell to the other party in the last election. "I want to say one thing, Bob," Bulger says. "Until a Republican was treasurer, no one in my family ever won the lottery." Some of the air leaves the room, now that Billy has brought up Whitey. Then he addresses everyone: "Remember, you can too. Just take out a pen and a piece of paper, and write down this number, and play 'the Game.' " As he closes, I hear someone say "He sure has a lively sense of humor."

Billy Bulger has been senate President for thirteen years, the longest tenure in the history of the commonwealth, and he sometimes behaves like a man who has crowned himself king. Few other legislatures across the country grant as much power to their leader as the Massachusetts senate has to its president. Bulger has the power to control virtually every aspect of senate life, choosing the majority leadership, assigning the members' offices, deciding the salaries of their aides, even appropriating the office expenses. He prides himself on being an enlightened despot, though. He has banished television from his elegant little house in South Boston, and he reads Latin and Greek works in the original—and quotes from them often, knowing full well how much that irritates his rivals. In a culture-free zone like the state legislature, however, his erudition must make him a little lonely sometimes. (It may also have provided an unexpected bond with the new Republican governor, William F. Weld, a summa cum laude Harvard classics grad.) A reporter I know was once summoned into Bulger's office for a getting-to-know-you session that turned into a heady literary discussion for which she was wholly unprepared. "Seeing that I was a reporter," she says, "he started on a high intellectual plane with me, but then he ratcheted down, down, down." Since Bulger knew my friend was Catholic, he began by talking about a socialist Catholic theologian she had never heard of, then dropped to Willa Cather, whom she had heard of but had never read, and finally descended to Tom Wolfe's *Bonfire of the Vanities*, which, fortunately, she *had* read. But once his intellectual airs had been cleared away, he was left largely with his prejudices, which are deeply felt. These consist largely of a lifelong antagonism toward the press—"men of unsleeping malevolence," he likes to call them—and toward *The Boston Globe* in particular, since the paper dismissed him as a troglodyte for opposing forced busing. In conversation with my friend, he seized on *Bonfire*'s slimy journalist character, Peter Fallow. "He found that so fascinating," the reporter recalls. "Because Fallow was a dissolute, irresponsible, drunken, craven, manipulative asshole. That's what he thinks about all of us." Whatever Bulger's intentions, it proved to be an awkward conversation.

Bulger has been pleased to take his place among the rulers of the city, not just the pols. He is a member of the Union Club, one of the prestigious gentlemen's clubs on Beacon Hill, but the Union, a bastion of old Yankee Boston, has not taken him to its bosom. "I doubt they're proud of him," one Brahmin told me. Bulger is a trustee of the Massachusetts General Hospital and of the Boston Public Library, and an overseer of the Boston Symphony. Although he has made a political cause of South Boston High School, he has sent most of his nine children to private schools, such as Winsor, and private colleges, such as Harvard. "Billy is very upwardly mobile," says one fellow politician. "He's not a guy who thinks his kids should be the same as he is." His oldest son, William M. Bulger Jr., served as his campaign manager in the last election but has no interest in a political career.

While Whitey leads a fly-by-night existence, Billy spends his days in nearly Augustan splendor. When the senate is in session, he governs the proceedings from the tall chair at the front of its marble bust-filled chambers. Otherwise, he holds court in his sumptuous office, which he had restored with $160,000 of the taxpayers' money. With its delicate inlays and gilded finery, the room looks as if it emerged from the pages of an Edith Wharton novel. He proudly shows it off to visitors, observing that the new rug was specially commissioned from the English manufacturer of the nineteenth-century original, and pointing out the portraits of his many predecessors lining the wall—Samuel Adams, Horace Mann and Calvin Coolidge, among them. The taciturn Coolidge is a "great favorite of mine," Bulger says. "I love the story of him coming out of church. 'What did the minister speak on, Mr. President?' 'Sin.' 'And what did he say about it?' 'He agin it.' " Bulger beams with pleasure.

For all his high-mindedness, Bulger has never entirely risen above the world of the down and dirty. The sharpest allegations leveled against him have to do with his role in the development of 75 State Street, a gilded marble office building in downtown Boston that was designed by Skidmore, Owings & Merrill. Bulger and his former law partner, Thomas E. Finnerty, each pocketed nearly $250,000 shortly after Finnerty had received $500,000 from the building's developer, Harold Brown, for few apparent services rendered. Brown claimed he was the victim of extortion, and it looked to many as if Bulger had taken part in a classic shakedown, a well-established practice in the city. Bulger has insisted that the money was merely an advance against an unspecified legal fee he was expecting. (He has always maintained a private law practice on the side.) Bulger repaid the money with interest, and no charges have ever been filed. This past January, the state attorney general, Scott Harshbarger, concluded his investigation by announcing that "no crime [had] been committed."

Still, suspicions linger, and Bulger is widely referred to around town as the "corrupt midget," a phrase coined by an early political enemy and then turned into a Homeric epithet by the *Boston Herald's* vituperative political columnist Howie Carr. In fairness to Bulger, the Bay State has never treated its legislative leaders very kindly. "You make a kind of bargain if you become a legislative leader in Massachusetts," says Congressman Barney Frank, who once served in the state's House of Representatives and who, though usually voluble, seems no more eager than anyone else to talk about the senate president. "You get a lot of government power, but you become the personal embodiment of the unpopularity of the legislature." No legislative leader in memory has succeeded in gaining statewide office, although several have tried. The state's anti-Bulger animus came to a head during the last election, when, in the voters' anger over the sudden implosion of the Massachusetts Miracle, Bulger was regarded as the ultimate insider haunting Massachusetts politics. One Republican ad compared him to Leonid Brezhnev. "HE Used to RUN A ONE-PARTY DICTATORSHIP," read the caption under Brezhnev's picture. "HE STILL DOES" were the words under Bulger's. Yet for all the fury he provokes, Bulger can be surprisingly demure, almost dainty, in person. When we first spoke on the phone to set up an interview, he compared himself to Greta Garbo. "I think I get more attention for my reticence," he said. "As somebody once said about Greta, 'Ah, but how she waits to hear those cameras clicking.' " He closed by saying that he was sure that if I met him, I would be disappointed. "You're going to say there's no there, there," he said, quoting Gertrude Stein. As he must have known, that only piqued my interest.

Trace the divergent paths of the Bulger brothers back to their source, and you come to 41 Logan Way, a South Boston housing project originally known as Old Harbor Village. Built in 1938, it was the second housing project in the country, and at the time, it bore little of the stigma attached to public housing today. It now looks like a project, stark and barren, with graffiti staining its red-painted brick and Astro-Turf laid down in the cramped front yard where grass won't grow. But the place was borderline respectable when the Bulgers moved in from nearby Dorchester the year it opened, and doubtless it was the border-line quality that made it all the more attractive to the children. Whitey and Billy were 9 and 4, respectively, when the family moved in, the second and third of six Bulger children. "It was a wonderful place to grow up," recalls Joe Quirk, a neighbor in those years and a lifelong friend of Billy Bulger's. "A combination of Tom Sawyer and Huck Finn, with a little bit of *West Side Story* thrown in."

The family qualified for public housing because the children's father, James Joseph Bulger, had lost his left arm in a railroad-yard accident as a young man and had been able to work only part-time, at the library and at the navy yard, since. He was a short, stoic figure, who always walked ramrod-straight, the empty left sleeve of his suit jacket tucked into the side pocket. Politics were his chief interest, and he was a passionate supporter of the New Deal. Billy Bulger remembers his dad's mocking Herbert Hoover's ardor for private contributions to make up for the wages lost in the Depression. "Gee, private charity," his father would say in his rumbling Irish brogue, shaking his head in disgust. Aside from his political enthusiasms, the father emerges from Billy Bulger's recollections as a distant figure. Both powerful and pow-erless, he must have posed a complicated role model for his sons. His wife, Jane, was the cheerful, outgoing one, always busy with house-work or the children. They are both dead now. "It's an odd feeling I have about my parents," Billy Bulger once told *The Globe*. "You think about it and get bluesy."

Whitey and Billy shared one bedroom with their younger brother, John, or Jackie; their three sisters shared another. Known to the family as Sonny, Whitey was always well-mannered around the house, and he was nice to the younger kids, like Joe Quirk, who were friends of his little brother Billy's. But as he entered his teens, he toughened himself up physically, and the courteous, dutiful Sonny side disappeared from general view. "Whitey was in perfect physical condition," Quirk recalls. "Not an ounce of fat on him. He had a body like steel." Whitey often asked the young Quirk to punch him in the stomach as hard as he could; when Quirk obliged—he says it was "like hitting a wall"—Whitey would only laugh and say "Oh, come on, you can hit me harder than that." Not content with proving himself to the younger kids, Whitey started to mix it up with the older, bigger, rougher teens from the neighborhood, who were never in short supply. "When he got into a fight, it was usually with a bigger person," Quirk says. "He was always looking for a challenge. He was macho, and he liked to show it."

Billy's childhood was more happy-go-lucky. He spent hours with Joe Quirk, hunting for matchbook covers to add to his collection, and was thrilled to coax an autograph from Ted Williams. He played stickball, hitchhiked with a parish priest to Provincetown and fell in with a neighborhood group called the Pirates, who played street games around the projects. Billy became a leader of the Pirates, just as he would later be captain of the high-school baseball team. While Whitey had to win people's respect with his fists, authority flowed automatically from Billy, just by the way he carried himself. "I don't remember his being involved with anything where he wasn't the top dog," says Quirk. Billy's pursuits were always innocent pastimes, just kid stuff. But in South Boston, especially down around the projects, one never has to go very far to find trouble. That is the amazing thing about the place: You can find whatever you want there, sin or salvation.

One evening, Billy and Joe Quirk spotted a bunch of toughs from nearby Mercer Street taking on another gang in a park a few blocks from the projects. As the two kids looked on, horrified, the teenagers lashed one another with leather belts tipped with sharpened buckles. "It was like warfare," Quirk recalls. "Those guys were really going at it." The two boys watched as long as they dared, then raced back to the safety of Old Harbor.

Whitey Bulger also watched these fights. But he had a different reaction. He joined the Mercer Street gang.

• • •

The two brothers moved in completely different worlds after that. Whitey started showing up at local police precincts on larceny charges, although none stuck. And he developed a showy side to his hell-raising. One time, he drove his car right down the tracks through the old Broadway elevated-train station with a blonde beside him, honking and waving to the startled crowd. At 20, he went off to the air force. No doubt his parents hoped the military would straighten him out. Instead, he was frequently AWOL, ending up in such diverse places as Oklahoma City or the Great Falls, Montana, jail as a suspect in a criminal case. Out of the service in 1952, he turned to crime with a vengeance, as if he was trying to make up for lost time. He went on a crime spree, robbing banks in Massachusetts, Rhode Island and Indiana, before he was grabbed in a Revere, Massachusetts, nightclub, in 1956, and sent away to federal prison for nine years.

Billy played it straight and hit the books. He stayed up so late, he was nicknamed Beam for the reading light that was always on. He didn't plan on being one of the losers who climbed the hill to South Boston High and thence went on to a lifetime of low expectations. He was determined to pass the special entrance exam to Boston College High, and he succeeded, even though going there meant an hour's trolley ride each way and work after school at a neighborhood meat market to make the $37.50 tuition each term. B.C. High led to B.C., then B.C. Law, making Billy Bulger a celebrated Triple Eagle.

Life for Billy quickened the year he graduated from law school, 1960. He married his first girlfriend, Mary Foley, whom he had met as a high-school junior on a cruise ship to Provincetown. And he decided on a political career, running for the Massachusetts house seat that had been vacated by Joseph Moakley, who also lived in Old Harbor Village, at 57 Logan Way. "But that was lower socioeconomic," Bulger teases now. "Ours was the high-rent district." It was his father who had set Billy on the political path, with the regular discussions of Mayor Curley and the New Deal, but it was also his father who tried to warn him off of it. "He thought it would be hard on me," Billy recalls. Then, typically, he opts for a more elevated way, of putting it: "I liken it to Themistocles, the great Greek politician, who was taken by his father to the seaside to discourage him from becoming a politician. He showed him the old fishing galleys on the beach, lying there, rotting away. He said, 'That's what the crowd does with its public men when it no longer has use for them.' "

James Bulger may have had another concern when he heard about young Billy's ambitions, and that was that the good son might be tarnished by the exploits of the bad. At the time, Whitey was in the federal penitentiary. But the voters of South Boston proved to be understanding, and they sent Billy to the house. Ten years later, Joe Moakley called to say that he was giving up his seat in the Massachusetts senate to run for Congress, and Billy went on to win it. By the end of the decade, he'd risen to the third in command, then was the only one left standing when the senate leadership was erased in a series of scandals. He assumed the presidency in 1978.

By that time, Whitey had settled down to life as a career criminal. Prison had been his B.C. He proved a voracious reader, and he developed a fascination with the strategizing of World War Two, devouring accounts of battles from both sides. This may have sharpened his mind for his own criminal campaigns to come. He also learned about drugs firsthand, when he participated in a three-year CIA program to study the effects of LSD. Billy claims that the drugs still give his brother nightmares, but, according to investigators, that hasn't kept Whitey from profiting from the sale of controlled substances to others. His prison term had the added benefit of keeping him off the streets when they were especially dangerous for a hot-tempered Irish hood. Through the Sixties, Irish gangs from Somerville and Charlestown were fighting it out in a vicious turf war, and sixty aspiring wise guys were snuffed out, their bullet-riddled bodies turning up in the blood-drenched trunks of stolen cars, if they were ever found at all.

When Whitey emerged from prison, in 1965, he quickly fell in with South Boston's Killeen brothers, who needed someone to enforce their gambling-and-loan-sharking operation. But Whitey soon transferred his loyalties to Pat Nee, a leader of the Killeens' archrivals, the Mullins gang, who would later emerge as a major marijuana smuggler in league with the IRA-linked Joe Murray, whose exploits were chronicled in the book *Valhalla's Wake*. In 1972, when Donnie Killeen was machine-gunned to death in his car, the police figured that Whitey had done it. No charges were ever filed, but the crime made Whitey's reputation. He began hanging with the Winter Hill gang in Somerville. He started out small, collecting loan-shark debts and putting the squeeze on hoods trying to make off with goods stolen from the docks of Charlestown and South Boston. But he did well. When Howie Winter was sent off to jail in 1979, he left Whitey Bulger in command.

Although each is a terrible liability to the other, Billy and Whitey have displayed an enduring loyalty to each other. The precise nature of Whitey's emotional ties to his brother can't be known, of course, but he has done his best to keep his criminal activities from damaging Billy's career. This effort apparently led to an attempt to stifle a member of the press. On one slow news day back in 1978, a *Boston Herald* crime reporter named Paul Corsetti happened to ask an organized-crime detective with the Boston police if he thought there was any connection between the Bulger brothers, a topical question since Billy had just ascended to the senate presidency. The detective didn't say much, and Corsetti never followed up on the idea. But the next Saturday night, he was having a beer at the Dockside, in Quincy Marketplace, when a man with unforgettably terrifying steel-gray eyes came up to him and asked if he was Paul Corsetti. Corsetti said yes. "Well, my name is Whitey Bulger, motherfucker, and I kill people for a living," the man announced. He added that he knew where Corsetti and his daughter lived and what kind of car Corsetti drove. Then he left. Corsetti bought a .22 to protect himself, and arranged for police protection for the next few days, but he never again heard anything on the matter. The lesson was not lost on him, however. He never did write anything about the Bulger brothers.

For Billy's part, he provided that custodial job for Whitey, hired him to drive a car during one campaign and named him godfather of one of his children. In the past, he has downplayed the reports of Whitey's criminality but offered no real rebuttals. He once told *The Globe* that his brother had "run off with the circus," unable to bring himself to mention Whitey's true calling.

I was warned that Billy hates to talk to the press about his brother, and I put off our interview as long as I could, but eventually I found my way to his statehouse office. While I waited for nearly forty-five minutes as Bulger was serenaded by a school choral group, I browsed through an edition of Vasari's account of various Renaissance masters, which had been left out for visitors' edification.

Finally, my palms moist, I was ushered into Bulger's presence. Because of his office's majestic proportions, Bulger seemed even smaller than his five-feet-six. Still, as we sat together in a pair of leather club chairs, he could hardly have been more courteous or pleasant. "This man is warming to me," he loudly declared to his secretary at one point. At first, the conversation was less a formal interview than a little chat. He was surprised to hear that everyone was too scared of him to speak on the record. "Really?" he said, actually yanking back his head in a gesture of amazement. "Well, I'll be all the more insufferable now." He pooh-poohed the idea that he was all-powerful, declaring that the power accrued only to his office and that it depended on his pleasing the majority of senators, who had placed him there. He seemed happiest when he could lift the conversation to a higher literary plane. "I assume that life is a constant effort toward greater self-education," he observed at one point, and he freely quoted Seneca, Cicero, Homer, Samuel Johnson and Seamus Heaney. Finally, before I missed my chance, I swung the conversation around to his upbringing, to his family, and to Whitey. I asked how his brother could have heard a different message at home than he had.

The playful, ironic bantering suddenly stopped. The words came slowly and painfully, as though each one had to be physically ripped from his body. "I have no explanation," he said. "Each person does what he desires to do."

Is it hard for him to be in his position, with Jim—as I knew Billy prefers to call Whitey—in his?

"When people are hostile, then everything is available as a weapon, and yet I don't think it counts."

Does he see Jim very much?

"As often as I can."

Who arranges the meetings?

"I seek him out, and I urge him to come by."

I tried to probe deeper: Does he think that Jim is really evil, as everyone says?

But Billy would go no farther. "Whatever I say, my critics will leap upon and distort, and so I prefer to leave the subject untended." With that, he would discuss his brother no more.

A little later, however, he gave a more revealing glimpse into Whitey. We had been going over a well-publicized incident in which he'd reduced the pay of a housing-court judge named E. George Daher for refusing to provide a job Billy had promised to the son of a former governor's councillor. Although the incident occurred ten years ago, Bulger's anger was still fierce as he recalled the part played in the affair by a reporter he refuses to name. "You have to bear in mind that the reporter who ran the thing and made it the big thing it was is a fella who at that time I would not speak to," he began, his language slipping from nearly Harvardian tones back into his native Southie diction. His voice dropped to a near whisper, and he bore in on me with his ice-blue eyes. Time slowed, the rest of the world fell away. "And one of the reasons I wouldn't speak to him was, he drank too much. One day, I came in and found him using the telephone in the lobby. I said 'I don't think you should use the telephone. I don't let the public do it. I don't think I should be allowing you to.' So he reached in his pocket, and he took out a dime. He was about to flip the dime to me, and I told him 'If you do it, you're going out of here and you're not coming back. Your newspaper will have to kill me before you come back.' "

By the time the senate president finished this story, I'd broken into a sweat. I'd heard Whitey Bulger speak.

• • •

The two brothers, so divergent in other respects, coalesce in this: Both have succeeded in leveraging a small base in South Boston into far broader realms. Both have uncanny survival instincts, knowing when to ride a trend and when to buck it. Both are loners. And, most important, both are absolute masters of power, exactly as ruthless as they have to be, no less and no more. "With both of them," says one of the few people in Boston who know both brothers, "if you step out of line, you get your head whacked." It's pretty well established how Whitey does his head-whacking. Interestingly, those who know Billy use the same language to describe his methodology. Senator David Locke, the state senate's minority leader and Bulger's sparring partner, says that Bulger succeeds by figuratively putting a gun to the back of your head. "It's an unseen power, but it's there," he says. Whitey may have offed any number of underworld rivals over the years. Billy is a far more selective assassin, yet his political hits have, if anything, reverberated far more than Whitey's. "I always liked that," Billy told me, smiling, "because it means you don't have to be a real villain." Only two stories ever come up. One is the Judge Daher incident; the other, curiously, involves Whitey's custodial job at the supreme judicial court: Billy froze the pay of John Powers, the former state-senate president, who later served as clerk of the court, after Powers had declared it unseemly to have a convicted felon on the payroll.

But there is a wider pattern of fierce determination that is more impressive than are the specific instances of dirty dealing. During the last campaign, Bulger faced a Republican candidate from the Back Bay named John de Jong, who had the unlikely profession of veterinarian and campaigned to "neuter Billy Bulger." One might think that Bulger wouldn't have taken him too seriously, but in the anti-incumbent political environment, Billy couldn't be too careful. De Jong claims that Bulger's staff threatened to withdraw funding for the Tufts Veterinary School, his alma mater, if De Jong pursued his candidacy, and arranged for Tufts president Jean Mayer, a Bulger loyalist, to tell De Jong so. During the campaign, De Jong received several threatening

Whitey-esque phone calls in the middle of the night, cautioning him to "watch your back." Merchants who placed De Jong signs in their windows found themselves facing unexpected questions from the board of health. And on Election Day, De Jong's poll watcher at Saint Monica's Church in South Boston reported being told by Bulger henchmen to "sit outside for a while" as Billy Bulger went into the polling place for a few minutes, alone. It could not be determined what, if anything, he did in there. Bulger himself recalls doing no more than "putting my head in." When he emerged, he clapped his hands and shouted to about a dozen associates "Go get 'em now." The men charged into the nearby projects, where Bulger himself had grown up, and pulled out voters two, three and four at a time.

Bulger won easily. He laughs about the campaign now. "Just because everything is going to the dogs," he says, "that's no reason to send in a veterinarian."

Are Billy's and Whitey's activities somehow linked? The question is almost too shocking to ask. And every person I spoke to immediately and emphatically dismissed the possibility of any criminal involvement on Billy Bulger's part. Still, one does wonder. Whitey Bulger has developed an uncanny ability to sense when the investigators are watching. Robert Long, the former state police detective, spent months compiling enough evidence to win a court order to place a listening device in the Lancaster Street garage, and then, practically as soon as the bug was in, the whole show mysteriously stopped. Long halted the investigation for a few months to let things cool down. By the time he resumed it, Bulger and his associates had shifted their operation to a bank of pay phones outside the Howard Johnson's on the Southeast Expressway in Dorchester. After state troopers had documented this behavior for another few months, they secured a court order to place a wiretap on the six phones. "It takes a lot to get a court order to tap one pay phone," Long says wearily, "let alone six of them." Finally, the taps were in place. "The day we got the court order, *the day we got the order*," Long says, "they stop showing up."

Someone told Whitey, but who? *The Boston Globe's* Kevin Cullen has advanced the theory that Whitey Bulger has avoided prosecution by serving as an informer for the FBI and cultivating the friendship of John Connally, a now-retired FBI special agent on organized crime who had previously racked up Jerry Angiulo. Bill McMullin, a spokesman for the FBI's Boston office, refused to comment, as a matter of bureau policy, on the allegation but did point out that, under the law, "informers are subject to prosecution like anyone else." And if the charge is true, that doesn't explain why other law-enforcement operations should have been compromised or why other mobsters haven't taken exception to Whitey's FBI involvement. Some people have suggested that the state police inadvertently selected a monitoring specialist with ties to the Patriarca crime family in Providence, who let Whitey know. Or maybe—although there is no evidence of this—Billy Bulger, who knows everything, let his brother in on the secret.

Or maybe the world is not as separated as we'd like to think. Maybe good and evil don't necessarily live in different neighborhoods. Maybe they come from the same family, grow up together, stay in touch, like each other. And maybe they are so intermingled that one can never drive the other out.

Woven through the Bulger story are a number of fringe players who, likewise, have brothers who took a different path—the mobster whose brother is a policeman, the Whitey associate whose brother worked on Michael Dukakis's presidential campaign. Such ancient, unfathomable loyalties hold Boston together, even as other ancient, unfathomable hatreds pull it apart. Either way, the struggle occurs on a far more fundamental level than conventional morality can ever reach. As Whitey himself said, "We're all good guys here." The first thing people say about Boston is all you need to know: It's a very small town. We're all brothers here.

from Tin for Sale

by John Manca and
Vincent Cosgrove

John Manca's family had strong mob connections—his grandfather worked for Lucky Luciano. John in 1954 joined the NYPD, where for nine years he behaved more like a mobster than a policeman. Vincent Cosgrove helped write Manca's 1991 memoir.

took the subway to the station house the first day, wore my uniform. I liked the way people looked at me when I got on the train. It made me feel special. Going to work that day was like a new beginning. I told myself everything that'd gone before—the way I was screwing around with women, some of the crazy stuff I was doing out of boredom—was over and done with and I had a clean slate. I wasn't going to mess up a good thing.

"My first beat was through wiseguy city. You couldn't walk half a block and not pass a place that wasn't somehow connected. It was probably one of the few parts of the city—with the exception of a couple army bases—where you never needed a cop. Who would be stupid enough to rob a joint belonging to a wiseguy?

"I was a very happy cop walking my beat that first day. Then the sergeant drove up and warned me off the card game. I spent the rest of my tour wondering about that. A card game didn't bother me. If I'd found out about it on my own, I wasn't going to bust it. A card game was no big deal. But getting paid off to ignore it was something else. I didn't want to be put into a position where some wiseguy was pushing money in my face. Three hours into the job and already I was dealing with corruption.

"I tried to forget about it. I went back to the station house. I loved the action in the place, and it seemed like there was always something going on. I didn't feel like heading home right away—even though I had a wife and a kid and I kept telling myself I'd turned over a new leaf. But I was too jagged-up to go home—hell, I'd just walked my first beat.

"I ran smack into the sergeant. He took me aside. 'Kid, I know this was your first day, but you're gonna have to learn sooner or later that life in the street ain't like life in the academy.' Now I didn't like being treated like some rookie, even though that's exactly what I was. I could feel myself getting mad—just like I had at the railroad cop who was going to report me when I was working the Long Island Rail Road job. But I kept my mouth shut this time. 'There are certain facts of life up here—and you can do a few things with them. You can accept them, which in my opinion is the smartest move you can make. You can turn your back on them and just let bygones be bygones. That's okay, but not smart for you in the long run. Or you can do something else, which would be very dumb—and dangerous. Nobody likes a cop who rocks the boat.' He gave me a big smile and walked away.

"So much for a clean slate. I couldn't get to sleep that night. I didn't want to take money. Christ, I could have taken a job with Joe Aiello or one of my grandfather's other wiseguy pals if I'd wanted to go that way. But I wasn't about to blow the whistle on anybody. A rat I wasn't. So I made up my mind to look the other way. Next day I'm on the beat and there's Joe Aiello and he welcomes me to the neighborhood with a big handshake and the promise he'll spread the word with his goombahs that I was an all-right guy.

"What the hell was I going to tell Joe? He'd been my father's business partner for years, even though that had ended when my father decided to open a liquor store up on Vermilyea Avenue. They were still friends. I'd known him since I was a kid. He'd given me my first base-ball glove.

"So far the only police activity I was involved in was writing out summonses for illegally parked cars. I didn't even give out any moving violations. The only actual illegal activity I saw was on hot days when the kids would open up the hydrants to cool off—and I wasn't about to bust chops over that. Sometimes I'd play stickball with them. I'd use my nightstick for a bat. I got a kick out of it and I figured it was good for community relations. But forget being a crimebuster. Not on that beat.

"A few weeks passed after my meeting with Joe Aiello. One morning Louie Peels comes up to me. I hadn't seen him since the night Dominick Vats shot the telephone in the candy store. He's very friendly; acts like it's only been a few weeks. He asks me if I like demi-tasse. Sure, I tell him. So he invites me to have a cup in the social club down the block. Why not? Where's the harm?

"It was a sunny day out, and when I walked into the social club I couldn't see anything, it was that dark inside—like going into a movie theater. Everyone seemed to be whispering, like they were in church. The air was cool, too, even though there was no air conditioning. A few guys were sitting around a table playing cards. An old man was reading *Il Progresso*. When he saw us come in, he went over to a long table with an espresso machine and poured two cups. He handed them to Louie, and we walked to the back and sat down on some folding chairs. I remember thinking how uncomfortable the chairs were. There was a back room and there were some guys in there but we didn't go inside. I learned later that all these places had a room like that and that was where the wiseguys conducted their serious business. All the years I was a cop, I never got into those back rooms.

"We had a nowhere conversation that started with him mentioning Joe Aiello and what a great guy he was. I told him how it was I knew Joe, and he acted like he thought that was real interesting. We talked a little about the neighborhood—he used to live there but now he lived in Queens. I finished my coffee and that was it. I told him I had to get back to my beat, and he said sure, but first there's something Joe Aiello wanted you to have. He went into the back room.

"I stood there thinking this is it, he's going to give you some money, and then what are you going to do? Make a scene in a social club filled with wiseguys? I thought about just walking out, but that would be an insult. So I stayed where I was.

"Louie comes out with a long, narrow box—the kind that ties come in from the department stores. He gives it to me and says this is from Joe, Joe wanted you to have this. Open it up. I do—and it's a tie, a silk tie with a very nice design on it. So what do I do now? Make a stink over a tie? I put the tie back in the box and ask him to thank Joe the next time he sees him. Louie Peels nods like I've said the right thing and takes me to the door. I spend the rest of my beat with the box in my hand wondering what the hell that was all about."

It didn't take John long to find out. A few days later, Louie Peels stopped him in front of the building with the card game. Louie invited him in.

"I told him I didn't think that was a good idea. He said there was nothing going on, the game hadn't started and no one was around. He wanted to talk to me. So I went in.

"The card game was played in a three-room apartment on the ground floor. Louie went into the kitchen and brought out a milk bottle filled with homemade red wine. We sat down and he poured two glasses. I took a sip, but I wasn't about to have any more. Not while I was on duty. That's how square I was.

"Louie suddenly reaches into his jacket, takes out two twenties, and puts them on a table next to my glass. 'Joe asked me to give this to you. He's sorry he didn't get a chance to see you the other day.' I stared at the money. Finally, I said I couldn't take it. Louie looked surprised. 'What'll I tell Joe?' he asked. 'Tell him I appreciate the offer but it's not necessary.'

"Louie can't understand this. 'Just take it, Johnny. You don't want it for yourself, put it in the poorbox. But you should take it. It don't look right otherwise.' I thanked him again and walked out. The money was still on the table.

"I called my old friend Kenny. I couldn't think of anyone else to go to for advice. I wanted to know how to handle this.

"We went to the same bar where we'd first talked, only this time it wasn't so crowded and there weren't too many women in it. By then lots of people had TVs of their own. Kenny and I took a booth and I told him about Joe Aiello and Louie Peels. He listened to everything I had to say. When I was finished he said, 'You got no problem, kid— you think you got one but you don't.'

"I'd known Kenny for a long time, and we'd gotten to be pretty close over the years. I never heard him once say anything about being a cop on the take. So I figured when he said I had no problem he was going to tell me to turn the money down—or even report it to the shooflies in Internal Affairs. I was dead wrong.

"Kenny told me to take it and be grateful I had the chance to make some money on the side. He asked me how much I made a week. I told him eighty-five dollars. 'How much you think those guinea thugs take home a week?' Kenny said, then he realized he was talking to an Italian and he apologized. 'Nothing personal, kid. There are Irish and micks and there are Italians and guineas. You know what I mean. Why shouldn't you take their money? It isn't from drugs, right?' I told him it wasn't, it was strictly from gambling. 'Then you got no problem. Take it. Everybody else does.'

"That was one of the great rationalizations of all time in the police department. If the payoff came from numbers or hookers it was clean and you could take it. If it was drug money it was dirty. I used that excuse for almost ten years—that it was clean money. The only problem is you got to buy the idea that the mob keeps all these separate piles of money—here's one from gambling and over there's one from drugs, and they only pay off cops from the gambling pile. Pure bullshit, but I believed it. It made taking the dough a lot easier. But I knew guys on the job who took lots of drug money with no problems. They'd say, 'Who's it hurting? Niggers and spics. Animals. Who cares?' And they'd take early retirement and move to Florida and buy real estate. When you want to, you can find an excuse to do anything.

"The night I saw Kenny he offered to take me around to some places in the precinct—places he knew I could score. I couldn't believe it. I had Kenny pegged as an upstanding guy—and in his own way he was. I told him I couldn't do it—maybe some other night real soon.

"I went home and tried to sleep. Couldn't. It'd be nice to say it was strictly because I was against taking money. I was, but I kept thinking about some of the things Kenny said, and I began to feel like a sucker. Part of me wanted the money. Part of me didn't. A few times over the next couple days I picked up the phone but I didn't call Kenny. Two weeks went by. I worked the night tour. First few nights everything was quiet. That changed."

One night John was on patrol when he came upon an argument in front of an Italian restaurant. It was the kind of mom-and-pop operation that served good food at reasonable prices and attracted a loyal clientele. John had peeked in once or twice, and the restaurant reminded him a bit of OK Tom's. A nice family place.

Only what was going on in front of the restaurant was nothing you'd want a family to see. A young wiseguy from the neighborhood was in a rage, screaming into the face of a smaller, middle-aged man. Off to the side stood the middle-aged man's wife. Both she and her husband were clearly frightened.

"The wiseguy was a punk named Vito. His uncle was a soldier in the Lucchese family. Vito was a flashy dresser, one of those guys still wet behind the ears who always seemed to have a smirk on his face. He had a rep for being a bully. He figured no one would touch him because of his uncle's connections.

"What had happened was Vito had double-parked outside the restaurant and gone in to eat. This older couple came out and found that their car was blocked. The husband beeped his horn to get Vito to move his car. That was all Vito needed to start a fight. He was really cursing at the guy, throwing out a lot of 'cocksuckers' and 'motherfuckers.' The husband didn't know what to do.

"That was when I came along. I got between them and managed to find out what was going on. I told Vito to back off. He told me to go fuck myself. I grabbed him and threw him up against his car. He took a swing at me, but it just glanced off my shoulder. I shoved the end of my nightstick into his gut and he doubled over.

"I reached into his jacket and got his keys and gave them to the husband so he could move Vito's car out of the way. As he's doing that, Vito gets his breath back and looks up at me. 'You made a *big* mistake, pal,' he says. 'You don't want to mess with me.'

"That was all I had to hear. I picked him up by the lapels and told him I was putting him under arrest for striking a police officer. He couldn't believe it. He starts in with the cursing and the threats. By this time, the couple are in their car and I wave them away. Then the patrol car from the precinct showed up.

"The two cops who got out were old-timers, real veterans. They knew everybody in the neighborhood—at least everybody who could make them some money. Right away they recognized Vito. As soon as they figured out I'm taking him in, one of them pulled me aside. 'Look, kid,' he said, 'this wop bastard's got a couple of hundred on him. What say we take that and forget the whole thing?'

" 'He's my collar,' I said.

" 'What are you? Some kind of crusader? It don't pay to be a hard-on.' "

John brought Vito to the station house, booked him, and put him in the holding pen until he could bring him down to the Foley Square courthouse for arraignment. Less than an hour later, John got a phone call. It was his father. He wanted to meet John right away.

"I had a pretty good idea what was going on. I told my old man to go down to Criminal Court. By the time I got there, he was sitting outside the arraignment part with Joe Aiello. I knew what was coming, and I remember thinking how it gave new meaning to the term 'criminal justice system.'

"Joe was an old friend of Vito's uncle. The kid's lawyer had called the uncle, and the uncle called Joe because he recognized my last name and knew that my old man and Joe were pals. Joe got up as soon as I sat down and said he had to make a call. He just wanted to leave me alone with my father.

"My father asked me to drop the charges against Vito as a favor to Joe. I told him I couldn't do that. My father asked me to do it for him. I told him I wasn't part of this bullshit. My father looked me straight in the eye, something he didn't do too often. 'You gotta understand, Johnny—we're all part of this bullshit.'

"Joe came back. I thought about how he had helped my old man after my grandfather kicked us out. I figured if I did this one thing, Joe and I would be even. When Joe heard I'd drop the charges he said he always knew I'd do the right thing. Then he went to look for Vito's lawyer.

"At the arraignment, the judge asked me if I'd be satisfied with an apology from the defendant. I said sure, wondering how much the judge had gotten. Vito turned my way and mumbled something. Case closed."

Outside the courthouse, Joe Aiello sat in his car and waited for John to come out. He called John over and tried to press a wad of cash into John's hand. John refused to take the money. He told Joe he'd done what he'd done out of friendship. He even declined Joe's offer to drive him home. He took the subway.

The longer he was on the job, the more corruption he saw. One morning he came upon two young guys unloading crates of liquor from a truck. He asked for a bill of lading. One of the guys offered him two bottles of Chivas Regal instead. When John indicated that they were breaking the law, the guy mentioned the name of two cops in the precinct. John knew better by this time to even bother checking with the cops. He resumed patrol.

He already felt compromised. The moment he ignored the card game he'd failed to do his duty, at least as it was taught at the academy. But this was real life, and cops were making good money on the side for doing what he was doing: looking the other way. He just wasn't on the take.

One night John went to see *On the Waterfront*, a movie everybody was talking about. He found himself identifying with Marlon Brando's Terry Malloy, the washed-up fighter torn between his loyalty to the code of the dockworkers and his growing realization that bosses like Johnny Friendly were exploiting the men. Brando in the end decides to tell prosecutors what he knows about corruption on the docks. John understood Brando's plight—but he didn't agree with his solution.

"You know what would happen to him in real life? He'd disappear, never be heard from him again. By the time I saw the picture I was leaning toward Georgie's viewpoint: why the hell not go on the take? You'd have to be nuts to pass the money up. I wanted to buy a house for me and my wife and daughter—and I wanted to have more kids. It'd take years just to save for a down payment on what I was making. So I decided I'd do what I had to do. I called Kenny.

"He didn't sound surprised to hear from me. We made plans to meet later that night in a bar near the station house. I wasn't wearing my uniform. Kenny's already there, nursing a scotch. Kenny introduces me to a little guy sitting next to him, a bookie named Sallie Bones. Sallie buys us a round. Kenny tells Sallie that I'm new to the precinct and I'm a good guy. Sallie makes a few comments, then says he's got to get going. He leaves two tens on the bar—one for me and one for Kenny. It was that easy.

"Kenny and I hit about six bars that night. Kenny told me to always have a stamped, self-addressed envelope when I was on the job. That way if I made some money on the side, I could stick it in the envelope and drop it in the nearest mailbox. If any bastards from Internal Affairs were to stop me, I wouldn't have any money on me to incriminate myself.

"When I got home I went into the kitchen and dropped the money on the table. There was eighty bucks there, all wadded up. I began to smooth out the bills just like my mother used to do with the money she made me turn over to her from my job delivering groceries. Then I looked under the sink and found an empty coffee tin. I stuck the money in the tin and put it in the back of my bedroom closet.

"That night I had trouble sleeping. Not from guilt, but from the adrenaline rush of getting all that money. I felt like a schmuck for waiting all that time.

"The next morning I was on the beat and a guy comes up to me, says he's a friend of Louie Peels. He runs a game nearby. Turns out to be the same building the sergeant had warned me off of my first day on the job. He makes small talk, then says he's got to get going and sticks out his hand to shake. What the hell? I shake his hand and he slips me a bill. He tells me he'll see me around and he takes off. I stood there like a kid with is hand caught in the cookie jar. This was different from the night before, because now I was in uniform. I felt like everyone on the block was looking out their windows at me. Of course, nobody was. I kept holding the money, not even looking at it, crumpling it up in my hand. No turning back now, I told myself, and I stuck the money in my pocket.

"At lunch I finally took it out. Ten bucks. Now I knew what a handshake with a wiseguy was worth on my beat. And I didn't feel bad at all. I went into a candy store and bought some envelopes and stamps. I put the money in an envelope and mailed it to my apartment. I remember thinking about *On the Waterfront* and what a sucker Brando was."

from Mobfather

by George Anastasia

Tommy DelGiorno—Tommy Del to his friends—was a good earner for Philly mobster Nicky Scarfo. Then Tommy got sloppy, which was bad news for Tommy and his two young sons, Tommy Jr. and Bobby. Reporter George Anastasia covers the mob for the Philadelphia Inquirer; *his book about the DelGiorno family was published in 1993.*

Nicky Scarfo was a mob boss for the 1980s: bold, brash and full of avarice. In the short term, this made him a very rich man. In the long term, it brought down his organization. While Angelo Bruno at least had paid lip service to the time-honored concepts of respect and loyalty, Scarfo ruled through fear and intimidation. There were no sitdowns with the mob boss to iron out disputes or clear up misunderstandings. Greedy and treacherous, Scarfo wanted it all. And he wanted it now. His was a slash-and-burn philosophy, not unlike the approach of the pinstriped outlaws who were ransacking Wall Street at this same time. It was more Attila the Hun than Machiavelli.

"When you get involved with him, you know . . . you take the good and take the bad," Tommy Del would say. "The good is you can run around a lot and have everybody in your circle afraid of you because you got him behind you. The bad is, once in a while you got to do him a favor."

Usually the favor involved whacking somebody. But on a few occasions Scarfo went for the money instead of the blood. This was the case when he heard that a group of drug-dealing loan sharks from Northeast Philadelphia were using his name as leverage to collect debts from their customers. Since Scarfo had nothing to do with their operation, he figured he was entitled to a fee—a commission, so to speak—for being a part of their merchandising campaign.

He sent a local bookie named Sparky to collect.

The scam was ingenious in its simplicity. Sparky asked to borrow $250,000, telling the loan sharks it was for a drug deal he was putting together. The guys from the Northeast, as Scarfo knew they would, called down to South Philadelphia to see if anyone in the organization would vouch for the bookie. Several members did. Sparky got his cash and began to make his weekly payments. The interest alone was several thousand dollars a week. But after three or four weeks, on Scarfo's orders, Sparky stopped paying. The guys from the Northeast, as Scarfo knew they would, called downtown again to ask those who had vouched for Sparky to straighten out the problem.

"They were told to forget about their money," an informant said later. "Scarfo had it and that was it. They were told to just be thankful they weren't dead. What were they gonna do?"

On another occasion, Ralph Staino, a member of DelGiorno's crew, stole one hundred gallons of P-2-P from a drug dealer who was paying the mob's street tax. Staino had found out that the dealer had the chemical contraband—a key ingredient in the manufacture of methamphetamine—stashed in an apartment in Germany, and he sent someone over to grab it. If the laws of the underworld were being strictly applied, Staino should have been ordered to return the P-2-P. And if he had refused, he should have been killed. Protection from rip-offs was what the street tax was supposed to be buying, particularly protection from members of the organization collecting the tax.

But Tommy Del, knowing Scarfo's lust for money, decided to look the other way. Instead of solving the drug dealer's problem, he manuevered his way into the scam, threatening to kill Staino unless he turned the P-2-P over to him. He then told Scarfo he had come up with a deal that would earn them two million dollars. Scarfo didn't want to know the details. He just asked when he'd see the money. Staino had already gotten fifty gallons of the stolen P-2-P into the country. At the going rate of twenty thousand dollars a gallon, that netted the organization a million dollars. Tommy's cut was two hundred thousand. Scarfo got five hundred thousand. The rest of the money went to several other mobsters involved in the transaction. The chance for another million was lost, however, when customs agents confiscated the second fifty-gallon shipment as a Staino associate tried to smuggle it into the United States.

Scarfo reacted in typical fashion. Instead of being satisfied with his first cut, he berated DelGiorno for losing his second half-million dollars.

Greed and arrogance had turned the diminutive mobster into an underworld despot who enjoyed belittling and mocking anyone he considered weak or ineffective. It was another way to flex his muscle, to show he was boss. Little Nicky had waited a long time for the power and wealth. And he wanted everyone to know that he had arrived. His house in Fort Lauderdale became a meeting place during the winter and spring for members and associates of the mob and also for New York Mafia figures who were in the Florida area. Early in January he would hold a New Year's celebration there, a catered affair not unlike the Christmas parties that were now annual events at La Cucina. And while Bobby and Tommy junior never made it to Fort Lauderdale, their father was a frequent visitor.

Ownership of the home was another one of Scarfo's scams. For tax purposes he had to show how he could afford to live in the six-hundred-thousand-dollar waterfront hacienda. So he had his lawyer set up a corporation, Casablanca South Leasing, Inc., and, for three thousand dollars each, several of his associates bought into a time-sharing plan that, on paper at least, entitled them to spend several weeks living in the home each year.

One of those buying into the plan, DelGiorno told investigators, was a popular Philadelphia disc jockey, Jerry Blavat. Blavat had been a longtime friend of Philadelphia mob figures, dating back to his days as a sometime driver for Angelo Bruno. Known as the "Geater with the Heater," he also owned a nightclub in Margate, New Jersey, near Atlantic City, where Scarfo and the others often stopped for drinks or a meal. Blavat ran legitimate businesses and, his lawyer maintained, was never anything more than a friend to Scarfo and the others. There is evidence to the contrary. Whether he took full advantage of his time-sharing, however, is something Tommy Del thought unlikely.

"One weekend we went down there," Tommy Del told New Jersey investigators. "It was on a Sunday and we were all in the house and Spiker [mob associate Anthony Gregorio] or one of them was making spaghetti and meatballs and [Scarfo] said that Blavat was coming. . . . Blavat came into the place around ten o'clock or something, 10:30 that morning . . . He came in, said hello to everybody. He went over. He went and sat down with Scarfo for a little bit talking to him. He went and he ate a meatball sandwich, came back to the table and said goodbye. And so when he was leaving, I said to Nicky, 'Where's he goin'?' He said, 'Back to Philly.' So I said, 'Wait a minute. You mean to tell me this guy flew to Florida to eat a meatball sandwich?'

"[Scarfo] said, 'No, no, no. He comes here because he's one of the guys that leases the house and he thinks that because he shows up that the surveillance will pick him up and if they ever ask him if he's really leasing he could say yeah.' "

Scarfo's role as lord of his Fort Lauderdale manor and gracious host of mob meetings and "confabs" there belied a current of unrest within the organization. In rapid succession, and for reasons that appeared based more in his own paranoia than in reality, the mob boss turned first on his old friend Salvatore Merlino and then on DelGiorno.

Merlino and his brother Lawrence, then a capo in the organization, were "taken down" at a meeting in March of 1986. Both men were reduced to the rank of soldier and lost all their authority within the organization. Salvatore Merlino, Scarfo said, had become a drunk and an embarrassment. In fact, one month earlier he had begun serving a four-year prison sentence after being convicted of trying to bribe a police officer who stopped him for drunken driving. Lawrence Merlino, more a contractor than a gangster, fell out of favor simply because he was Salvatore's brother. At a raucous mob meeting at a private room in a Sea Isle City, New Jersey, restaurant, Scarfo denounced both Merlino brothers, threatening to kill them and their families unless they shaped up. He then promoted his nephew, Phil Leonetti, to underboss, and elevated Tommy Del and Faffy Iannarella from acting capos to capos. With Salvatore Merlino away in jail and with Scarfo and Leonetti operating primarily in Atlantic City, DelGiorno and Iannarella became the top mob figures in South Philadelphia.

Whether it was pressure from the added responsibility or simply the constant fear brought on by the double-dealing and treachery that had become the trademarks of the organization, Tommy Del began to spend more and more time looking at life through the bottom of a bottle of booze. And when he drank, he often became nasty and belligerent.

"My brother and my father never really got along," Bobby said. "They were always arguing. My brother never really liked what he did. He used to tell me I was crazy for wanting that kind of life. My brother, he just wanted a job and to be left alone. One night me and my brother were out drinking with a couple of his friends and we ended up at my father's bar, the J&M. My father and a few of his friends came in, all drunked up. My father tends to talk too much when he gets drunk, you know. He aggravates and gets on your nerves. It was Nicky Whip [mob solider Nicholas Milano], little Joey Merlino, my father and Faffy. They had been out drinking. My father calls my brother over and then he turns and puts his arm around Nicky Whip. Then he said to Tommy, 'This is a real son. This is what you call a real son.' My brother really felt bad. He just gave my father a dirty look and walked away. I thought he was ready to cry. I think he wanted to kill my father, that's how mad he was.

"My father really took his friends first . . . He treated them first.

Nicky Whip was young, in his twenties. He was a gangster. A killer. He's treatin' him better than he is his own son.

"The next day, my brother wouldn't go over my father's. But my father, he acted like nothing had happened. That's the way he was. If something happened, the next day he just forgot about it. He thought money or things would make it up. . . . He always took the side of his business partners over his family. One time I got in a fight and he took the other kid's side before he even heard my story because the kid's father worked for him. I didn't go over to his house for, like, three weeks. When I finally did go over there, I sit down in the kitchen. My brother was there too, watching a ball game or something. My father was sittin' on the other side of the table and before I even got to say anything, my father reached in his pocket, grabbed a hundred-dollar bill, crumbled it up and threw it at me. He says, 'This is what you came for, ain't it?' I wanted to kill him. He made me feel so small. Like I was just after money. I had come to apologize, to make up. But he just had that way about him, like everybody was after his money, like he was somebody because he had all this money.

"So I got up and I said, 'I don't want your fuckin' money.' And I threw the hundred-dollar bill back in his face. I said, 'Stick your money up your God damn ass.' And I ran out the door. He sent my brother to run after me, saying he was only kidding around. I didn't think that was very funny at all.

"That's cold, you know. When it gets down to all you could think about is money. And I was gettin' that way, too, toward the end. He had me so brainwashed, I was startin' to think like him. . . . I just wanted to do everything he did and be just like him. . . . His money and his friends always came first. And he always would make an excuse. He'd say, 'I gotta make a livin', don't I?' "

Tommy Del's world began to unravel in the summer of 1986, even as his wealth continued to grow. The stolen P-2-P deal was causing problems for the organization. A partner of the drug dealer who was ripped off was threatening to go to war with the mob over the two million dollars he lost. Scarfo didn't like that kind of aggravation.

And another scam, involving a corrupt Philadelphia city councilman and an attempt to extort one million dollars from a developer, blew up when the developer ran to the FBI. This was a deal involving a Delaware River waterfront project called Penns Landing, which the city had been trying, for years, to get off the drawing board. Finally, in 1986, a company had been selected to begin the first, seventy-million-dollar phase of the project. Using their ties to the corrupt city councilman as leverage, the Scarfo organization tried to shake a million dollars out of the deal by threatening to tie up two key pieces of legislation needed before the project could move forward.

But Nicky Crow Caramandi, the point man in the extortion plot, got picked up trying to extort an FBI undercover agent posing as the developer's project manager. The city councilman, his legislative aide and Caramandi were all indicted. Scarfo, who had approved the scam, began to worry. DelGiorno, who was supposed to be supervising Caramandi, worried even more.

That summer, the New Jersey State Police tapes coming from the wiretap and electronic bug in the Ocean City condo contained more and more outrageous, drunken monologues from Tommy Del, who would rant and rave about the organization and the people who ran it. On one tape, which later made its way into newspaper reports, DelGiorno belittled Scarfo and Leonetti and the rest of the mob leadership. "They're all pussies," he said. "Four Irish guys from Northeast Philly could run the mob better."

Several mob soldiers in DelGiorno's crew began to complain about him to Scarfo and Leonetti, claiming he was often drunk and irrational and that he berated them for no reason. "He would get drunk and make a list up," Leonetti said later. "[Telling his soldiers] that I'm going to kill you. I'm going to kill you. He'd say, 'Remind me tomorrow, I'm going to kill all you guys.' Real sloppy."

Tommy DelGiorno had become a problem. Nicky Scarfo decided to deal with him in typical fashion. In July, in the midst of the investigation into the extortion plot and with the drug dealer still issuing threats, Scarfo sent word to DelGiorno that he was "taken down," reduced to the rank of soldier. He would now report to Iannarella. Even more ominous from Tommy Del's perspective was Scarfo's decision not to divvy up earnings from the bookmaking operation that he, DelGiorno and Joey Pungitore shared. Usually they split the profits every three or four months. In August, they had more than three hundred thousand dollars sitting in their kitty. But when asked, Scarfo said to let the cash sit for a while.

DelGiorno saw that as an obvious indication that he might not be around much longer.

"That was much too much money to keep up," Tommy Del subsequently told a jury. "So I had suggested that we split some of it. And Scarfo said, 'Nah, let's hold it up.' Knowing him, he would never leave that kind of money up when it wasn't necessary. That gave me a hint.

"See, he figured wait a couple more months and I would be dead, then he'd only have to split it two ways," Tommy explained. "I know the way this guy thinks, how he operates . . . I had seen guys who he had killed and I knew the way it was done."

It was Scarfo's greed that tipped Tommy off. On the surface, the tyrannical little mob boss was telling Tommy to straighten out, to cut out the drinking and carousing and to reestablish himself within the organization. But in reality, DelGiorno knew Scarfo had already decided to kill him. It was just a matter of time. His demotion was permanent and, if Scarfo had his way, it would be terminal.

Tommy Dell also began to notice that guys he bet with were holding back. "Everybody stopped paying, you know. You don't do that unless you are a guy who is going to get killed." DelGiorno had been on the other end of the gun often enough to read the signs. Clearly he had a problem. Late that summer the situation intensified when two detectives from the New Jersey State Police paid a visit to his South Philadelphia home. Their message was short and to the point. They said they couldn't tell him how they knew, but it was their obligation to warn him that there was a murder contract out on his life. The contract, they said, came from his boss, Nicky Scarfo.

Tommy Del played dumb to the detectives, but the visit shook him up. He thought about running away, just taking as much of his cash as he could get his hands on and leaving the city. But he hesitated. Then he toyed with the idea of firing first, of taking out Scarfo. Through what remained of that summer and into the early fall—even while he showered money, presents and jobs on his two sons—Tommy Del lived on the edge. Now, like Johnny Calabrese and Salvie Testa before him, he was the one looking over his shoulder. He was the guy who ducked meetings and never followed the same routine. He was the hunted.

Bobby picked up on the problem shortly after he started working full-time for his father. One night early in the fall of 1986 he was out drinking in a club on South Street with some friends. South Street was a trendy strip of funky boutiques, restaurants, bars and after-hours clubs where people partied every night. Most of the younger members and associates of the Scarfo crime family frequented the area. While standing at the bar, Bobby spotted the son of another mob figure and offered to buy him a drink. The kid brushed him off, first ignoring him and then telling him, "I already got a drink."

"The guy treated me like trash," Bobby said. "So the next day I go over to my father's house and tell him what happened. My father tells me he's having some problems with his business partners, that he got 'taken down' by his boss. And he told me to stay away from his friends' sons, not to trust any of them."

Tommy Del said nothing about a murder contract, but Bobby knew he was worried.

Sunday morning, November 2, 1986, as a steady rain fell on Broad Street, two men in trench coats knocked on Tommy Del's door. It was 9:30 a.m. DelGiorno recognized the two as the New Jersey State Police detectives who had visited him in August, Sergeant Ed Johnson, who was spearheading an organized crime investigation into the Scarfo family, told him they were there to talk again about the plot to kill him. This time Tommy said he wanted some proof. Johnson pulled two cassette tapes out of the pocket of his coat.

"I'm here to play these tapes," he said.

Tommy Del was stunned. For a few seconds he didn't say anything. Then, recovering, he asked two questions. Where were the tapes from and whose voices were on them.

Johnson was short and to the point. The tapes were made in Ocean City, New Jersey, he said. One was Tommy Del's own voice. The other was an interesting conversation between Faffy Iannarella and Sal Grande, the ruthless young hit man who two years earlier had killed Salvie Testa.

Tommy Del invited the two detectives in. He was clearly agitated. Nervous. He told them to hurry up. He wanted to hear the tapes, but he said he was expecting some people over the house in a little while. Johnson, taking charge of the situation, said it wasn't a good time or place. He said they'd need at least an hour. He then suggested that they meet later in the day in a hotel out by Philadelphia International Airport. Tommy Del agreed. Johnson said he would call when everything was set up.

From Broad Street, Johnson and Detective Charlie Crescenz, another member of the Organized Crime Intelligence Bureau, drove out to the airport and booked Room 308 at the Marriott Hotel. The room was nothing fancy. There was a bed, a television and a sitting area—two chairs and a small couch around a coffee table. Johnson set a cassette player on the table, telephoned DelGiorno and then started a pot of coffee. Tommy Del arrived about fifteen minutes later. He had regained his composure and was once again the South Philly tough guy.

"I'm not interested in cooperating," he said.

Johnson said that wasn't the purpose of their visit.

"We just want to inform you of the grave situation you're in with your boss," the detective said.

DelGiorno took a seat on the couch and Crescenz handed him a cup of coffee. Johnson picked out the first tape, a short conversation made on August 16 in a condo rented by Sal Grande in the same complex in Ocean City. The state police had a bug in Grande's place all summer long.

Tommy Del listened intently, leaning forward so as not to miss a word. Grande and Iannarella were discussing the fact that DelGiorno had been "taken down" by Scarfo. Iannarella wondered about Tommy's fate. Then DelGiorno heard Grande's response. The phrase seemed to hang in the air of the hotel room. Tommy could almost see the smirk on the young hit man's face.

"Ain't nothin' gonna happen to him . . . yet," Grande said.

Johnson just looked at DelGiorno. Then he removed the tape and put the second one in the cassette player. Now DelGiorno heard himself talking about Scarfo, Leonetti and the rest of the mob. His words were somewhat slurred. He was obviously drunk. Tommy listened for ten minutes, then told Johnson to turn off the tape.

"You don't have to play anymore," he said. "I remember it vividly . . . I remember the day."

But Johnson was taking no chances. He reminded Tommy Del what else he had said on that tape.

"Do you remember the remainder of the day you were drinking and you started to get very loose-lipped," Johnson said. "You identified yourself as a superior in this organization, and then you went on to identify a number of other people."

"Yeah, I remember," Tommy Del said as he reached under the sweater he was wearing and began to massage his chest with his right hand.

"Now your predicament," Johnson continued, "is that tomorrow New Jersey is going to indict you, Scarfo, and the others. And eventually, this tape is going to be turned over to the defense attorneys in the case and their clients, the guys you were belittling, will hear it all."

The meeting at the Marriott lasted for two hours. The state police had built a major gambling and loan-sharking case against DelGiorno, Scarfo, and fifteen other members of the organization based largely on some eight-hundred hours of conversations recorded over two summers in Ocean City. Already in trouble for the drug heist and the Penns Landing waterfront extortion, DelGiorno knew that the New Jersey indictment would seal his fate.

The next day, DelGiorno, Scarfo and the others were arrested. Word of the secret state police tapes surfaced, and DelGiorno moved to the top of Scarfo's hit list.

"Everybody got rounded up," Bobby said. "Nicky Scarfo and Philip Leonetti were arrested in Jersey and the others, my father, Faffy, all of them, were picked up in Philly. So I had to go bail my father out. The bail was set at $250,000, so we had to come up with $25,000 in cash— 10 percent—to bail him out. My father had money hidden in the ceiling of his house. I go over and Roe goes downstairs and in the ceiling is all this money. She takes it out and counts out what she needs.

"So I drive my stepmother over to bail my father out. We waited, we musta waited about two hours because all these people, whoever was bailing Faffy, Grande, Joey Pung out, they all brought cash and the cops had to count it all out three or four times. It was all in twenties and tens and fifties. It took a long time. But they all got bailed out.

"That night, after my father is home, I drive back to Gladstone Street in my father's car. I used to take it for him, clean it, get it washed. It's one of the things he had me doing when I started working for him. The next day I was gonna take it to the car wash, shine it all up and bring it back to him.

"So the next day, it musta been ten o'clock, ten-thirty in the morning. I'm taking the car back. I pull around the corner at Broad Street and I look over to my left and there's this car with three guys in it, just waiting there. I couldn't see who they were. They all had hats on. They were just sittin' there. It was a Lincoln Towncar. So I'm driving down Broad Street and here this car starts following me.

"As I pull in front of my father's house, I jumped out and I looked and there was Tory Scafidi [mob soldier Salvatore Scafidi] in the passenger side. He tried to turn his head, but I seen him. So, he like, waved to me as the car went past. The other two guys had hats on and the one in the back slouched down and I really couldn't tell who it was. It mighta been The Whip [Nicky Milano]. I'm not sure. . . . So I was wondering why they didn't stop."

Bobby went into the house and told his father what had happened.

Tommy Del, sitting at the kitchen table drinking a cup of coffee, went cold with rage.

"Those motherfuckers," he said. "They want to fuck with me."

"What's the matter?" Bobby asked.

"You were driving my car?" Tommy Del said, ignoring Bobby's question and telling him to again recount, in detail, what had happened.

"Yeah," Bobby said. "Remember. I took it home last night."

Tommy Del sat quietly for a few minutes, staring at his coffee cup. Then, in a voice laced with both fear and anger, he told Bobby, "I think they were gonna kill me. But then they seen that it was you, so they just drove by."

"Then he started talking," Bobby said. "For the first time, I heard him talkin' serious. It was him talkin'. It wasn't this mob guy that he was, or that he thought he was. It was him as a person. He don't have his army no more. He's all by himself. He's got nobody to turn to. . . . He said, 'They're gonna kill me. It's all bullshit. The boss thinks I drink too much. The only reason is, he [Scarfo] wants to make more money by cuttin' me out.'

"Now he's talking to me," said Bobby "asking me for advice. He never, ever, asked me for advice. I'm sittin' there confused. He says, 'I have two options. I can go and try and kill Nicky [Scarfo], but that would be crazy . . . or I could turn informant.' But he says that that's just something he's thinking about and he tells me not to tell anybody.

"Then he tells me he's got a couple hundred thousand put away and he says we could start over. And he asks me whether me and Tommy would go into the witness program if he became an informant. I said, 'Dad, I don't know.' And he says, 'But Bob, they're gonna kill me.'

"I felt bad. I was confused. I shoulda said no right from the beginning. Here's a guy, all my life, he thought he was a king. He was on top of the world. He thought it would never end . . . I never seen him nervous like that. Scared. Very scared."

Two days later, Detective Ed Johnson again called DelGiorno and set up another meeting. This one would take place in the parking lot of the airport hotel the following Sunday, November 9.

Once again it was raining. Johnson was waiting in his car when Del-Giorno pulled up. The detective walked over and sat in the passenger side of Tommy's Cadillac. He suggested they rent a room and have another discussion. Tommy, who had already been figuring the angles, said he wanted to talk, but he wanted the feds there as well. Johnson was agreeable. He said he'd set the meeting up for the following night but that Tommy had to give him something to bring back to his superiors.

"What can I tell them they can expect from you?" he asked.

"Everything," Tommy Del replied.

Maryann lost her two sons on November 11, 1986. Even now, it is a date circled in black on the calendar in her mind. The night before, in a room in another hotel near the airport, Tommy DelGiorno finalized a deal with the government. In exchange for protection for himself and his family and a plea bargain to all the crimes which he had committed, DelGiorno agreed to testify against the organization. He was the first made member of the Philadelphia mob ever to strike such a bargain.

Bobby and Tommy junior, after discussing the matter for hours, had reluctantly agreed to go into hiding with their father, stepmother and two half brothers. Both boys thought they'd be gone for six months to a year. Then they hoped—and Tommy Del let them believe—they'd be able to return to South Philadelphia.

All that remained, on the night when they were to leave, was one last visit to the house on Gladstone Street.

Maryann was in the kitchen cooking when Bobby and Tommy junior walked in.

"Sit down, have some dinner," she said.

"No, mom, we can't," Bobby said. "We gotta talk to ya. Come on in the parlor and sit down."

Maryann sat on the couch in the tiny living room with her husband. She could tell from her boys' expressions that something was wrong. Just how wrong, she couldn't have imagined. They quickly told her that their father was going to be a witness for the government and that there was a contract out on his life. Then they said there was a chance they might be killed and that they would have to go into protective custody with their father.

At first, Maryann didn't understand what they were saying.

"Why?" she said. "You two live with me. That's not possible."

"Mom," Tommy junior said softly. "We have to leave."

Maryann began to shake and then to gag. She could not catch her breath. Tears welled in her eyes.

"I knew it, I knew it," she screamed. "It's all blowing up in his face. I knew it would come to this. That's why I divorced him."

For Maryann, it was a nightmare. She had fought to keep her sons away from their mobster father and now he, with the help of the government no less, was taking them away from her. Joe Fisher reached over and tried to comfort his wife, but Maryann could neither hear what he was saying nor take any solace from his presence.

"Where is he?" she screamed, her tears turning to a bitter rage. "I'm gonna kill him. I'm gonna kill him."

Bobby and Tommy junior tried to calm her down. Both insisted that this was just a temporary move, that after their father had finished testifying they'd be able to return home.

"When are you going?" Maryann said between sobs.

"Tonight. In a little while."

"Where are you gonna stay?"

"We can't tell you."

"How can you go and not tell me where you are? What am I supposed to do? I'm your mother. . . . That son of a bitch."

For more than an hour, the boys and Joe Fisher tried to console Maryann. Then it was time to leave. She sat sobbing quietly on the couch as they walked out the door. Memories flooded back of her babies, of her struggle to bring them up with little or no help from their father, of the sad and happy times on Gladstone Street. Of Broadway Eddie. Of the Christmas presents. Of Halloweens and graduations and birthday parties. She was always there, while Tommy Del was nowhere to be seen. God, oh God, how could this be? The only things of value she had ever taken from her first marriage were the boys. They were all that mattered to her. Their big shot father with his money and his guns had proven to be the coward that she always knew he was. All his talk about the mob and all his gangster bullshit meant nothing. He could shoot people in the back. But when it was time to defend himself, he turned and ran. The hell with him, Maryann thought. But God, oh God, how can he take my babies?

That night, shortly before midnight, a Winnebago camper pulled out from behind a home in the twenty-nine-hundred block of Broad Street in South Philadelphia. There was an unmarked New Jersey State Police car in front of the camper, and another behind it. Inside, with his wife and his four sons, was the man who would bring down Nicodemo "Little Nicky" Scarfo.

The DelGiornos had packed hurriedly, throwing clothes and other necessities into green trash bags and a few suitcases. The state police promised that the rest of their belongings would be sent once they were permanently situated. Tommy Del clutched a blue gym bag that contained cash and jewelry. Bobby guessed that his father had close to $200,000 on hand, although later police would say DelGiorno took about $137,000 with him into hiding. Tommy Del had also slipped Tommy junior a handgun, telling him to hide it. They might need the gun in the future, he said, if he decided "to go back to the old ways."

Teary-eyed members of the family hugged and kissed Roe, Danny and Michael as detectives looked on. Bobby and Tommy junior, still reeling from their emotional goodbyes on Gladstone Street, looked on in stunned silence as their paternal grandparents and Roe's family tried to cope with the forced departure of their loved ones. Tommy junior's fiancée, Chrissy, begged to go along, but the state police refused to take her with them.

No one quite knew what to expect as the caravan pulled out of

South Philadelphia. Danny and Michael, then just ten and eight years old, were excited. To them it was the start of a great and mysterious adventure. But the rest of the DelGiornos wore more somber expressions. Tommy Del had crossed over a line that meant living the rest of his life with a Mafia murder contract on his head. Roe, as any young mother would be, was concerned about her family, especially her, two young boys. Bobby and Tommy junior, sitting in the camper as it headed north, were literally and figuratively in the dark.

In the days leading up to their secret departure they had been repeatedly told that protective custody wouldn't be that bad, that it would be like a vacation, that in six months or so they could return to South Philadelphia. They hoped that was true. But within a week, they came to believe that, in Bobby's words, "it was all bullshit."

Casually at first, but on a consistent basis, the troopers who were guarding the family began to make it clear to the two older boys that they would be better off breaking all ties with the past.

"There's nothing back there for you but trouble," they would say, emphasizing that to return to South Philadelphia was to return to the lair of the mob.

Their father was the biggest mob informant in the history of the Philadelphia Mafia. There was already a contract out on his life. And Scarfo had made it clear that he wasn't above holding family members responsible for the sins of their fathers, sons or brothers.

Joseph Salerno, Jr., an Atlantic City plumber who had testified against Scarfo in the 1980 murder trial of cement contractor Vincent Falcone, was a prime example. This was the case in which Scarfo, Leonetti and Lawrence Merlino were acquitted. But the jury verdict wasn't enough for Scarfo. He thought he had to make an example of the plumber. The problem was that Salerno was in hiding under the Federal Witness Protection Program. Salerno's father, Joe senior, however, was living in South Philadelphia and traveling to Wildwood Crest, New Jersey, every summer, where he owned and operated a small motel.

On the night of August 10, 1982, a man wearing a designer sweat-suit and ski goggles knocked on the motel office door. When Salerno answered, the man pulled out a pistol and pumped a bullet into his neck. The elder Salerno survived the attack but a long-held Mafia tradition was shattered.

"Based on the past, Joseph Salerno senior had little reason to be frightened," the Pennsylvania Crime Commission noted. "[Because] tradition held that the mob did not harm an innocent relative or member of an enemy's family—a brother, a sister, a father. It just wasn't done."

Nicky Scarfo changed those rules, and thumbed his nose at the authorities while doing it. A day after the Salerno shooting, Scarfo and several of his henchmen were spotted walking around Atlantic City wearing the same type of designer sweat suit as the gunman who shot Joe Salerno senior.

Now Tommy Del was the guy Scarfo wanted looking down the barrel of a Mafia gun. But anyone in DelGiorno's family would be an acceptable substitute. This was the bind that Bobby and Tommy junior found themselves in. They were paying a price—a steep and unreasonable price, they would, eventually decide—for their father's life of crime. Both the FBI and the state police were insisting that they would be targeted by Scarfo's hit men because of their father's decision to become a government informant. Bobby, who had gloried in his father's role as a macho mobster, wanted to help his father. But he was being asked to give up his life—his family, his home, his friends, his very identity—to do it.

On the one hand the detectives were telling him if he went back to South Philadelphia he would be killed. On the other, South Philadelphia, the place and the people, meant everything to him. He couldn't imagine living anywhere else. He couldn't imagine never seeing his family and friends again. Sometimes he thought he'd be better off dead, that maybe he should just go back home and take his chances. At other times he and his brother would rail against their father for the spot he had put them in.

"Why doesn't he stand up like a man?" Tommy junior would ask. "All his life he told us never to be a rat. Now what is he?"

"Yo, Tom," Bobby would say, trying to calm down his brother and at the same time avoid the undeniable truth in what he was saying. "This is Daddy we're talking about. They were gonna kill him. What could he do?"

But for the first time, somewhere deep in his subconscious, Bobby began to question his father's way of life. For the first time he began to ask himself if the money, the cars, the clothes, the "easy living" of a mobster were really worth it.

Bobby, even more than his older brother, chafed at the confinement and restrictions that the state police imposed upon him. He was used to coming and going as he pleased. Now he had to ask permission to go outside. And a trip to the store or the movies required security clearance and an escort.

Their father took thousands of dollars into hiding. He had his wife and his two young sons with him. Bobby and Tommy junior liked their half brothers, but their relationship with their stepmother had deteriorated to little more than mutual tolerance. Their friends and family were back in South Philadelphia. And as each day went by, South Philly seemed farther and farther away.

Less than a week after their clandestine departure, the DelGiornos were set up in a state police "safe house" in northern New Jersey. The house, in a small town in the north-central part of the state, was on a large, fenced-in estate. There was a swimming pool in the back yard and beyond the fence was a wooded area. The closest neighbor was a half mile down the road. Danny and Michael adapted immediately. For a time they didn't even have to go to school. They were with their mother and father, enjoying an extended vacation. There was a large yard to run around in and, once the weather warmed, there would be a pool to swim in. Their house on South Broad Street in Philadelphia was nice, but nothing like this.

Adding to the younger boys' excitement was the constant presence of detectives with guns and walkie-talkies and cars equipped with two-way radios and shotguns. Danny and Michael were too young and too naive to realize what Bobby and Tommy grasped almost instantly. They were prisoners. There were no bars, but this was a jail. Their every move was monitored. Any time they left the house, a detective would have to go with them. They needed permission—and an escort—to go anywhere.

Tommy junior would grow more hostile as the weeks went by with no indication of when—or if—the confinement would end. Bobby, who clung to the belief that he was engaged in an effort to save his father's life, fought off a foreboding sense of homesickness, denying at first what Tommy said was the reality of their situation: that they'd never be able to go back to South Philadelphia.

For Bobby, that was incomprehensible.

Even before they made it to the safe house, he was dreaming about home. On the very first night, after collapsing in nervous exhaustion on a bed in a motel somewhere in New Jersey, Bobby thought about home. The tension and pressure had drained him, left him numb. All he wanted to do was close his eyes and sleep and hope. Maybe, he thought, this wasn't really happening.

"There was a state trooper driving the Winnebago and there were troopers in cars in front of us and behind us. We drove for about four hours that night. We finally pulled into this motel. There were three more undercover police cars there waiting for us.

"We all got out of the camper and walked up to the second floor. I asked one of the troopers what room was mine. He says, 'Well, Bob, we got the whole second floor, so pick two if you want.' I was so tired I walked into the first room, fell on the bed and passed out.

"I still remember what I dreamed that night. I dreamed that I was home, waking up in my own bed, running down the stairs; and my mother's in the kitchen cooking breakfast. I run up to her, give her a big hug and say, 'I'm never gonna leave you, Mom. I had this terrible dream that I left.' And my mother says, 'I'll never let you leave.' "

Then Bobby woke up.

And he started to cry.

In the months that followed, as he and his brother grew bored and tired and angry while living in the safe house, that dream would come back to haunt Bobby's nights. He couldn't shake it. He would go for three or four nights without it, then a piece would return. He'd see himself in his room, or in the kitchen. He'd smell the eggs cooking and see his mother at the stove. He'd hear her voice. And then he'd wake with a start and there'd be that empty feeling in his stomach.

He was nineteen, and he was away from home for the first time in his life. Really away. This wasn't a vacation at the shore or a trip to Florida. He missed his mother, his grandmother and grandfather. He missed his friends. He missed the schoolyard where he used to hang out and the neighborhood he grew up in. He missed being able to walk out of his house on Gladstone Street and see, sitting on a stoop two doors away, Anthony Forline, the guy who was as close to him as his brother. He missed the Saturday night beef-and-beer parties that would bring together everybody from the neighborhood. He missed being able to walk two blocks to his grandmother's house. He missed climbing out his bedroom window at night and sitting on the roof of his mother's tiny row house and looking up at the stars and dreaming about the future.

There weren't any dreams in Jersey—only nightmares.

The DelGiornos spent their first two days in hiding at that motel. Security was so tight that when the boys wanted to go out and play football in the parking lot, they had to get clearance. It took an hour to get the okay.

"This is the kind of trouble we had to go through just to play a game of football," Bobby recalled. "First we had to wait for the okay from the supervisor who was in charge of the guard detail. Then we had to wait for him to assign two of his troopers to stand outside with us. When we finally got to play outside I felt like a little kid. There was a cop at each end of the parking lot, like they were babysitting us.

"There was nothing for us to do but play football and eat. We stayed at that motel for two days, until my father started to complain. Then they moved us to another hotel at a ski resort. It had an indoor swimming pool, weight room and a game room for my younger brothers. But we only stayed there one night because the state police said a lot of Mafia people from New York came to that resort. That's when Roe threw a fit. She started yelling, 'I'm not living this way, going from one hotel to another. Tell 'em I wanna be put in a house or else I'm going back to South Philly.'

"Roe was right. We were being yanked around like yo-yos, moving around like gypsies."

Five hours after Roseanne DelGiorno's outburst, the state police told Tommy Del they had found a "safe house" where they'd be able to stay on a permanent basis. They all piled back into the Winnebago. The two state police escort cars, one in front and one in back, fell in line, and they headed out.

The house had six bedrooms, five bathrooms, maid's quarters, a den, playroom with a ping-pong table, a weight room for exercising and a swimming pool and cabana out back. There was a two-car attached garage and a two-car detached garage. There were security cameras set up all over the estate, along the winding driveway that led from the road to the house and along the back and side yards. The den on the first floor served as the state police office, where a bank of television cameras allowed a trooper to scan the grounds.

Somebody rich owned the place, although Bobby never found out who. Nor did he learn how the state police got access to it.

The DelGiornos settled in as best they could.

Tommy Del would be away from the home for days at a time, attending debriefing sessions or court hearings where his testimony was being used to substantiate the charges that had been lodged against Scarfo and the others and to build several other cases that state and federal authorities hoped would bring down the mob.

For the law enforcement agencies that had been battling the Scarfo organization—with little success for more than five years—Tommy Del was a valuable and lethal weapon. Not so, his family. For the New Jersey State Police and, later, the FBI, the DelGiornos were a source of constant aggravation. And no one was more aggravating than Bobby.

A week after moving into the safe house, Bobby took off. He had been planning the move for two or three days and was amazed at how easy it was just to walk away. The night before, he took fifteen thousand dollars in cash out of the blue gym bag where his father had hidden all the family funds. The money was from Bobby's loan-sharking and bookmaking operations, all the cash he had saved up over the past three years. He had given the money to his father to hold onto the night they left Philadelphia. Tommy Del had put it in the bag with the cash and jewelry he took into hiding.

The money and the clothes he was wearing were all Bobby took with him when he left.

It was a Friday around 11:00 a.m. After breakfast he started for the back door when his younger brother, Danny, ran up to him.

"Where you going, Bob?"

"Out back in the woods to look for deer," Bobby said.

"Can I come?"

The two headed out the door, past one of the detectives who asked where they were going.

"Out to look for deer," Danny replied.

Once in the back yard, Bobby told his younger brother to climb up into the tree house and keep watch.

"If I'm not back right away, that just means I've gone deeper into the woods," Bobby told him. "You stay up in the tree."

Bobby climbed through the fence that separated the grounds of the estate from a clump of woods and then headed out, moving in the direction of what he thought was a roadway. Ten minutes later he was out of the woods and moving toward a gas station. He asked a young girl there if she could call him a cab.

"A cab out here, are you crazy?"

It was then that Bobby realized how out of touch he was with reality. He didn't even know where he was. All he knew was that this was North Jersey, not far from New York City. And now he also knew he was somewhere without taxi service; somewhere a long way away from South Philadelphia.

"Is there a bus or a train around here that I can get to Philadelphia?" he asked.

"There's a train," she said, "but it goes to New York."

Bobby had to control his emotions, to think clearly. He had been gone less than ten minutes, probably not long enough for anyone back at the house to get suspicious. But he was running out of time. He had to get to the train station, get to New York and then connect with a train to Philadelphia. He thanked the girl and, breaking into a trot, headed off in the direction she had indicated.

The train station was nothing more than a commuter stop, an outdoor platform that filled up each morning with office workers on their way into the city. But shortly before noon, the platform was practically deserted, adding to Bobby's feeling of isolation and contributing to his growing anxiety. For thirty minutes he sat on a bench clutching a train ticket, expecting that any moment the gravel parking lot behind him would be filled with state police cars, sirens screaming, red lights flashing. He fingered the ticket like a rosary bead and prayed to God that the train would be on time.

Five hours later, he was getting off another train at Thirtieth Street Station in Philadelphia. There he had no trouble hailing a taxi. A broad smile lit up his face as he jumped into the back seat and told the driver, "Take me to Second and Ritner."

Bobby had the cab driver drop him off about a block from the neighborhood schoolyard where he and his friends always hung out. It was nearly 6:00 p.m. when he stepped out of the taxi. The sun had gone down. What had been a bright fall afternoon was turning cold. But Bobby felt a warmth that was beyond description as he began to walk the sidewalk in his neighborhood. He was home.

He turned a corner and looked across the street toward the schoolyard. It was like he had never left. There, under the lights, stood John GQ, Jimmy, Mark Pop, all his friends from the neighborhood. Bobby moved toward them, but stayed in the shadows. He scanned the streets around the schoolyard, looking for a car that might seem out of place, a car with someone sitting in it, watching. Satisfied that wasn't the case, he moved in closer. If this was a typical Friday night, the guys would be drinking beer in the schoolyard and planning what to do for the rest of the evening.

"They each had a quart of beer in their hands and they were leaning against the wall of the school," Bobby said. "I hollered over to them, 'Hey, you faggots, you got a quart of beer for me?' Everyone looked up, but they couldn't see me because it was dark and they were standing under the schoolyard lights. As I walked closer, Mark Pop yells, 'It's Bobby. It's fucking Bobby.' Then he runs up and lifts me in the air and he's hugging me and the other guys come running over, hugging me and asking me all kinds of questions.

" 'I thought we'd never see you again,' John GQ says. 'All the newspapers are saying you, your father and your whole family's been put under protective custody.'

"While this is going on, Anthony Forline comes strolling around the corner. He sees me, runs up and jumps on me. Then he says, 'Bob, I gotta talk to you. The FBI's been to my house. They think me and you planned your escape and I was going to drive somewhere and pick you up with the fifty thousand dollars. They say you stole fifty thousand dollars. Your mother's going crazy. She don't believe 'em, but she's real upset.' "

Forline, in his excitement, had gotten his story somewhat twisted. It was the New Jersey State Police, not the FBI, that had questioned him.

"State Police, FBI, what the fucks the difference," he said when Bobby asked him to repeat the story. Also, it was fifteen thousand, not fifty thousand, and the money wasn't stolen, it was Bobby's to begin with. This was, to Bobby's way of thinking, just another example of how the authorities take a piece of information and distort it to suit their purposes. Bobby had begun to see them do that with his father—detectives would offer subtle suggestions to Tommy Del, suggestions that Bobby and his brother later suspected were designed to ensure that their father's testimony would conform with evidence and other testimony the prosecution planned to present.

It was all a game.

Now Bobby decided he was going to play.

He sent Jimmy around the corner to check out his street. Sure enough, Jimmy spotted two plainclothes detectives sitting in an unmarked car on the corner. Nobody, however, was watching the alleyway that ran behind his mother's house.

Now Bobby sent Anthony Forline back to knock on his mother's door.

"All the attention will be on you," Bobby said to his best friend. "Once you get in the house, make sure you keep my mother occupied. Make sure you keep her downstairs."

Anthony headed off for Gladstone Street. Like a quarterback in a pickup football game, Bobby started handing out assignments to the others. His plan was to sneak in the back window to his bedroom. Under a floorboard in the closet was a .357 magnum, a gun he had bought two years earlier from a local drug dealer. If Bobby was going to be walking around South Philadelphia with both the state police and the Mafia after him, he wanted to be armed.

"If anybody's gonna come up behind me and try to put some bullets in my head," he told Anthony and the others, "I want to be holding something besides my dick in my hand."

They gave Anthony a two-minute head start so that he could distract the detectives who were watching the street. Then Bobby, Mark Pop and Knave, another one of the guys, headed out. Knave was supposed to stand at the entranceway to the alley. If anyone came around, he would whistle. That would be a warning for Bobby and Mark Pop.

John GQ stood in the schoolyard with a puzzled look on his face.

"What about me?" he asked.

"You?" Bobby said. "You got the hardest job of all. Here's twenty bucks. Go to the bar and bring back two cases of beer. Make sure it's Bud."

"And make sure it's cold," said Mark Pop.

"Me and Mark Pop started down the alley. We got to my house and both of us climb over the fence. Mark gives me a boost onto the roof that was near my bedroom. I look down and tell him, 'If you hear any yelling, just go back around the schoolyard.' As I'm walking across the roof I'm praying the window isn't locked. I pulled on it and it opened, so I climbed in. I could hear Anthony talking to my mother, but at this point I'm most interested in gettin' the gun. I open the closet door, lift up the rug and move the floorboard and there it is. I just look at it for a few seconds, feeling so powerful. I grabbed it and, at that point, I wasn't afraid of anything or anybody. No Mafia. No nobody. I just sat there holding that gun.

"Before I go back out the window, I creep over to the top of the stairs to see what my mother was saying. I could tell she was crying. I hear her tell Anthony that she hopes I'm all right. Anthony's telling her, 'Maryann, I know your son. Bobby can take care of himself.'

"At that point I'm thinking how, here I am, right dead in the middle of everybody's life except my own. I felt like running down the stairs and just hugging my mother. But I knew if I did that, she would turn me over to the police for my own safety. The last thing I wanted was to go back to that safe house where there wasn't anything but trees and grass."

Bobby was living his nightmare. This was his house. This was his bedroom. The sounds, the smells, the feel of the place were all familiar, comforting, solid. His mother was right downstairs, sitting at the kitchen table talking to Anthony. It was a common, ordinary scene. A piece of his past. Bobby headed for the window. He knew if he stayed any longer, he'd start to cry. All he wanted was to come home.

Five minutes later he was back in the schoolyard with Mark Pop, Anthony and the others. They each had a beer in their hands and were planning their next move when a girl from the neighborhood walked up.

"Bobby, what are you doing here?" she said.

"I live here, remember?" he said.

"But I heard there's a bounty on your head."

"And I heard there's a bounty on your ass," Mark Pop yelled, chasing her away.

"What was that all about?" Bobby asked.

No one answered.

"What's she talking about, Ant?" Bobby said.

"The word on the street is one hundred thousand dollars," Anthony Forline said. "That's how much for whoever kills your father or you or your brother."

The reaction of the New Jersey State Police during the twenty-four hours that Bobby was "free" indicated just how valuable law enforcement considered Tommy DelGiorno.

State police detectives swarmed all over Bobby's South Philadelphia neighborhood, correctly surmising that a nineteen-year-old who was born and bred on the concrete sidewalks around Second Street would head for home. Cops staked out the neighborhood. They sat in unmarked cars on a half dozen corners. They had surveillance posted outside his grandmother's home and, of course, they were inside and outside his mother's.

In the end it was a tearful and despondent Maryann Fisher who found Bobby and talked him into returning with the state police. But that would not occur until the morning after Bobby got his gun.

He and his friends, full of bravado after polishing off both of the cases of Bud that John GQ had brought back to the schoolyard, headed for a beef-and-beer party at the Irish Club on Second and Muffin that night. With detectives staked out all over the neighborhood, Bobby and his buddies partied past midnight with about two hundred people. Then Bobby, drunk but still alert enough to realize he was being looked for, crashed at his friend Jimmy's house.

"They'll be looking for me at Anthony's or Mark Pop's," he told Jimmy through the drunken haze that had enveloped them all.

"You could stay with me as long as you want," Jimmy said.

A state police detective was at Jimmy's door the next morning. Word had filtered back about the party and the police were questioning every one of Bobby's friends. Jimmy tried to hold the detective off, basically playing dumb while Bobby listened from a back room.

"Listen, you punk, this isn't some street-corner fight, this is a life and death situation," the detective said.

"Who's life you talking about?" Jimmy shouted back. "Bobby's? Are you kidding? You could give a fuck. All you care about is that if Bobby doesn't go back, his father won't testify."

Then Bobby heard the slam of another car door and his mother was inside the house, pleading with Jimmy.

"Please tell me where Bobby is," she said, her voice full of fear, anger and sadness.

Bobby walked out. He and his mother embraced. Tears filled his eyes. They streamed out of hers. Bobby was in a daze. He couldn't quite focus. In the background he heard the state police detective suggest that they all go somewhere for a cup of coffee. Somewhere where they could talk. Bobby went willingly.

The somewhere was the New Jersey State Police office in Bellmawr, New Jersey, just across the Walt Whitman Bridge from South Philadelphia. It was the only place they could be sure they were safe, the detective explained.

Bobby, his mother and two detectives sat in a small office discussing the situation.

"Look, Bobby, we know it's rough," one of the detectives said, "but try to go along with us on this. We'll give you whatever we can. We'll find you a job. I understand you've got family out in Oregon. We can relocate you there. We'll pay for everything. Set you up real nice."

The only Oregon Bobby was interested in was Oregon Avenue in South Philadelphia.

"You're so busy playing cops and robbers, you're missing the whole point," Bobby said. "Don't you understand? Where I want to be is home, with my mother, with my family, with my friends."

Bobby fought to hold back the tears welling up again; this time they were tears of anger and frustration.

"How would you like it if you had to leave your family and friends and was told you'd never see them again? Tell me what you would do."

Like the night before at the schoolyard when he first asked about the murder contract, no one answered. Then one of the detectives asked the other to take Bobby's mother to another room for a few minutes. When she had left, the detective sat down behind his desk and stared directly into Bobby's eyes.

"Do you know how serious this situation is? Do you know your father has already admitted to committing fourteen murders? Do you know what they're going to do to him if he doesn't testify?"

The implication was clear. If Tommy Del reneged on his agreement to cooperate so that his family could return to South Philadelphia, then the state would prosecute him for the murders he had admitted committing. And while the detective might have been exaggerating slightly—Tommy Del would eventually admit to his own involvement in five gangland murders—that did not change the fact that Bobby's father could face life in prison or the electric chair.

The irony was that if Tommy Del did testify, then he and his family would have to remain in hiding because they were already under a death sentence from the Scarfo organization.

It was a no-win situation for Bobby.

And for Maryann.

All she had been thinking about for the past twenty-four hours, from the moment the state police called and told her that Bobby had fled, was her baby turning up dead in the gutter, tortured horribly and shot in the back of the head by some Mafia goon. Now she had found him, but she couldn't protect him. For his own safety, she had to send him back to his father and the state police. She had to be content with an occasional call or letter from God knew where. She had to live her life without knowing where her boys were or what they were doing.

As she sat pondering the situation in the state police office, the phone rang. It was Tommy Del. He wanted to talk with Bobby.

"He'll talk to me first," Maryann said, grabbing the receiver from one of the detectives.

Bobby, from the other room, could hear his mother screaming and knew immediately that it was his father on the other end of the line.

"This is all your fault, you son of a bitch," Maryann said. "Now I have to convince him to come back. If I do, I don't want you to lay a hand on him. Do you hear me? I don't even want you to raise your voice to him. You caused all this. If I knew where you were, I would get a gun and blow your fucking brains out. You're nothing but a coward. Why aren't you dead?"

Quickly, one of the detectives grabbed the phone out of her hand.

"Maryann," he said, "we can't let you issue death threats. I understand how you feel, but this is a state police office here. You threaten to kill somebody, you're breaking the law. Please, try to calm down."

Bobby was handed the phone in the other room and listened while his father begged him to come back.

"Bob, they're gonna kill you if you stay in South Philadelphia," Tommy Del said. "Come back and I'll make sure you can have visitors, whoever you want, whenever you want. Who knows. In a couple of years, when this is all over, you could probably go back home."

"I'll come back," Bobby told his father. "But when this is over, I'm coming home for good."

After he hung up the phone, the state police detective told Bobby he had done the right thing. Bobby just stared at him.

"Your family's gonna come out on top of this," he said.

"The only people who are going to come out on top are you guys and the FBI," Bobby shouted. "I don't know who's worse, the mob or the police."

Bobby spent another thirty minutes alone with his mother. They hugged, and she squeezed him tight. He told her he would be back as soon as his father had finished testifying at all the trials. He said the state police would arrange for her to visit with him. He said to tell grandmom and grandpop that he would see them soon. Then he was gone, whisked away in an unmarked state police car for a trip up the New Jersey Turnpike to Newark.

There another detective in an unmarked car was waiting to take him back to the safe house. The detective was about six foot two and weighed nearly 250 pounds. He wore jeans, a sweater and a black leather jacket. His hair hung down around his collar. He had an earring. He was unlike any of the other members of the state police Bobby had met.

"My name's Jim," he said, reaching out to shake Bobby's hand.

"Bob DelGiorno," Bobby replied with what must have been a quizzical look in his eye.

"I work undercover, narcotics. That's why I look like this."

For the next three months, however, Jim was going to work the detail guarding the DelGiornos. Bobby liked him immediately. Even more so when they were alone in the car driving from Newark.

"Listen," Jim said, "I grew up in Jersey City so I know what it's like to be away from the city. Most of the guys on this detail don't know the difference.

"So, if you wanna get laid or just go out drinking or whatever else, just name it and we'll try to figure out a way to do it. Just do me one favor."

"What?" Bobby asked.

"Don't run away on my shift," the detective said.

Bobby smiled. Finally, he thought, an honest cop.

The Sting

by Elizabeth Gilbert

Elizabeth Gilbert's (born 1969) profile of a federal investigation gone Hollywood has the makings of a movie itself.

A round the time that George Moffly gets himself all tangled up with the Mafia, the FBI and the International Brotherhood of Teamsters, he's 27 years old and living in Boston. George is producing cheap television commercials for a living. He has recently filmed an effective ad campaign for a weight-loss center, showing fat people trying to cram themselves into packed elevators and snug airplane seats. He's also filmed a whole series of commercials for the Wonderland Dog Track—"A Bettor Place to Play." George Moffly is good at commercials, but he's bored. What he really wants to do with his life is produce movies. He thinks he would be excellent at this, not only because he loves movies but also because he's pathologically well organized, compulsively frugal and unapologetically dictatorial. And he's certainly smart enough; he went to a fancy college and all that. And he's a tough little bastard, too. George Moffly may be skinny and Episcopalian, but he comes from six generations of lawyers and he knows how to say in three different languages, "I will sue you so fucking hard it'll make your fucking head spin."

In short, he has everything it takes to be a good movie producer. All he needs now is a movie to produce.

So, in September 1988, George Moffly starts sniffing around Boston to see if any features are coming to town—any small-time features, willing to give a small-time guy like him a chance. And that's when he hears about an independent filmmaker named David Rudder. Seems this Rudder character has been scouting out Boston recently, looking for a crew to shoot a $1.3-million movie called *The Knockdown*. George phones Rudder, and the two men agree to meet at the Regal Bostonian Hotel. George Moffly is nervous. He's aware that his résumé is thin—*The Wonderland Dog Track? Jesus Christ!*—but this is his big chance to produce something *real*.

On the morning of the interview, David Rudder makes an intimidating impression. Six feet four. Frighteningly Aryan. Dark blue suit. Intense. Odd southern accent. Rudder asks George some normal questions—*What films have you done? How well do you know Boston?*—but then the conversation takes a decidedly odd turn. David Rudder wants to talk about the Teamsters. Specifically, he wants to know whether George has ever "dealt" with Boston Teamster Jimmy Moar, vice president of Local 25.

The question is not totally out of the blue. Many states require that movie sets hire union labor, so all movie producers have to negotiate with the Teamsters eventually. And negotiations with this powerful union can often become dicey. Film producers must figure out how many Teamster truckers they can reasonably afford to hire at $1,600 a week each, not counting overtime and welfare benefits and the "donation" to the Teamster Scholarship Fund. Producers also need to know how to manage threats if the Teamsters aren't happy with the offer. They also need to know how to sometimes just hand the Teamsters a fat envelope of cash to walk away and let the movie be shot in nonunion peace. George Moffly knows all this. He's tussled with Teamsters before. He's even heard of Jimmy Moar. But he's never engaged in any negotiations with the guy. And he's certainly never handed the guy any fat envelopes of cash. George considers being honest about this, but then, he really, really wants this job. So he lies. He says he's "handled" Jimmy Moar before, sure. Loads of times.

Good enough. George Moffly is hired. His salary is set at a handsome $2,000 a week. He is given his very own copy of *The Knockdown*. Which is truly the most putrid script George has ever read—a tits-and-ass action comedy about a historic preservationist trying to save an endangered landmark building with the help of a buxom young realtor. Dreadful, but whatever. The money is real. And Brian Dennehy and Rebecca De Mornay are apparently "all excited" about playing the leads. George Moffly is all excited, too. He thinks he has finally become a movie producer. How very surprised he would be to learn what he has really just become: a federal employee.

David Rudder, you see, is not actually a filmmaker. He's not even David Rudder. George Moffly's new boss is Federal Bureau of Investigation special agent Garland Schweickhardt. And Garland Schweickhardt has set into motion—with George's unwitting help—Dramex, or Drama Exposé, the code name for a sting operation whose primary purpose is to catch and arrest Teamster leaders across New England who have been fleecing the hell out of the motion-picture industry in recent years. Intimidation, coercion, extortion—the works. Since the days of Jimmy Hoffa, Teamsters have had some trouble recognizing the difference between the terms *organized labor* and *organized crime*, so the Feds have reason to suspect the Mob might also be involved in this profitable corruption. Specifically, the FBI wants to prove a connection between Boston's Teamsters and the Patriarca crime family—the New England satellite of the worldwide Sicilian Mafia empire known simply as La Cosa Nostra.

The only question has been—how to catch the bad guys?

It's 1987 when Los Angeles–based FBI agent Garland Schweickhardt goes before the FBI's Undercover Review Board in Washington, D.C., and proposes that the bureau create an independent film production company with Schweickhardt posing as president. While planning the production of a movie, Schweickhardt will offer cash bribes to Teamster leaders, who will accept the money (while under FBI surveillance) and share it with their friends in the Mob.

Now, this is surely one of the stranger pitches in show-business history. But operating on a this-just-might-be-crazy-enough-to-work syllogism, the FBI approves the sting. And so it comes to pass that 49-year-old FBI veteran Garland Schweickhardt—who's never been undercover before and who has spent much of his bureaucratic career pushing paper through the Freedom of Information Act office—becomes a filmmaker. He gets himself a new identity: David Rudder. He sets up the offices of David Rudder Productions in Santa Monica, California. He visits Paramount Studios and asks if he can borrow a dud archived script. A studio executive hands over a turkey called *The Knockdown*. Schweickhardt takes his wretched script and goes off to the UCLA film school for one semester to study under a "really wonderful" teacher named Jonathan Krane. When the semester is over, the new filmmaker David Rudder is as ready to make a movie as any first-time Hollywood mogul could ever hope to be. He has his training, his offices, his investors, his script and his enthusiasm. He even has his location—the unusually corrupt city of Boston. All he needs now is a producer.

When he meets George Moffly, he believes he has found his man. Here's a "very impressive, very organized" young producer who not only knows Boston well but also knows the Teamster Jimmy Moar extremely well. And Jimmy Moar is one of the FBI's prime targets right now. If George Moffly can get Jimmy Moar to trust David Rudder enough to accept a cash payout? Why, the Dramex sting could be a huge success. A blockbuster, even.

Autumn 1988. George Moffly is eagerly trying to get *The Knockdown* produced. But he's having trouble getting his boss to move forward. Whenever they have production meetings, all David Rudder seems to want to talk about is the Teamsters. George certainly worries about labor issues, too, but he does feel there should be other concerns. He keeps asking, "Who's your director, David? Who's your gaffer? Who's your cinematographer?"

But Rudder hedges and hesitates. George Moflly is starting to think this guy doesn't know very much about movies. Then again, Rudder has openly admitted to George that this is his first venture into Hollywood. After all, he's just a conservative financial adviser by trade who's making this film as an investment for "a small group of doctors and dentists in the greater Alexandria, Virginia, area." George Moffly has never heard of dentists as movie investors before. But George Moffly hasn't worked on that many movies, so what does he know?

In fact, Garland Schweickhardt has not hired a director because he suspects he might be able to bribe Jimmy Moar during preproduction negotiations, thereby nailing the Teamsters without shooting a single frame of film. So he sends George Moffly off to begin negotiating with George's old buddy Jimmy Moar. He authorizes George to hire no more than seven Teamsters for the vaguely upcoming production and hints that George might suggest "alternative measures" if Moar balks.

So George goes forth, for the first time in his life, to meet Jimmy Moar, the beefy, irritable vice president of Teamsters Local 25. The discussion turns sour fast. George explains that he can afford only seven Teamsters. Jimmy demands that George hire nineteen. George tries to offer some "alternative measures," but Jimmy won't bite. Nineteen Teamsters is the final offer, or George can take his fucking movie to Toronto. George Moffly, who has zero tolerance for swindlers or pricks, loses his temper now. Fine, he says, *The Knockdown* will hire nonunion truck drivers instead. And with the money saved, George promises to hire armed Pinkerton guards and order them to "shoot to kill" any labor agitators disrupting the set.

"How's that sound, Jimmy?" he asks.

"Get out of my fucking office!" Jimmy Moar explodes. "Nobody tells me how many Teamsters are gonna work. Get the fuck out of here before I break both your fucking legs and dump you in the fucking river!"

George has no more luck in subsequent conversations with another high-powered Teamster honcho, Billy Winn. Winn not only won't discuss "alternative measures"—claiming the climate's too hot because of a rumored FBI presence in Boston—but he also threatens to rip George's legs off. George Moffly isn't turning out to be such an effective negotiator after all. But neither is his boss. Rudder can't get the Teamsters to accept the bait, either. Jimmy Moar and Billy Winn hate George Moffly's fucking guts, and they don't know who this David Rudder fuck is, wandering into town with no director and no shooting schedule and looking for shady deals.

The Dramex sting, in other words, is a failure.

Special agent Garland Schweickhardt returns home to Los Angeles and calls George to tell him the movie's off. George feels let down, but he also feels like a loser, convinced that the deal fell through because he couldn't negotiate union peace. Rudder assures George that it's not his fault. The problem, Rudder says, is much more fundamental: The investors have simply pulled out.

Fucking dentists.

Months pass. Garland Schweickhardt gets back to his routine work at the FBI headquarters in Los Angeles. Then one day in January 1989, something wonderful falls in his lap. And that wonderful something is a vengeful mobster with a twenty-inch neck named Robert Franchi.

Robert Franchi is a minor figure associated with the major Patriarca crime family. A small-time Boston hood, Franchi is also a compulsive gambler who's gotten himself into trouble with the Patriarcas by borrowing money he could not later return. Trying to escape a bad situation, Franchi has moved to sunny California. But back in Boston, a senior Patriarca soldier named Dennis "Champagne" Lepore has started threatening Robert Franchi's mother about her son's debts. Franchi is outraged. He hates that fucking bully Dennis Lepore. When Franchi was 16 and working as a waiter in a North Boston café, Lepore once threw a cup of steaming cappuccino in his face, complaining the drink was too cold, and then stuck a knife into the boy's nostril for fun. That was bad enough. But this business about harassing Franchi's mother!

Franchi considers killing Lepore. Then he comes up with an even better idea; he'll put the bastard in prison instead.

And so, one fine afternoon, Robert Franchi strolls into the Los Angeles branch of the FBI and announces that he would like to become a federal informant, please. Franchi lays out his credentials— his contacts with La Cosa Nostra—and thereafter makes some promising tape recordings of New England mobsters boasting about their connections to New England Teamsters. ("Anything union," Dennis Lepore brags, "I can do anything the fuck I want.") The tapes find their way to Garland Schweickhardt, who flies back to Washington to try to persuade the FBI to let him attempt the Dramex sting again, only using Robert Franchi's invaluable help this time. Things will be very different with a good informant on the team, Schweickhardt promises. This time "David Rudder" will be contacting the Teamsters through the Mafia itself, with a Mob insider making introductions, negotiating payoffs and swearing that Rudder is a trustworthy guy. The FBI gives the nod.

Garland Schweickhardt knows he's gotten a reprieve here, and he feels the weight of his whole career riding on the sting. He refuses to let it fail simply because he doesn't come across as a legitimate filmmaker. This time he's actually going to make this movie. Lights, cameras, action—the works. It is with such thoughts in mind that Schweickhardt decides he needs George Moffly again. Only as a real producer this time. He likes George anyway. Admires his hustle.

Meanwhile, George Moffly is in New York City, working as the location manager on a low-budget picture called *The Ambulance*, starring Eric Roberts. He's standing in the production office one afternoon when David Rudder calls. The investors are back in! Would George step back into his old role of producer?

George agrees—he's still dying for a producer's credit—and shortly thereafter Rudder flies him out to Los Angeles to talk about the movie.

This is a thrilling day for George, because he's never been flown any-where for work. And he's even more thrilled when David Rudder picks him up in a shimmering bronze Rolls-Royce. George Moffly has never been in a Rolls-Royce before. (He's certainly never been in a convicted drug kingpin's federally seized Rolls-Royce before, but he is, of course, ignorant of the car's previous ownership.) Rudder drives George through Beverly Hills. The sun is shining. The palm trees wave seduc-tively. George is starting to feel a little intoxicated. It's Hollywood!

Then Rudder pulls the Rolls-Royce into the parking lot at 2811 Wilshire Boulevard. He parks in a spot that is "Reserved for David Rudder Productions" and escorts George inside. George Moffly's intox-ication diminishes speedily. The signs on the doors of the building read VASCULAR IMAGING, BIO-CHRONO THERAPY and DERMOPATHOLOGY. This is not a place you come to get a lucrative movie deal; this is a place you come to get a biopsy.

George follows Rudder up to his office, a grim suite of orange car-peting and cheap furniture. On the walls hang framed posters of movies that David Rudder Productions clearly did not produce. *Biloxi Blues? Clan of the Cave Bear?*

George, still wondering what kind of guy drives a car like *that* but has an office like *this*, decides it's time he started acting like a real pro-ducer. He firmly declares that he's willing to work on this movie again, but only under one condition. *The Knockdown* must be rewritten, because it's a ludicrous piece of shit. To his surprise, David Rudder agrees. George then asks for $5,000 to hire a screenwriter to rescue the script. Rudder blanches. George explains that five grand is a scant sum to pay for a rewrite—truly the least you can get away with—but money well spent if it can resuscitate *The Knockdown*.

Special agent Garland Schweickhardt listens carefully. He's con-cerned about spending $5,000 of taxpayer money improving a script that is really only bait. On the other hand, a more legitimate script would make David Rudder Productions look like a more legitimate company. Besides, George is right. *The Knockdown* is a ludicrous piece of shit. And Schweickhardt is a proud man. He doesn't want his name—even a fake name—attached to some ludicrous piece of shit. So he approves the expense and the rewrite.

"Let's make a movie we can be proud of, George," Rudder says, and they shake on it.

Meanwhile, Robert Franchi, the FBI'S mob informant, has been in friendly contact with his old mortal enemy, the mobster Dennis Lepore. Franchi has worked off his gambling debts, so the two guys are buddy-buddy now. Franchi has casually mentioned that he has a good friend—an independent filmmaker named David Rudder—who's been trying to make a nonunion movie back in Boston but keeps getting static from the Teamsters. Franchi asks if Lepore might be able to use his Teamster contacts to smooth things over. There's easy dough in it, Franchi promises. If David Rudder can save money by shooting nonunion, he'll pay off anybody.

Dennis Lepore is strapped for cash at the moment, and the deal sounds good. He discusses the proposition with his partner in crime, a mobster named Thomas Hillary. And now we are getting somewhere in La Cosa Nostra. Tommy Hillary is Mafia royalty—an intelligent, slick and totally connected gangster who makes the FBI's mouth water. He's in an entirely different league than Dennis Lepore (a hot-tempered thug who once boxed a man's ears with bricks for "taking up too much space" on a public sidewalk). Tommy Hillary is nobody's fool, so he grills Robert Franchi—who is recording every word—for more details on this movie deal.

> HILLARY: What do they want us to do?
> FRANCHI: Well, I was talking to them, and they asked me if I knew some people there (Massachusetts]. I said, "Well, sure, I know some people." And they said, "We're gonna do some business up there."
> HILLARY: In other words, they want to do movies out here, but they want to be connected. They don't want no problems with the Teamsters, all that shit.

FRANCHI: Yeah, they mentioned something like that.

HILLARY: What kind of movie are they making?

FRANCHI: A documentary. I don't know what it is.

HILLARY: Documentary.

FRANCHI: It's a documentary, but they've got everything. They show me scripts about this, scripts about that. To the point that I don't know what the fuck's going on.

HILLARY: What's it about, this documentary?

FRANCHI: I don't know.

HILLARY: I hope it ain't organized crime.

Great news! George Moffly has found someone to rewrite *The Knockdown* for cheap. It's a young acquaintance named Jody O'Neil, who's been working on low-budget movies, but who secretly aspires to be a screenwriter. Jody enthusiastically accepts the rewrite job, which he sees as *his* big Hollywood break. The only problem is, he doesn't have any screenwriting experience to speak of. He also doesn't have a word processor to speak of. He slugs out his draft on a shabby Brother manual, and when the new, improved *Knockdown* is delivered, it's such a mess of typos and pasted-on corrections that it looks like a ransom note.

George Moffly is beginning to suspect that *The Knockdown* may be beyond salvation. So he flies back out to L.A. with a bolder plan. Over drinks at Chateau Marmont, he asks David Rudder for $20,000 to go out and buy a brand-new script. Rudder hesitates, but George explains the arithmetic. If they can actually make a decent picture, they can market it later to film festivals, cable TV stations, airlines, overseas venues. . . .

"Let's do it right, David," he says, "or let's not bother doing it at all."

Again special agent Garland Schweickhardt listens keenly. He's starting to thoroughly enjoy these conversations with George Moffly about movies. He really admires George's moxie and his facile expertise with casting and location scouting and Hollywood's exotic gossip. And what George is saying makes perfect sense. Why waste money on a substandard product? Anyhow, all this business about making a profitable movie plays into the larger scheme Schweickhardt has been hatching lately. He's started to dream of producing phony films all over the country, of bribing and nailing corrupt union officials in cities across America—one movie at a time. The profits from one film could go toward financing the production of the next film, just like in a real Hollywood studio. And he wants George, his show-business "mentor," to be his producer every time.

Now, Schweickhardt knows the other agents in the FBI are dubious about his plans. He knows they think he's losing sight of judicial objectives. He knows they're jealous that he's gallivanting around Hollywood hot spots and reading *Variety* while, as one Justice Department lawyer bitched, all the other guys are out there "kicking down doors on a search warrant." Schweickhardt knows the other agents resent him, but that's only because they don't have any *vision*. They don't see how huge a crime-busting empire this phony-movie business could potentially become.

Inspired, Schweickhardt authorizes George to scrap *The Knockdown* and go find a brand-new script. George is thrilled and flattered. It's nice to be working with someone who really listens to your ideas. Nicer still when you can express those ideas over cocktails in Hollywood's toniest bars.

"Think of it, George," Rudder says one night over martinis. "We could actually win an Academy Award for this movie!"

Through the introduction of the FBI informant Robert Franchi, filmmaker David Rudder has finally met the mobsters Thomas Hillary and Dennis Lepore. Rudder is also introduced to Frankie Salemme Jr. (son of Frank "Cadillac" Salemme, who once blew off the legs of a prominent Boston attorney with a car bomb). Frankie Salemme Jr. is a good-looking young stallion who doesn't just have an arrest record full of assault-and-battery charges against police officers; he also has a few acting classes under his belt. Frankie loves Hollywood. Swears he'd drop the whole New England crime scene "in a New York second" if David Rudder ever made him an offer to stay out in Los Angeles.

The other mobsters privately refer to straitlaced David Rudder as "Goofy," but they do like his cash, and they are drawn to his Hollywood patina like magpies. They want him to introduce them to movie stars, to take them out to hip restaurants in L.A. Even the elusive godfather, Raymond Patriarca Jr., wants to get involved and has offered David Rudder the use of his speedboat for the making of this film. And all the wise guys want Frankie Salemme Jr. to play the speedboat driver.

George Moffly, meanwhile, has found a decent script for David Rudder Productions. It's called *Car Tunes*. It's a comedy about a female band manager named Sam who's on tour with her mediocre heavy-metal group when all her musicians suddenly dump her. Stuck in Arizona, Sam cobbles together a new band, composed of deadbeats and a lounge act from this small desert town, and she takes them on the road. George sends *Car Tunes* to David Rudder, who loves it. Rudder has only two teensy changes to suggest on the script: *(1)* Instead of being set in the Arizona deserts, could the story be relocated to Providence, Rhode Island? *(2)* Could the writers possibly add a scene with a speedboat?

September 1989. David Rudder flies to Boston on business for the movie. George Moffly swings by his boss's room at the Charles Hotel, but when he walks in, he encounters a most unsettling scene. There's David Rudder, talking on the telephone. And there, sitting on a chair next to Rudder, is the most fear-inspiring man George Moffly has ever seen—a colossal man, with a head the size of a medicine ball and a neck to match. George says, "David?" The colossal man leaps up and crosses the room in two strides. Towering above, the colossal man passes his index finger slowly in front of George's face, like one swipe of a mighty windshield wiper.

"Shhh," he warns. "David's on da phone."

George shushes. The colossal man sits back down. Silence. When David Rudder finally gets off the phone, he introduces George to "Robert"—no last name given—"my associate." George's hand vanishes into Robert's grip. The three men order drinks and stare at one another

Awkwardly, George tries to bring up some casting business. George and Rudder have been seeing some very good actors in auditions (the ancient Dennehy–De Mornay lie, of course, has long since turned to vapor), and some decisions need to be made. David Rudder wants John Lithgow for the male lead, but George has his heart set on the Broadway actor Tom Noonan. Bebe Neuwirth and Carol Kane have both auditioned. Rudder is crazy about Carol Kane. (Sure, he admits, she's too old for the part as written, but she's just "so wonderful.") Normally, Rudder loves talking about casting, but today he seems distracted. He finally tells George he's very sorry, but he must run. He has important negotiating meetings with the Teamsters all weekend. And, no, George is not invited. Although the mysterious Robert is going along.

Hearing this, George Moffly feels hurt and even jealous. He's the producer here; he should be negotiating labor deals. And why is Rudder acting so nervous? And who is this Robert, this thug, this enforcer, who suddenly gets David Rudder's private time? What gives?

What gives, exactly, is that "Robert" is Robert Franchi, the Mob informant, and today is D day—the day the bribe money will change hands. The mobsters have come through for their new friend David Rudder; they've promised him an illegal deal with Boston Teamster bosses Jimmy Moar and Billy Winn. The wise guys are there to supervise the payout and take their cut.

An internal FBI document chronicles the day's events:

> HILLARY then took WINN and MOAR in to meet RUDDER. . . . MOAR said there would be no problems with the union. . . . Shortly after the meeting concluded, HILLARY and SALEMME JR. met with FRANCHI at Charlie's Kitchen, across the street from the Charles Hotel, to receive the agreed-upon $25,000 payoff from RUDDER. FRANCHI gave the cash to SALEMME JR. in the second floor of the restaurant and the money was split up by SALEMME JR right there. HILLARY questioned sarcastically if the three of them were going to be arrested now.

• • •

The filming of *Car Tunes* is slated to commence in the early spring of 1990. George Moffly flies to Providence to join David Rudder for location scouting. He's waiting at the airport gate to meet his boss's flight when he notices nearby a small clutch of what he can only think of as extras from *GoodFellas*—four guys who all look as if they have the middle name "the." David Rudder's plane lands, and Rudder steps into the waiting area. George Moffly rises to greet him but is paralyzed when he sees the group of gangsters break into grins and rush into David Rudder's arms, embracing him and slapping him on the cheek affectionately with the backs of their hands, Mafia-style.

Rudder spots George, calls him over. He introduces George to his new pals. George is hit with a flurry of names like Johnny, Tommy, Frankie, Joey. Who are these people?

Investors, Rudder explains. Associates of David Rudder Productions.

George Moffly's guts turn to ice. Why is his boss "associating" with these scary fucking goombahs?

George is now in serious preproduction on *Car Tunes*, having hired a crew of about fourteen people, but Rudder's "associates" are crawling all over his goddamn set. Gangster types hang out at the local coffee shop, boasting to anyone who will listen that they're Hollywood movie producers. And then there's this Robert character (whom George has privately started calling "Robert the Neck"), who won't leave David Rudder's side for a single moment. And then there's Frankie, a studly punk who always hangs around the production office, bragging that he's "gonna be in da movie" and hitting on George's innocent little sister, Kate, whom George has hired as production coordinator. Frankie scares Kate so much that George finally confronts him about his behavior.

"If you ever harass any woman on this set again," George barks, "I will slap you with such a sexual-harassment lawsuit you won't even know what fucking hit you."

Frankie screams, "Don't you fuckin' talk to me like that, you piece of shit! You don't know who the fuck I am! You don't know who my fuckin' father is! I'll fuckin' kill you!"

For Frankie Salemme Jr., the phrase "I'll fuckin' kill you" is not merely a colorful expression; it's also a family motto. And that very night Frankie comes back to George Moffly's hotel with every intention of throwing the producer of *Car Tunes* out a window. He is stopped from this act only by the intervention of the FBI's mob informant, Robert Franchi, who tackles Frankie Salemme Jr. in the hallway of the Omni Biltmore Hotel and reasons him out of homicide. George, diligently at work on the shooting schedule in his hotel room, knows nothing of this disquieting incident.

But George is unsettled by another incident that occurs a few days later. George has been trying to convince David Rudder for months that he needs to open a bank account for the production. George finally drags him into the Fleet National Bank in Providence to get the job done. They sit down with a bank manager. David Rudder asks, "What's the most money I can put in an account each business day before you have to report it to the federal government?"

"Ten thousand dollars," the manager replies.

Rudder pops open a nondescript attaché case. Stacked inside—just like in the fucking movies—are bricks upon bricks of freshly minted, neatly bundled $100 bills. Rudder counts out $9,000 as George and the banker stare, aghast.

The FBI, it turns out, hasn't officially cleared this phony movie budget with federal bean counters, because Schweickhardt and his bureau partners feel "it's just a lot more paperwork to let the IRS know what you're doing." So Garland Schweickhardt is keeping all the transactions in low cash figures, to make sure that his sting operation stays under the tax man's radar. The big cash display shocks the hell out of George Moffly. He tries not to obsess—*What do I care who this guy is? I'm getting my producer's credit*—but he still can't sleep well. He gets up in the middle of one particularly insomniac night to drink at the hotel bar, and he finds David Rudder and Robert the Neck there, engaged in some intimate conversation of whispers. They stop talking as George approaches. *Typical*, George thinks sulkily.

Rudder and the Neck have a lot to talk about. Their sting franchise is failing. Rudder's been flying out to Las Vegas recently with the mobster Tommy Hillary as a guide, trying to get criminally cozy with the Nevada Teamsters. But Rudder is coming on too strong, and the Vegas Teamsters don't buy his ruse. Worse, they have even got Tommy Hillary and his Boston cronies worried that Rudder might be a Fed. As Frankie Salemme Jr. gripes about David Rudder on tape to Robert the Neck, "You gotta really emphasize to this fuckin' jerk that he put everyone on the defensive like it's some big Abscam or somethin'."

All this suspicion worries Schweickhardt and puts Robert the Neck under enormous stress. He has to vouch for David Rudder, after all, and if the Mob starts to suspect a frame-up? Unthinkable. What's more, the Neck is actually suffering from a crisis of conscience about this whole sting operation. He's been watching young actors pack the David Rudder Productions office to audition for bit parts, and it makes him feel horrible, seeing all these innocent people putting their hearts and hopes on the line for a fake movie. All this deception doesn't seem right to the Neck. And now here comes George Moffly, strolling clueless into the hotel bar in the middle of the night. Another pathetic stooge.

The Neck reaches out and pats George's arm.

"Don't you worry, Georgie," he says. "David's taking care of everything. He's a good guy. The movie's gonna be great."

David Rudder adds, "One of these days, George, I'm going to tell you what this was really all about."

It is two weeks before the filming of *Car Tunes* is set to begin. George Moffly and David Rudder are at their usual spot at the hotel bar when Rudder tells George the bad news.

"The investors have pulled out again," he says. "They lost confidence in the project. *Car Tunes* is over."

Rudder rails bitterly against the investors, defaming them for having "no imagination!" In truth, special agent Garland Schweickhardt *is* upset. He thought he had a go picture here. But someone important in the U.S. Justice Department recently learned about Dramex and has shut it down. Justice fears that if the American public ever found out that the FBI tried to make a movie, it would be a humiliation to law enforcement everywhere. Schweickhardt tries vainly to defend his baby. No, he insists, *Car Tunes* is going to be good! It won't embarrass anyone! But the Feds are also worried about the dicey ethics of letting Rudder hire legitimate actors to star in a sham movie. Schweickhardt fights this charge, too. "They're just actors!" he says. "They're happy to get work. They don't care who funds it!"

But no amount of pleading can save Schweickhardt's movie. And now it's all over. Rudder is despondent. George Moffly is pissed. Twice he's been burned! And now Rudder plans to sally back to L.A., leaving George in Providence to clean up the mess, settle the bills and fire an entire crew. It's a sucky job, but George complies. He flies to Hollywood one last time to deliver the final accounting. And then— exhausted, angry and genuinely puzzled about what happened to him—George escapes to a derelict motel in the middle of the California desert. He sits by the pool as the sun sinks, drinking margarita after margarita, documenting frantically on a yellow legal pad every detail he can recall of the last two years. He can't make sense of any of it. He scribbles in one margin, "I know there are clues everywhere, but I just can't see them."

Before passing out completely,, he scrawls across an entire page: WHO ARE THESE PEOPLE?

Fifteen months pass. George Moffly is working nonstop. He does *Chain of Desire*, with Malcolm McDowell and Linda Fiorentino. He makes *The Obit Writer*, with Mira Sorvino. He works on a miniseries called *A Woman Named Jackie*. And then, one day in June 1991, he gets a phone call at his home. It's David Rudder, and he wants to see George one more time.

Intrigued, George goes to meet Rudder at the Paramount Hotel in New York on Wednesday, June 12, 1991. He enters Rudder's suite, shakes his hand and considers once again how huge and hulking his old boss is, and then Rudder says, "George, I have to tell you something: My name is not David Rudder. My name is Garland Schweickhardt. I'm a special agent with the organized-crime division of the FBI."

George Moffly goes deaf. The floor and walls seem to fall away from him. He can't feel his legs. Then the FBI agent starts spinning some dizzying confusion of words about indictments, secret grand juries and the protection of witnesses from La Cosa Nostra.

Garland Schweickhardt says, "You're not in trouble, George. We're not after you."

But this is not comforting. Not at all! George reels; the Fed talks. The extraordinary thing about this meeting is how quickly it ends. No more than ten minutes pass before George is led on shaky legs to the door by David Rudder. Or Garland Schweickhardt. Or whoever the fuck he is. George Moffly looks this familiar stranger straight in the eyes and says, "Meet me for a drink downstairs at the hotel bar tonight." Old habits die hard.

At the bar that night, George says to special agent Garland Schweickhardt, "Tell me everything. You owe me that."

And, amazingly enough, Schweickhardt does tell George exactly how the whole sting operation was executed—every detail, every nuance. He says, "I hope you didn't pay taxes on any of your earnings from me, because we never really reported that money." Schweickhardt even reassures George about what a terrific producer he was, what a great film they could have made together, if only they'd been given the chance. George is calm. He gets riled only once, when Garland Schweickhardt explains that he'd "many times" thought about confessing the truth to George and then asking him to wear a wire for the investigation.

"Just out of curiosity, George," he asks, "would you have worn a wire for us?"

At this, George Moffly's numbness is shot through with an energizing bullet of rage.

"Would I have worn a fucking *wire*? On my fucking *body*? For the fucking *FBI*? To record my conversations with the fucking *Mafia*? Are you out of your fucking *mind*?"

"Yeah," Schweickhardt admits sadly. "That's kind of what we always figured you'd say."

George Moffly does not want to testify against the Teamsters or La Cosa Nostra. At the moment, he would rather let a dozen crooks go free than endanger his safety by helping a Justice Department that has used him as a hapless stooge for two years. George Moffly feels he's already served the United States government plenty, thank you. But the Justice Department disagrees and tries hard to get him on the stand. Very hard. A half-dozen times they try serving him with a subpoena, but George continually refuses to sign for the papers.

"I'm not George Moffly," he declares to anyone, who comes near his door with legal documents. "Go away."

He finds the whole thing so disconcerting that he quietly slips off to Ecuador for a few months to live with his Peace Corps girlfriend. He is chilled one afternoon to pick up the ringing phone in her cheap Quito apartment and hear Garland Sweickhardt's familiar voice on the other end.

"George," Schweickhardt says, "were getting the feeling you're trying to avoid us."

But there's no way to avoid the full weight of the U.S. Justice Department, and when George returns to the States he is served his final subpoena by two armed federal marshals, who inform him that they are "not horsing around." He is flown to Boston and delivered to the federal courthouse, where he is interrogated for hours by government lawyers. They keep reassuring George that he isn't their target, but he sure starts feeling like a target after about the seventh hour. George is smart enough to realize that "I don't know" and "I don't remember" are always good answers, but the Feds don't buy it. To spur George's memory, a prosecutor finally slams down on the desk a cinder-block-thick pile of documents. Transcripts of George Moffy's telephone conversations from the last few years. When George stares down at the appalling sight of his own words, transcribed as neatly as a screenplay, he's not sure if he's going to vomit or start crying.

What do these people want from me?

What the Feds want, it becomes clear, is for George to help establish on the witness stand the previous criminal intent of the Teamster Jimmy Moar. After all, George Moffly, in his initial job interview with David Rudder, had boasted of bribing Jimmy Moar in the past.

But George Moffly had never bribed Moar! He only pretended that he had because he wanted a producer's job!

When the government prosecutors learn about this lie, they are mightily disappointed. Furious, even. There's some shouting, some threatening. One of the Justice Department prosecutors calls him a "slippery bastard." But George—who is now passing *frightened* and entering *angry*—shouts and threatens right back ("Let's both tell our stories to *The New York Times*, shall we?"). And in the end the government decides that George Moffly wouldn't make such a cooperative witness, after all. So he is released from the federal courthouse on Friday, November 15, 1991, shaken but heartily satisfied to have left the Feds helplessly fuming.

With the exception of FBI special agent Garland Schweickhardt, who harbors no hard feelings about George's little lie.

"Hey," he says later, "that's how this business works. They tell the story of Henry Fonda. The first time he ever tried to take a job on a Western, they asked him if he could ride a horse. He'd never been on a horse in his life. But he lied and said he could do it, just to get the job. Sometimes you have to represent yourself that way, in order to advance."

The trial, which commences in 1994, is a rather wussy affair. Two Teamsters (Jimmy Moar and Billy Winn) and three mobsters (Dennis Lepore, Frankie Salemme Jr. and Tommy Hillary) are indicted on labor and racketeering charges. But the results are disappointing. Jimmy Moar is flat-out acquitted. Billy Winn is convicted but dies before he can be sentenced. The studly Frankie Salemme Jr. dies before he can even be tried. (Some say cancer; some say AIDS.) The slick gangster Tommy Hillary turns state's evidence and goes into the witness protection program, where he still lives today. ("It is an incredible story,"

Tommy admits, speaking from somewhere deep within his new existence. "Somebody oughta make a fuckin' film. But who would play me? I think Harvey Keitel.") Dennis "Champagne" Lepore is the only one sent to federal prison for any substantial amount of time, which no doubt brings peace to his old enemy, Robert the Neck.

Robert is still among us, but he's hiding from the Mob somewhere in Middle America. He was offered a spot in the witness-protection program, but he ultimately refused it. At the last minute, Robert learned he would have to euthanize his pet cat, Rusty, before entering the program, just in case someone from his past recognized the kitty.

"What about my fish?" Robert apparently asked the supervising FBI agent, who replied stonily, "The fish has to go, too."

The Neck took a pass on federal protection.

As for George Moffly, he's a successful producer now. Works constantly. His only professional legacy from the Dramex sting is a big hole in his résumé from 1988 to 1990. Personally, the legacy is more complicated. For years George didn't tell anyone about what happened to him. He was too scared to mention it. Two years after he refused to testify George Moffly was audited by the IRS, and he couldn't help but wonder if the audit was some kind of message from the Justice Department: *Never forget that we are huge and you are puny.*

And as for Garland Schweickhardt? He's retired from the FBI. Spends his days driving his young daughters to piano lessons. Schweickhardt is proud of the deterrent legacy of the Dramex sting—everyone from federal prosecutors to George Moffly concedes that the days of the fat-envelope pay-offs are over. Still, Schweickhardt admits he "always wonders" how good a movie he could have made with George. He gets a little upset when he sees movies on HBO that aren't any better than *Car Tunes* might have been. But there's no use dwelling on the old David Rudder days. Garland Schweickhardt is done with show business, he swears. Although he does still live in Los Angeles, practically in the shadow of the famous Hollywood sign. And parked in front of his nice house is his 400-series Mercedes-Benz, as white and gleaming as a starlet's smile.

The license plate reads DAVID RD.

by Joey with David Fisher

Writer David Fisher (born 1946) and mob hitman "Joey" collaborated on this 1974 account of the killer's 29th murder. The victim, a small-time hood and gambler named Joey Squillante, had robbed a numbers boss. Squillante was set up as follows: A mob acquaintance hired him for a job and told him to go to a parking lot and wait for a "friend"—someone he'd recognize—who would give him instructions. The friend was Joey.

started walking toward the car. Slowly at first, then I speeded up just a bit. The total distance between the building and Squillante's car was no more than 30 yards, a distance I can normally cover easily in less than 30 seconds. I have no idea how long it took me that night, but it was quite a bit longer.

Jackie Sweetlips, left sitting in a puddle inside the hallway, was forgotten, a part of my distant past. Everything was now, this moment.

Mentally I divided the 30 yards into three separate areas of concentration. The first ten yards I looked to my sides and behind me, trying to locate either the Chevy with the two punks in it, or pick up anybody that might be coming up on me from the rear. I couldn't find the Chevy, and I began to think the hoods just took off. There didn't seem to be any other movement behind me.

I walked right into a big puddle I never even noticed. My shoes and socks soaked right through and I knew this was going to add to my unhappiness.

I spent the second ten yards surveying the area in front of me. I made visual arcs, as I learned in the army, each arc just a bit wider and deeper than the one before it. If anyone was going to come out of the park toward me I wanted to pick him up very quickly.

The last ten yards were all Squillante's. I walked toward the car at a steady pace. I was not in any hurry to get there. I had absolutely no idea what was going through his mind as I made this walk. I had to assume he was scared. Scared to be there, scared to be meeting somebody, scared to be holding a loaded gun in his hand.

I had no doubts he was holding the gun and ready to use it. I just wanted to make sure I could startle him briefly. That would at least prevent him from shooting on sight. If he did that I didn't have a superwonderful chance of walking away unhurt.

I reached my left hand into my belt and pulled the new .38 free. I kept it inside my coat, completely concealed. I took one quick look over my shoulder, again trying to pick up the Chevy. If they weren't there, I could simply blast him and walk away. If they were there, they were watching me make this walk. I already know they can't stand up to pressure—they talked quick enough when the Fat Man asked the questions—so I know they're going to talk if some high-powered detective is doing the asking. I could not afford any witnesses.

Squillante realized I was coming when I was approximately ten yards from the car. I could see him watching the rear-view mirror at that distance and, as I got closer, he shifted his body so he was facing the passenger door. I knew his gun was sitting in his hand.

I made sure I stayed as close to the car as I could. When I was briefly hidden by the dead visual spot between the back window and the rear side window on the right side of the car, I stuck my right arm as far away from my body as I could, pointed the flashlight right where I guessed Squillante's head was going to be, and turned the beam on.

There was no shot. I eased up a little on my breathing. Normally if an individual is in a state of panic and a light goes on quickly and unexpectedly, he'll fire away at it. As long as my body isn't behind it, I won't get too badly hurt. And the beam from the light will cause him to become temporarily blinded, making him an easy target.

But he didn't fire. I reached the car and opened the door very wide. As I thought, he was holding his gun in his right hand, pointing it more or less in my direction.

"Whattya say, Joe?" I said as calmly as I could, then slid into the passenger seat. It'd been a long time since I was looking down a gun barrel first.

He looked at me almost blankly. He knew who I was, yet didn't know what to make of my being there. He *knew* I was a hit man, but he didn't know if I was there to hit him. So he did nothing. He sat and kept that thing pointed right at me.

Moving very easily so as not to upset him, I took my right hand and pushed the gun away from me. "Watch it," I said, "those things hurt people when they go off." I also took my left hand off my gun, but left the .38 loose inside my jacket, so I could get at it very quickly.

He seemed to come out of the daze. "Hey Joey," he said almost brightly, "I didn't expect to see you here."

I agreed. "Yeah, it's sort of a surprise party."

He still didn't know whether to believe that he was the intended or not. If it had been me sitting in his seat I would have plugged me as full of holes as there were bullets available. But he wasn't used to the gun, so he hesitated, and hesitated. "Who's gonna be surprised?" he asked.

What was I gonna tell him? "You'll see," I finally answered. Then I sort of gave him a command. "Listen, put that thing away and let's go."

"Where?"

"Just drive, I'll tell you where." I think I finally got through to him. He put the gun inside his belt and turned frontwards. He started the car.

"What's with the flashlight?" he asked as naturally as he could, but still with some strain.

"It's dark out. I wanted to make sure it was you in this car." I paused for effect. "What's with the gun?"

He tried to be casual about it. "Oh, you know. It's dark, it's late, I didn't know who I was meeting. And . . . well, I've had some problems with some people and I just wasn't sure that you weren't one of them."

"Problems?" I asked, as if I didn't know.

He did not elaborate. "Problems," he said. As he started to back the car up I took a good long look in the rear-view mirror. About 40 yards behind us a pair of headlights flashed on and off, then stayed on. The boys of night had indeed returned.

In my mind I was trying to figure out two problems: one, how to drop the tail and two, where to take him. "Just head downtown," I told him, I knew I'd come up with something. I also knew it shouldn't be too difficult to lose a tail that didn't want to stay attached. The hoods knew that the Fat Man held their lives in his hand, so I knew they weren't going to be too serious about tailing Squillante, especially after it became obvious he was trying to lose them. I just had to give Squillante a reason to want to lose them. They had done their job—they had gotten Squillante to his appointment.

"Yeah," I said as easily and friendly as I could, trying to set something up, "I know what you mean about problems. I got problems too. That's the real reason for the flashlight."

"What sort of problems did you have?"

"Just problems," I said. We both laughed. I think he was beginning to feel more comfortable with me.

We rode silently down through the Bronx as I tried to figure a location Squillante would find believable. My first choice was under the Williamsburg Bridge, where I first met with Petey, but I knew Joe would never go for that. He's supposed to point somebody out, that's the story, and I knew he wouldn't expect to find a crowd under the bridge at midnight.

Where would he find a crowd? The answer was obvious: at a restaurant. Outside a restaurant would be okay. In a big parking lot. In the back of a big parking lot. I started to think of restaurants I knew in Brooklyn or Queens with big parking lots. Then I thought of one. A big place in Queens, right on the water. "When you reach the Fifty-ninth Street Bridge," I told him, "take it to Northern Boulevard."

He nodded.

I was trying to make small talk. Now that I knew the spot, I wanted to get rid of the tail. How? "How's your mother doin'?"

"Better," he said. "The doctor said it wasn't a heart attack really, just a warning."

"That's scary enough," I said.

He agreed. "You know, Joey," he said after a pause, "we really haven't been that friendly over the years, but I'm glad it was you out there tonight. I have to tell you something. I was nervous as hell sitting there. I really thought it was a setup. I felt better when I saw it was you."

These were all nice words, but I knew they were bullshit. If he felt so good about seeing me he would have released the tail. He was trying to lead me into some sort of corner. "Yeah, well, I was glad when Jackie told me it was you who was gonna be here tonight, too," I agreed.

I leaned forward and looked in the mirror. "Listen babe," I said, "I don't want to scare you or anything, but I think we got company."

He made a big show of leaning over and looking in the mirror. "You sure?"

"No, not exactly. It's just that there's a car that's been right behind us the whole trip."

"I doubt they're following us."

"Not us," I said, "me. I told you I had some problems. Well, I think somebody is trying to solve them tonight."

Squillante simply did not know what to do. He couldn't admit that the boys on his tail were his because this was a legitimate job for him and he could be in real trouble for bringing other people on business. "I don't think they're following us," he tried to bluff.

"Let's find out. Make the next right." It was 112th Street in Manhattan. I had him make the standard four rights in succession. The Chevy stayed right behind us. "I told you, those fuckers are after me," I said as convincingly as I could.

"Son of a bitch," he said almost as believably.

"Okay, let's lose 'em," I cheered.

He didn't seem to want to do that. "How?"

"Like this." Without a warning I leaned across and jammed my left foot down on top of his right foot, sending the accelerator to the floorboard. The car jerked forward and then took off.

"TAKE YOUR FOOT OFF. TAKE YOUR FOOT OFF!" I took my foot off. We were going about 50 down the street when I moved back. Squillante understood what I had in mind. He also understood that I wasn't kidding around. He made a few quick turns, made a few yellow lights, and lost the Chevy someplace in the wilds of Spanish Harlem.

We were alone.

The silence got louder and louder as we drove toward the bridge. "What are you gonna do to this guy when I point him out?" he broke in.

I shrugged my shoulders. "Nothin' tonight. I just want to know who he is."

"I'll tell you why, 'cause if you're gonna burn him, I don't want any part of it. I'm not a getaway driver, I'm a controller."

I reassured him. "Don't worry, Joe, you won't be driving any getaway car tonight." I paused. "And what makes you think I do heavyweight work?"

He kind of edged his head from side to side. "Well, you know, the word around the neighborhood was, you know, that you did. And things I hear from people now and then, you know, you got a reputation. I mean, like, I don't really know, but I *know*."

I chuckled. What he knew was going to hurt him. "Yeah, I guess so. The word gets around, doesn't it?"

He agreed that it did.

"Then how come you didn't fire when you saw it was me? I mean, how did you know I wasn't sent by whoever you pissed off?"

"I didn't. I just took a chance." Bullshit. He chickened out. "I just couldn't pull the trigger when I saw it was you." That I believed.

As we drove over the 59th Street Bridge, the Queensboro Bridge officially, I wondered what was going on in his mind. Did he know? Did he suspect? I stared at his head and picked out one small spot, just behind his right ear, that I would fire at. Normally I don't like to be this close to my target, three feet is usually plenty close enough and I was less than two feet away. In fact, if I reached my arm out, I would be at point blank range. I didn't want his head to explode all over me, that would make getting away clean a little more difficult.

I reached my hand into my jacket and checked to see that the silencer was still attached tightly to the gun. It was. Squillante was babbling on about the old neighborhood. I should have killed him just for being boring.

". . . gamble," he said. I wasn't paying attention, so I only caught the last word. "Do you?"

"What?" I asked.

"Lose a lot when you gamble? Get way behind?"

"I can't afford it. Make this right here," I said, and then I told him exactly where we were going. I named the restaurant. "You ever been there?"

He said he hadn't.

"You should try it someday," I told him. "It's a whole meal for one price. All you can eat. And the food is pretty decent. You should take the old lady there some day."

"I will." We both were lying. I knew he wasn't going to live long enough ever to go there. He thought he would be leaving for Europe two days from now.

I really couldn't imagine him in Europe. When mob people run they almost always stay in the country. Very few leave these hospitable shores. I doubted if he would make it over there even if he had lived to get away. I laughed inside. Here I was sitting next to this guy who was breathing, who was alive, and already I was thinking of him in the past tense.

The last hour had been a tough one for a man in my profession. I like things orderly and absolutely nothing had gone right. And worst of all, I had lost the killing emotion, I was relaxing. Now, as we got closer to the restaurant, I started letting it build up inside me, just staring at Squillante.

"You know, I was thinking that . . ." he started to say.

I stared right at him. "Not now, huh? Just shut it for awhile."

He looked at me and then looked straight ahead. I think that at that moment, for one brief second, just an instant in time, he knew. Then he denied it to himself.

We reached the restaurant just past midnight. "Pull way in the back of the lot," I told him. He drove to the rear and started pulling in next to another car. "Not here," I ordered. "Move it over there, in that dark spot. I don't want anyone to know we're here."

He started to protest. "Nobody knows this car."

"Just do it, huh? That's what you're being paid for right? To listen to me? So listen to me."

As he moved into the parking spot I reached into my jacket and got a good solid grip on the new .38. I was looking around the parking lot quickly, my instincts once again sharp, trying to spot someone, anyone, who might be a potential witness. One car was just pulling out of the place, all the way on the other side of the lot. No way they could spot anything. The lot itself was well lit, but the spot we moved into was shaded and dark.

I kept the gun inside my jacket until he had stopped the car, put it in park, turned the engine off, turned the lights off, and then turned to face me. Then I took it out and pointed it right at him. He saw the gun and froze. I mean froze solid.

Panic strikes people in different ways. Some individuals immediately understand the situation, realize the hopelessness, and accept it as the final irony. Others start to scream. Some try but nothing comes out. From Squillante I got fear. In the one split second before I started to pump bullets into his head he crunched his body up, leaned hard against the door, and stuck both his hands out toward me as if in an effort to ward off the bullets. He knew. At the last second he knew.

"So long, Joe," I said in that brief moment. I don't know why I said anything. I can't remember ever saying anything on a job before, but I can distinctly remember myself saying, "So long, Joe," to him. It was the only sound before the shots and the words sounded tremendously loud.

Then I started firing into his head. The spot I had selected was turned away from me when he cringed, so I just fired randomly into his skull. The .38 made a muffled "pop" as I fired, the silencer almost completely covering the gunshots. No one standing outside the car could have heard anything.

The force of the first bullet drove his head to the left and against the window. The second bullet and the third bullet made his body jerk, but I'm quite sure he was dead when the first bullet smashed into his brain. All three hit their mark because, at that distance, it would have been impossible to miss.

There was no great spurt of blood all over the place, but a hard, steady stream flowed down the front of his face, running alongside his nose and then veering off to the side of his mouth.

After I stopped firing the momentum of the bullets made his body slump down, straight down, then against his door. For a slight moment I thought he was going to hit the horn, which was something I neither needed nor wanted, but he missed the steering wheel completely.

I sat in the car and unscrewed the silencer. I put it in one pocket and the fired .38 in the other.

Before getting out of the car I made sure Squillante's body was lying low enough so that no one who wasn't standing right next to the car could see it. Then I turned around to see if there was anybody in the parking lot. There was a group of four people walking into the restaurant. I sat there and watched as they disappeared inside the rear entrance. Then I got out of the car and, staying in the rear of the lot, keeping to the shadows, I walked away.

I never looked back.

Getting the job done was only half the fun. Even a well-executed hit is going to bring little satisfaction if you get caught before getting rid of the evidence: in this case, the new .38 and the silencer.

There are some people who do not pay too much attention to getting rid of the piece they work with. They heave it in the woods or throw it in the water or hide it behind their underwear in their top drawer. In the trade we have a word to describe people who do things like that: convicts. Guns have a way of coming back to haunt you. Not too many people know it, but the New York City Police Department has a special squad of skin divers that do nothing but look for things like guns. I can assure them they will never find one with my fingerprints on it.

I know that the only thing that can connect me to Squillante is the .38-with-silencer I have tucked in my jacket pocket. I'm not going to get rid of it simply and risk some kid accidentally finding it, I'm going to destroy it completely and for good. Once the job itself is done, that is my primary objective.

As soon as Squillante slumped over on the front seat I stopped thinking about him. He was finished as far as both of us were concerned. I walked out of the parking lot, trying to figure a way to get back to Manhattan and my own car. I wasn't worried about the car I left back at Bronx Park. There was nothing in it to connect it with me. I was going to drop it anyway, now I would just leave it there. Let the police find it.

As I walked I did my best to check my clothing out in the bad light. I wanted to make sure I hadn't ended up with any of his blood on me. I hadn't.

My problem was getting back to New York City without meeting anybody. I certainly couldn't hitch, I didn't want anybody picking me up anywhere near the parking lot. And I didn't want to grab a cab in the middle of nowhere. Most cabbies will remember if they pick somebody up walking along the road late at night, and I didn't want anyone remembering me. So I walked toward lights. I really didn't know the neighborhood too well, but I figured if I could find an open bar I could call a cab and the driver wouldn't think anything about it. My first choice would have been the subway to Manhattan, but I was a long way from any subway station.

I walked about 20 minutes. The whole trip I was thinking how this was just another foul-up in what had been the worst hit I ever made. And then, just to top everything off wonderfully well, it started raining again.

I found my bar and I sat down and had a quick beer before doing anything. Then I called a local cab company that had its name pasted on the phone and ordered a taxi. It arrived about ten minutes and a second beer later.

I took this cab into mid-Manhattan, then I grabbed a second cab back up to the all-night garage in the Bronx. Finally, almost an hour and a half after burning Squillante, I got into my own car. All I wanted to do was get rid of the weapon, as far as I was concerned I had been holding it too long already. The first thing I did after pulling out of the garage was turn the radio on. Music calms the savage beast—and it also relaxes the hell out of a hit man. I headed back down into Manhattan, toward the lower tip, the Battery. I had very specific plans on how I was going to get rid of the gun and silencer.

I took the East River Drive downtown because I was pretty sure I wouldn't have to fight traffic at that hour. I tend to get uptight and angry when I'm caught in a traffic jam, and uptight and angry was something I didn't want to be. On the way down I reviewed the job once again. It wasn't the smoothest in the history of the world, but it was done. I wondered if Jackie was still struggling to get his hands free. I doubted it very much. I knew my treatment was not going to increase his great love for me, but there really wasn't very much else I could do under the circumstances. I figured I might hear some nasty words from the Fat Man, but business, as they say, is business.

By the time I reached the Battery it was almost two-thirty in the morning. New York City is really a beautiful place at that hour, especially after it's been raining for awhile. All the grime and dirt is hidden by the dark or washed away and the lights from the buildings reflect on the water. It really is an ideal, mystic time, a time for romantic people, of which I am not one.

I figured with good luck Squillante's body would not be discovered until the next morning. With bad luck somebody leaving the restaurant had to take a piss and went near the car and found what was left. I figured as long as I got rid of everything before Sunday noon I would have no problems. I knew there was a slim chance I would be hustled by the cops. Every time there's a gang hit they round up some "knowns," so the papers can make it look like they are doing something.

I parked my car in the lot right near the ferry landing and waited to board the boat to Staten Island. I wasn't nervous or upset at all. Also, interestingly enough, I wasn't the slightest bit cold, even though it was much colder down by the water than it had been in the Bronx. In fact, I felt one long bead of sweat wind its way slowly down my spine.

The ferry left for Staten Island on the hour. Most of the people on the boat were kids, couples taking a traditional Saturday night ride on the ferry. There was one couple in particular I didn't understand. A real faggy looking guy, skinny, long hair, bell-bottomed trousers, rings on almost all his fingers, and he was with this super-beautiful chick. This broad had a body that would stop a war. I couldn't understand what a looker like that was doing with a skinny nothing like him. Little did I know then, in 1968, that the fag look was going to get so popular. I stared but I didn't really care, to each his own.

I stood by myself near the railing. Nobody paid the slightest attention to me. When we were halfway to the Island dock I reached into my pocket and pulled out the silencer. Plunk! I dropped it casually into the river and watched as it sunk right to the bottom. If the million-to-one shot hits and the police find the silencer, what do they have? A rusty silencer and no gun to connect it with.

Why did I bother to throw the silencer away after spending good money for it? I just don't want the thing to be found around me after I've used it. Especially after the law discovers somebody got hit in the parking lot of a busy restaurant, and since nobody heard the shots, they got to figure they're looking for a silencer. It's really just another safety precaution for my own piece of mind. I knew the currents would eventually pick it up and deposit it far away. The gun, which is a lot heavier, would have laid there longer. I held onto it. I had plans for it.

I got off the ferry for a minute and then got right back on. At that hour there are a lot of people who do exactly that, people just out for a boatride, so nobody pays any attention. Under normal conditions five minutes on Staten Island is too long, and these were certainly not normal circumstances. When we docked at the Battery, I picked up my car and headed back up to the Bronx.

My exact destination was the South Bronx. A friend of mine has a small machine shop to which I hold one key, to be used on just such occasions as this. The place wasn't big, but it was spooky quiet. I get more nervous in places like this than I do before gunning an individual. The quiet bothers me. I like noise, I like people, I like things happening. In this case, all I wanted to do was finish my work as quickly as possible.

The only light I put on in the place was the fluorescent lamp he had over his workbench. From the outside no one could tell it wasn't an interior light left on all night to scare away burglars.

The first thing I went to work on was the barrel. I grabbed an electrical hack saw and cut it right off at the base. Then I cut it in two pieces the long way, down the seam. Next, I took each of those pieces and cut them in half, lengthwise again. Now what was once the barrel was just four long pieces of metal.

Then I went after the hammer. I was right at home with these tools. I always had the ability to work with my hands and make nice things in the shop. The few times I've seriously thought about retirement I always end up looking for something to do with tools.

I propped the piece up on the workbench, opened the hammer and then smashed the shit out of it with a heavy hand hammer. There was absolutely no way that gun was going to come back to haunt me. I smashed the firing pin because, even if the coppers come up with the cartridges, without a firing pin there is absolutely no way they can match it up to a gun. I finally had the whole thing dismantled.

I took all the pieces and put them in a paper bag. I got back in my car and started touring the Bronx, looking for sewers. Looking for sewers in the Bronx at 2 a.m. Sunday morning is not my favorite occupation in the world, so I tried to make it brief. Every time I found another sewer, I would carefully wipe all fingerprints off one individual piece and deposit that piece into the sewer for posterity. I threw the cylinder in one place. The stock went in another. Then each part of the barrel. There simply ain't no one in the world who could find all those pieces and put them back together.

This all sounds like a lot of trouble and it is. But after making a hit, especially one with all the problems that this one had, you are all keyed up anyway and you really need something to do to keep busy. Some men are able to go out and eat dinner, some guys get laid. Me? I take my time getting rid of the weapon. Then, if it can be arranged, I go out for dinner and get laid.

The whole disposal operation, from the moment Squillante died until I finished spreading the gun, took about four hours. It was getting to be toward morning when I finally finished my labors. Now I could go home and try to get some sleep. Sunday was supposed to be a work day. My cigarettes were arriving and I planned to be at the warehouse.

I really felt tired when I laid down, but I just could not get to sleep. My wife was dead to the world when I got home and, as promised, I didn't wake her, but I couldn't get to sleep myself. Normally I have no problem putting my head on the pillow and zonking out, but I guess the tension of the night was taking its time unwinding.

About 6 a.m. I really made a second effort. I remember tossing and turning for awhile and then I guess I drifted off into a semisleep. I did not dream about Joseph Squillante. This ain't the movies.

Acknowledgments

Many people made this anthology.

At Thunder's Mouth Press and Avalon Publishing Group:
Thanks to Tracy Armstead, Will Balliett, Sue Canavan, Kristen Couse, Maria Fernandez, Linda Kosarin, Shona McCarthy, Dan O'Connor, Neil Ortenberg, Paul Paddock, Susan Reich, David Riedy, Simon Sullivan, Michelle Rosenfield, and Mike Walters.

At The Writing Company:
Nathaniel May did most of the editorial research. Taylor Smith oversaw permissions research and negotiations. Nate Hardcastle and Wynne Parry took up slack on other projects.

At the Portland Public Library in Portland, Maine:
The librarians helped collect books from around the country.

Finally, I am grateful to the writers whose work appears in this book.

P e r m i s s i o n s

We gratefully acknowledge everyone who gave permission for written material to appear in this book. We have made every effort to trace and contact copyright holders. If an error or omission is brought to our notice we will be pleased to correct the situation in future editions of this book. For further information, please contact the publisher.

B i b l i o g r a p h y

The selections used in this anthology were taken from the editions listed below. In some cases, other editions may be easier to find. Hard-to-find or out-of-print titles often are available through inter-library loan services or through Internet booksellers.

Abadinsky, Howard. *The Mafia in America: An Oral History.* New York: Praeger Publishers, 1981.

Anastasia, George. *Mobfather: The Story of a Wife and a Son Caught in the Web of the Mafia.* New York: Zebra Books, 1993.

Capeci, Jerry and Gene Mustain. *Gotti: Rise and Fall.* New York: Onyx, 1996.

Cramer, Richard Ben. "Men of Honor". Originally appeared in *Esquire,* June, 1993.

Gilbert, Elizabeth. "The Sting". Originally appeared in *GQ,* March, 2000.

Grann, David. "Crimetown USA". Originally appeared in *The New Republic,* July 10 & 17, 2000.

Joey with David Fisher. *Hit 29: Based on the Killer's Own Account.* New York: Thunder's Mouth Press, 2003.

Joey with David Fisher. *Joey the Hitman: The Autobiography of a Mafia Killer.* New York: Thunder's Mouth Press, 2002.

Kinkead, Gwen. *Chinatown: Portrait of a Closed Society.* New York: HarperCollins, 1992.

Manca, John and Vincent Cosgrove. *Tin For Sale: My Career in Organized Crime and the NYPD.* New York: William Morrow and Company, 1991.

Nelli, Humbert S. *The Business of Crime: Italians and Syndicate Crime in the United States.* New York: Oxford University Press, 1976.

Pileggi, Nicholas. *Wiseguy: Life in a Mafia Family.* New York: Pocket Books, 1987.

Puzo, Mario. *The Godfather.* New York: Signet, 1978.

Sedgwick, John. "Blood Brothers". Originally appeared in *GQ,* May, 1992.

Stratton, Richard. "Life of Crime". Originally appeared as "The Man Who Killed Dutch Schultz" in *GQ,* September, 2001.

Exciting title from Adrenaline Books

MOB

STORIES OF DEATH AND BETRAYAL
FROM ORGANIZED CRIME

EDITED BY CLINT WILLIS

The sixteenth title in the Adrenaline Books series offers 13 terrifying windows on the brutal and mysterious world of organized crime. Here you'll meet characters who make Tony Soprano look tame, from murderous Dons to undercover agents risking their lives to break the Mob's most powerful syndicates. The picture that emerges from their stories is astoundingly complex and all too human: a world of warped desire and violent consequences that is at once shocking and fascinating. $17.95 ($29.95 Canada), 352 pages

PRAISE FOR MOB

"An anthology crime buffs can't refuse."—*Kirkus Reviews*

"Platefuls of stick-to-the-ribs tales of gangland murders, wise guys, heists and stool pigeons...the engrossing fiction and true crime tales collected here will whet many readers' appetites."
—*Publishers Weekly*

"All of these pieces make for spellbinding reading, and, taken together, present a far-ranging and intimate view of life on the wrong side of the law."
—*Library Journal*

adrenaline classics ®

"Chilling and compelling—A must-read."
—Former FBI agent Joe Pistone,
aka Donnie Brasco

JOEY
THE HITMAN
THE AUTOBIOGRAPHY OF A MAFIA KILLER

BY "JOEY" WITH DAVID FISHER

SERIES EDITOR CLINT WILLIS

Adrenaline Classics brings back the classic *New York Times* best-seller (originally published as *Killer*) that anticipated the new generation of unromanticized mob stories, from *Donnie Brasco* to *The Sopranos*. "Joey"—a journeyman Jewish hitman, numbers king, and loan shark—collaborated with David Fisher to lay out organized crime in gripping detail. The quality of the writing, the frank intelligence of the subject/writer, and Joey's convincingly matter-of-fact, regular-guy tone made this the unique bestseller it became.

$14.95 ($24.95 Canada)
288 pages

adrenaline classics ®

HIT #29

BASED ON THE KILLER'S OWN ACCOUNT

By "Joey" with david Fisher
Series editor Clint Willis

Soon to be a major motion picture from Paramount, *New York Times* bestseller *Hit #29* is a true-crime classic by a real Soprano. Readers are taken along on a stranger-than-fiction journey of one actual hit taken on by Jewish hitman, numbers king, and loan shark "Joey." But the 29th contract hit Joey has taken on— without a conviction—turns out to be a lot more complicated than it first appears. As recounted in Joey's patented matter-of-fact, regular-guy tone, the target, a low-level numbers "controller", turns out to be an old acquaintance from the neighborhood, the client is a man who once tried to have Joey hit, and there are enough twists and double-backs—not to mention fascinatingly cred-ible mob details and color—to keep *Soprano* fans up all night.

$14.95 ($24.95 Canada)
240 pages

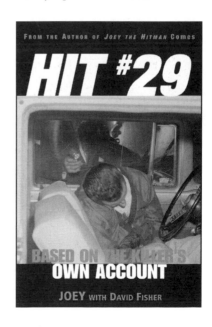